WOMEN WORLD LEADERS PRESENTS

SURRENDERED

YIELDED WITH PURPOSE

VISIONARY AUTHORS

KIMBERLY ANN HOBBS & JULIE T. JENKINS

World Publishing and Productions

Surrendered: Yielded With Purpose

© 2022 Women World Leaders

ISBN: 978-1-957111-09-4

Contents

Introduction

What does it mean to surrender to God? As you read the stories and teachings throughout the pages of this book, it is our prayerful desire that you will walk with an encouraged heart and a stronger understanding of the meaning of surrendering to God and yielding to Him for His greater purpose in your life.

Our world as we live in it is a battleground. Satan has waged holy war against those God has called with purpose. As a human race, we are born into sin from Adam's fall. *When Adam sinned, sin entered the world. Adam's sin brought death, so death spread to everyone, for everyone sinned.* (Romans 5:12 NLT)

We all have choices to make. We must choose to live life following our own sinful inclinations or look beyond ourselves and seek God. God promises that when we seek Him, we will find Him. And when we find Him, we must then decide to continue living on our own or surrender to His will, understanding that He is in ultimate control.

The title of this book is *Surrendered*. Surrender is a term used in battle; it implies giving up all our rights to a conqueror. Surrendering to God works the same way. As God's children, we can surrender to Him, understanding that His ultimate plan for our life is far better than our own. We are able to humble ourselves, realizing God has our best interests in mind. *"For I know the plans I have for you,"* declares the Lord, *"plans to prosper you and not to harm you, plans to give you hope and a future."* (Jeremiah 29:11 NIV)

The contributing authors in this book share their stories which, together with the teachings presented, will shed different levels of light on the word surrender to help strengthen your relationship with God. When we let go of our own attempts to earn God's favor and rely upon Jesus Christ, we receive a deeper intimacy with Him, and He allows us a greater power to serve Him. These stories and teachings provide examples and inspirations that coincide with that truth through scripture.

> *They conquered him completely through the blood of the Lamb and the powerful word of his testimony.* (Revelation 12:11 TPT)

> *Yet to all who did receive him, to those who believed in his name, he gave the right to become children of God.* (John 1:12 NIV)

> *God made him who had no sin to be sin for us, so that in him we might become righteousness of God.* (2 Corinthians 5:21 NIV)

Can you attest that you have areas, empty rooms in your heart, that need to be filled with the Holy Spirit? I know I can. In your hands, you hold readings that will help you fully surrender to His filling. May your heart ask God to lead you and guide you His way so you can be a victorious conqueror over self-desires through His Son, Jesus Christ! The more you surrender your old self-worshipping nature to God and replace it with God's total reign over every aspect of your life, the more the Holy Spirit will fill those vast areas of your soul.

> *"Whoever wants to be my disciple must deny themselves and take up their cross and follow me."* (Mark 8:34 NIV)

We pray that by reading *Surrendered: Yielded With Purpose,* you will see from the accounts within and how they are shared that lives surrendered to God are also pleasing to Him. This becomes the greatest human fulfillment there is. If you are looking for encouragement and a tool to help you on the battlefield of life, this book will provide access to ways to conquer defeat through Christ. So, get ready to be stirred. By surrendering strongholds that hold you captive to your old, sinful state of living, you will begin to move. You will progress in confidence, understanding that a life of peace is ahead of you, knowing God has you in His care and that ultimate rewards in heaven are coming.

> *"I have been crucified with Christ and I no longer live, but Christ lives in me. The life I now live in the body, I live by faith in the son of God, who loved me and gave himself for me."* (Galatians 2:20 NIV)

We are confident that through its encouragement, this book will inspire you to give your life over to the authority of the winning side. When it comes to struggles of the flesh, surrendering to God is more effective than striving on your own. We urge you to take a humble position in an act of faith and learn ways to keep hope alive by surrendering things of the flesh. You, too, can defeat death by walking with Christ, letting go of control, and trusting God. While you are in the process of reading Surrendered, we ask that you regularly focus on praying over your life, spend time in the Word of God daily, and continue doing what God has told you to do in obedience to Him. Turn your battlefield over to God completely. Let go of your own plans and allow God to take over and direct your path. Trust Him and release your past. May we all surrender before Him as a sacrifice to our Savior and King.

Kimberly Ann Hobbs

As the Founder and co-CEO of Women World Leaders, a worldwide ministry empowering women to find their God-given purpose, Kimberly Ann Hobbs oversees all elements of the ministry, including *Voice of Truth* magazine. Kimberly is also the co-CEO of World Publishing and Productions and an international best-selling author, speaker, motivational leader, and life coach.

As part of *Women World Leaders' Podcast,* Kimberly hosts *Empowering Lives with Purpose,* interviewing beautiful women from around the world. She also shares daily devotions on the WWL Facebook group and website, www.womenworldleaders.com.

Kimberly has been a guest speaker on Moody Bible Radio Stations and made appearances on Daystar Television, sharing her passion for bringing women to a closer walk with Jesus through encouragement. She is an artist, with much of her work reaching worldwide, and sits on Kerus Global Education advisory board, helping raise support for South Africa's orphaned children.

Kimberly supports her husband, Ken, in his ministry: United Men of Honor - Unitedmenofhonor.com. Together they serve in missions and ministry and run their own financial coaching business. They have children and grandchildren whom they love very much and a home-life "Tiki Hut Ministry" in South Florida.

A Night of Transformation

By Kimberly Ann Hobbs

When God invokes His favor, the heart rejoices. The floodgates of heaven pour in, and the blessings shower down. With prayer, worship, and reading the Scriptures, our lives come into alignment with God, and by giving God full surrender of our hearts, He has room to be the beneficent victor, to conquer us and bless us. And the more we surrender to God, the more room there is for the filling of the Holy Spirit.

In prayer and preparation for authoring this book, God led me to scripture which allowed me to hone my understanding of and identification with the word "surrendered." The further I prayed upon the revelations He imparted to me, the more God placed it on my heart to share them. And I will. But first, let me tell my own story of surrender, the heart of which came down to one pivotal life-changing moment in Israel, inside the Garden of Gethsemane. A complete transformation took place there that changed my life forever.

Nothing transforms my life more than the Word of God; they are His holy scriptures that are alive and most powerful to me. The portion I read before I wrote this chapter was not a coincidence. God brought me to the Garden of Gethsemane, where Jesus prayed.

> *"Father, if you are willing, take this cup from me; yet not my will, but yours be done."* (Luke 22:42 NIV)

This scripture became a constant reflection to me during the joint mission of writing *Surrendered: Yielded With Purpose*. Whenever we submit to the Father's will for our lives, He gives us more than we can imagine. God provided me the strength I needed to conquer a battle, just like He provided Jesus the strength He needed before He went to the cross.

> *An angel appeared to him and strengthened him.* (Luke 22:43 NIV)

When Jesus submitted His will to the Father, God provided the strength He needed to go on. It was God's will that Jesus would die to pay the price for my sin. This scripture revealed that what I would do in that sacred garden, far away from my home, would be transformational. What changed my destiny would not be from my own strength, but from God's. What seemed impossible for me became possible because of God. I saw the nature of Jesus come alive in His powerful prayer. Jesus taught me this: if you love your life, you will lose it, but if you care nothing for your life in this world, you will keep it for eternity. I did not want to lose my life or lifestyle back then, but I was headed down a road where it could have certainly happened.

My Surrender

In the winter of 2009, I went on a trip to Israel. There, I was accompanied by my fiancé, my daughter and son-in-law, and an exceedingly small group of about thirty people from a church I attended. That trip changed my life forever. It was the last night of the trip when I was sitting in the Garden of Gethsemane on a bench in a circle with thirty other people. A message was spoken by one of the pastors on that trip. When it concluded, we prepared our hearts to take communion. It was so quiet and serene that night. Was my life ready for what was about to happen? No, not at all. I knew I could not take the holy sacrament at that time. I could, and no one else would know the wiser, but inside I knew my life was riddled with sin. But if I did not take from the plate as it came by me, others would wonder why I was abstaining. The peaceful quietness of the evening disappeared in that moment. I became restless in my mind.

I wanted to take communion, but I had not confessed my sin. Repentance to God would mean turning 100% from my sin—a heart-motivated change followed by action. Action which, up until then, I had not taken. God knew my heart at that moment. If I said I was sorry, would I only be pretending so as not to look bad in front of the others?

I had just been through nine days of profound messages spoken by pastors at various sites through the Israel journey, and the convicting moments of what I heard were now setting in on my life. Although it was my second trip to Israel, this one was different. On my first trip to Israel, I was there to dedicate an underground playground in honor of my Jewish fiancé, who paid an exorbitant amount of money to have it built near the Gaza Strip. It was specifically built in that location to protect the children and give them a safe place to play from the constant bombings. Because we were amongst Christian friends on our current trip, I felt God would use this occasion to claim the heart of the man who was my fiancé as he found Jesus as his Savior. That was my true intention in asking him if we could take this trip. Back home, I had family praying for his salvation. I felt Mort's acceptance of Jesus would change my life. Instead, my heart was pierced and convicted on that trip. And my heart changed forever.

I had asked my fiancé if we could attend this historical Christian pilgrimage offered to only thirty people. He knew I never asked him for anything, and this opportunity was a noticeably big deal to me. He agreed we could go. He made provisions for the trip but also added another leg to the itinerary. We would leave from Israel and pick up a yacht to head to the French West

Indies and enjoy more of a luxurious time away. He felt this Israel trip would be rather boring for him, so he added on a better conclusion.

This man, Mort, was my fiancé, and we were living a life of extreme. He gave me total worldly abundance, but in grasping it, I was not honoring God. I was divorced and now engaged to Mort and living with him. My life lacked nothing during our relationship due to his extreme wealth. He had everything the world could offer, but he did not have Jesus. He shared the world's treasures with me, my family, and my friends. He held nothing back from any of us. Mort was extremely generous, but with his generosity came a high price tag: ME. He did it all to keep me captivated in a lifestyle I would never desire to leave. In the world's eyes, I had it all. I was a global traveler on private jets, first-class trains, yachts, and submarines. I had the "most of" and "best of" what money could buy and lived in the lap of luxury with jewels, exotic cars, mansion homes, and prestige. I wore a 7-carat diamond engagement ring showing I belonged to someone, but I did not belong to the One who genuinely loved me. Someone else owned my life. The more I was given, the emptier my life became. I watched my life slip away as I compromised everything I had, even my Christianity.

Attending the Israel trip was truly a miracle for me because it was a Christian-based trip. It was the first time in my seven-year relationship with this man that I would make such a request and have it granted. To take a trip like this was not our "norm." It meant Mort would have to become a common person. Life was all about fulfilling his wants, and I simply fit his needs.

God was going to do something on this trip; I just knew it. I felt that my fiancé, who was Jewish, might accept Jesus, so I prayed hard. Mort had denied Christ's deity, and his agreeing to go on this Christian trip led me to believe God was showing favor on me. I believed Mort would finally accept who Jesus really is, and when he did, it would make everything "right" in my life. Mort's acceptance of Jesus as his Messiah was my answer to happily ever after. I relied on this trip and other people to reach his heart since I had lost my voice to speak up for what I believed in. I grew silent in a world of opulence and over-abundance. Getting my needs satisfied made my identity vanish. But now, there was hope because Mort was willing to take this "Christian Historical Tour." Others could be the influence to bring on his belief.

Then, on the very last night of this 10-day experience, something powerful took place. In seven years of having a relationship and being engaged to this man, the purpose of this trip came down to one pivotal moment. But the purpose was for me, not him. The importance of the will of God and the will of God for my life was upon me. Until now, God was in my quiet life but was not a detailed part of my life. And I had accepted that God was nowhere to be found in this relationship.

People may ask God, "Where are You in my life? What is Your will for my life? What is Your purpose for my life?" I asked those very questions and did not know the answers.

Even though I had everything, I wondered if I was supposed to unlock a specific code to find out what God wanted for my life. This trip brought the answer. I began to understand that the will of God does not have to do with what I possess and where I am in life but with who I am, whose I am, and who I am becoming.

The apostle Paul instructed the church in Thessalonica when they wanted to know God's will for their lives.

> *For you already know the instructions we've shared with you through the Lord Jesus. God's will is for you to be set apart for him in holiness and that you keep yourselves unpolluted from sexual defilement. Yes, each of you must guard your sexual purity with holiness and dignity.* (1 Thessalonians 4:2-5 TPT)

God's will for me is to be sanctified, and I was not! What does it mean to be sanctified? To be transformed into His likeness. But how would I do that living the way I was? How could I expect God to change someone else when I was the one who needed to change?

I felt flutters of fear swarming around me as I heard the messages of Jesus spoken throughout that week. Anxiety rose within because I was out of alignment with God, and I felt it. I needed to confess my sin and surrender my life to God. And there I was in the Garden of Gethsemane, experiencing a defining moment in my life as communion began to take place.

Looking back, it is interesting that as we all sat down on the last night of the trip together, my fiancé received a phone call from the United States. He hadn't missed a single pastoral message up to that point. But because of the urgent phone call, he chose to step away from the circle, leaving me alone for the duration of the message. Alone with God, I no longer wondered how Mort would process the message as he was not there. Initially, I was disappointed he left, but God was working. God was in control. God would not be speaking to my fiancé's heart that night. Instead, He spoke directly to mine. My transformation had begun.

There will be times in our flesh when we will not want to face things, and this was one of those times. I wanted someone else's heart to change, but mine needed to change.

God was revealing that the key to discovering His will for my life was willful surrender. A battle began raging in those last moments before we were to fly off to our next adventure. After hearing that penetrating sermon, it seemed I silently sat in that garden forever, listening to God speak to my heart. I faced taking communion, but I knew that first, I needed to have a conversation with God about the condition of my heart.

Then God spoke into my heart in the quietness of that moment. "Do you love me? Do you trust me? If you do, then walk away from this lifestyle and who you are living with and repent."

Would I repent? An inner struggle raged.

My fiancé was so giving to me. I never asked for anything, and he gave me everything, but I was a kept person. I was provided for in every worldly way! I struggled to let it go. Deep inside, I knew Mort did not have intentions to marry me. The seven-carat diamond I wore had only been a facade to keep me content, and I wrestled with facing that as fact. Would I lose it all if I decided to surrender my heart?

I needed to make a willful choice. Would I surrender everything to Jesus before taking communion? Could I confess my sin—my life of living with someone unmarried and being unequally yoked? Was I allowing myself to be used to provide extravagant things for my children, my family, and my friends? Did I sacrifice myself to someone other than God? Could I turn completely away to a newness of life with Christ and become dependent on Him? Could I let go of my old life and never look back? How could I do this? How would I do this?

Simply put, I did it!

I surrendered everything to Jesus that night before I took communion. I prayed, "God, if there could be any other way, please let it be. I am so afraid, God, I will have nothing, nowhere to go, but I am going to trust You, not knowing what is ahead. It is not my will God, but Your will be done." I prayed this with all my heart, knowing what I was about to do was NOT going to be easy. Surrendering all of me to Jesus would be my deliberate choice.

I took communion, and God heard my heart. I asked Him to forgive me for all I was doing and how I was living. I had once called myself a Christian yet now compromised everything that word meant. I was not an example to anyone of the God I claimed to love and follow. I accepted living with a man I was not married to for the riches of this world.

God provided the strength I needed to walk away from a life that gave me everything. He led me into a life of blind faith, serving Him. I did not know what my new life would look like, but I would not look back, which meant trusting Him completely. Right there in the Garden of Gethsemane, where Jesus prayed, "Not My will but Thine be done," I fully surrendered.

In that moment, an angel from heaven strengthened me just as God strengthened Jesus. My life changed forever as I bowed before God in humility. In lowliness, I confessed before God everything I knew. In complete surrender, I consecrated myself to Him in trust. In repentance, I gave God all my sin, flesh, and partnership with worldliness that hindered my relationship with Him.

Was it easy? NO. Did it mean acting on my faith? YES.

Surrendering something your flesh loves and craves can be the trickiest thing you may ever do. For me, the luxuries of the world had a grip on me. I knew I would have to stand my ground, especially when others would oppose me and call me crazy for giving it up. But I knew I needed to be stripped of the residue, and God gave me the strength to endure it. My surrender meant that my life would change drastically, but the lives of others would also change.

Surrender will not only affect your life, but it may also affect the lives of others. We must trust God when this happens. The decision to submit to God means trusting He will work it all out.

> *And we know that God causes everything to work together for the good of those who love God and are called according to his purpose for them.* (Romans 8:28 NLT)

I did not know it back then in the Garden, but God was calling me to do something great. My obedient choice in that transformational moment before communion would affect my eternity and my whole future to serve God. Looking back, I shudder to think where my life would be right now if I had chosen differently. I cannot even go there. There is one thing I think of often. If I chose to ignore God's conviction in my spirit that night, would Women World Leaders be here today? But God knew all along what my choice would be.

I would love to share this takeaway with you. When God is pressing on you to surrender something you cannot let go of, even if it means fearing your uncertain future, please turn yourself in! Surrender your heart! Remember Jesus said, "Not my will but YOUR'S be done." Surrendering to God brings no end to what God can do for you in the form of blessing.

God took over for me that day. And He worked in me every hour of every day that followed. He never let go. He knew my heart was fully yielded to Him. I was committed. I told the pastor and others who supported me of my decision for accountability reasons. They watched me leave it all and empowered me to run after God. My body, which is God's temple, is just like King Solomon's temple. It is surrendered to God, fully dedicated for His service, and God resides inside. I exited the ungodly relationship, separated myself, and drew close to God.

If you believe in Jesus Christ as your Savior, submitting your body to Christ in absolute surrender opens your heart to allow God to dwell inside your temple. God then begins to work through His miraculous power inside you. The Holy Spirit claims you in your submission of your "yes" to Him. When yielded, your heart surrender and walk of obedience allow God to work His blessings in your life.

God accomplishes our surrender.

All my searching, longing, and hungering for what I was missing in a worldly relationship (despite that the outside world thought I had it all) came down to one defining circumstance: the possession of my heart. Now I can fully profess that God has it, and I am free. Does He have yours?

God works in the secret places of your heart. He urges you by the hidden power of the Holy Spirit. Yield to Him with purpose. Give God all your imperfections, your impurities, and your doubts; release them all. They will disappear as God takes possession inside you and you trust in Him.

You may not realize that God has already begun the work of surrender in your life. You are reading this book for a reason.

Being confident of this, that he who began a good work in you will carry it on to completion until the day of Christ Jesus. (Philippians 1:6 NIV)

Saying "I surrender" to God means something; it is what He is listening for, expecting, and what He died for. He wants us to surrender our will to Him completely. So please, do not block the blessings that may come by holding on to that one "tiny" thing you think is okay. There may be something you have not yet yielded, but you will never know the full blessings of God that await you on the other side of surrender unless you commit to yield to Him.

When you fully surrender your life, your heart, and your will to God, life at its best begins. Trust Him with your yes and give Him your all. Your purpose begins when you surrender.

Surrendering Your Addictions

By Kimberly Ann Hobbs

Addictions can enslave and harm us but thank God that He gives you the power to overcome any addiction. It takes hard work, but the Bible tells us:

> *I can do everything through Christ who gives me strength.* (Philippians 4:13 NLT)

God uses the word "everything" here to make it known to us that He includes "all things." This includes all your bad habits, labels that others put upon you, and all you have settled into believing about yourself. God says, "all things."

Addictions are a bondage of the heart and body that produces immediate pleasure or relief. At one time in my life, I had an addiction so strong I knew in my heart it would mean destruction to everyone around me, including myself if I did not break that habit or the need I so desperately depended on. I craved it. I looked for the sexual relationships of men to fill a need of loneliness that only God could fill. I became addicted to the lust and desire that rose from the pits of hell to satisfy my need to never be by myself. Unfortunately, I was lying to myself that I "needed" someone to be with, therefore suppressing the truth that all I needed was God. By suppressing truth, we disconnect from God and turn to the temporal fix.

When we become enslaved to something, we are addicted. We exchange the good God intends for us for unholy and self-ruling choices. The created thing that enslaves us, in turn, allows us to become cold to God.

How did I personally conquer this? I surrendered my addiction and invited the stronger power to rule over my life. God and God alone became my dependency.

I prayed daily because, in my own power, I could master nothing. I pursued Christ with all my heart. I cried to Him and acted. I surrendered and confessed my addictive thoughts as sin each time they entered my mind. I repented, which meant I turned 100% away from my addiction and addictive thoughts. You cannot go halfway—you need to totally eradicate an addiction. Get rid of it. STOP IT. Just that simple - S T O P. Your mind is a very powerful thing, and by renewing your mind in Christ Jesus every day, you can do all things through Jesus Christ, who gives you the strength.

God has given you everything you need to live a godly life. His divine power within you calls us His own. Surround yourselves with believers that can help you be accountable and free.

> *"For where two or three gather in my name, there am I with them."*
> (Matthew 18:20 NIV)

You can be victorious over any addiction. Remember Philippians 4:13 says, "all things" but it's not you-yourself, it's God who gives you the strength as you surrender to Him.

. . . .

Julie T. Jenkins

 Julie T. Jenkins is the co-CEO of Women World Leaders and World Publishing and Productions. She loves giving her time and talents to our Lord. Julie is partnered with Kimberly Hobbs to oversee WWL. She guides the ministry coordinators, writes for and leads the editing team of *Voice of Truth* magazine, and hosts "Walking in the Word" – the weekly biblical teaching episode of the *Women World Leaders' Podcast*. Additionally, she is a Bible teacher and best-selling author. Through WPP, Julie is honored to serve as a writing coach and editor for those called to share their God-story with the world.

Born in Indiana and raised in Ohio, Julie earned her Bachelor of Communications at The University of Tulsa and her Master's of Biblical Exposition from Moody Bible College. She traveled with *Up With People,* was a long-time *Bible Study Fellowship* leader, and has completed multiple biblical and leadership training programs.

Julie and her husband, Michael, have been married for 26 years, live in Jupiter, Florida, and own and operate *J29 Marketing* – a full-service digital marketing company. They have three children, of whom they are immensely proud.

Julie can be contacted at julie@womenworldleaders.com or julie@worldpublishingandproductions.com

Surrendering to Alzheimer's; Trusting Love

By Julie T. Jenkins

Linda Worland.

That name might not mean anything to you, but to me, it means love. And I know it does to God, too.

Linda is my mom. She was born Linda Ruth Burks, the daughter of Bob and Molly Burks, on December 31, 1940. As the oldest of five children, it was her lock of hair that her father carried with him when he served in World War II. From the beginning, her very existence was a source of love and inspiration.

Molly, my grandmother, was a practical woman who was always busy doing what needed to be done. Bob was a good provider and a soft, gentle man who spent hours in his home art studio—painting, making stained glass, and working with metal. My mom picked up attributes from both of these amazing individuals—she did what needed to be done with a gentle, nurturing side and a flair for art.

Both Bob and Molly were sold out to God, raising my mom in a loving, Christian home. As the oldest of five siblings, Linda was often held responsible for walking the younger children to school and keeping them in line. She loved reading, and from a young age, her favorite book was *Little Men* by Louisa May Alcott. Longing to be like Jo, the main character, she dreamed of one day being the mother of twelve sons.

After high school, where she spent hours following in her dad's footsteps creating art, Linda went to nursing school. Along the way, she met my dad, Don Worland, who happened to be from the "wrong" side of town. His story of growing up was not quite so storybook, but my mom saw his heart and understood that he was a good man. They fell in love, and she chose to marry him instead of finishing school and becoming a nurse. She never swayed from wanting those twelve boys, which made my dad throw his head back and laugh.

Don and Linda built a life together that was admired by many. Their first three children were daughters. Linda used her artistic skills to sew them beautiful clothes. Don was a good provider and clung to God as he strived to learn to become a good dad and husband. They named their oldest daughter Mary, and when they finally had their first son (on the fourth try!), they named him Joseph. Three more children followed, for a total of seven, of which I am the youngest—with only two boys in the mix.

My mom was an all-in kind of mom. She used her artistic bent to decorate the house to the hilt for each holiday, teach crafts at the elementary school, make hundreds of costumes for grade school and high school musicals, and create fantastic prom dresses—and later wedding dresses—for each of her five daughters. She made banners for church, religious stoles for my dad (who became a deacon), and designed and sewed a special heirloom quilt for each of her children when they went away to college.

My mom cooked every meal and changed every diaper, as my dad was of the generation who thought the "woman of the house" took care of all that.

She magically stretched a small food budget into plenty of good, healthy meals, with enough treats on the side to delight us. Each year, she planned, packed for, and cleaned up after a two-week summer camping trip. For Dad and us, those two weeks were a vacation, but I have no doubt that, for Mom, the work went on—and was even more challenging—as she cared for eight others away from home. And yes, I count my dad in the eight!

My parents were a blessing to so many in our church and community. They led pre-marriage retreats out of our home several times a year. As kids, we had to stay out of sight, but I often hid on the stairs and soaked in the teaching. Their marriage was far from perfect, which taught me even more. I learned that a relationship could be imperfect and still be used to glorify God.

Mom taught me the important things in life.

She taught me that my presence was meaningful to her. She would get so tired at the end of the day and often head to bed before my bedtime. As she lay in bed reading, I would sit in her doorway, just to be near her. That made her smile.

She taught me that I was worth listening to. And oh, I asked endless questions! When I wondered out loud if a baby who was being aborted could feel the pain inflicted on him, she assured me he could. When I told her I had a tough day at school with a teacher I didn't like, she helped me realize that if I contemplated even a bad situation, I could learn from it.

She taught me about loving others. Among her few loved possessions was a beautiful crystal bowl. One day, someone visiting was helping her wash the dishes when the crystal bowl dropped to the floor, shattering. The visitor was humiliated. Mom brushed it off, assuring the woman that the bowl was just a thing—not important at all. Sparing the woman's feelings was more critical to my mom than the crystal bowl she had cherished just moments before.

She taught me balance. My second oldest sister had many health challenges and was often hospitalized. But somehow, although the hospital was over an hour from our home, my mom never missed any of her kids' important events.

And she showed me her love for God. She wore a necklace inscribed with "70 x 7." When I asked, she explained it reminded her to forgive others, like God had forgiven her. (Matthew 18:22) We never missed a Sunday at church. And she reverently recognized the importance of Good Friday, insisting all seven children stay quiet from noon until three while she attended service. Of course, we were invited to go with her, and with my dad serving on the altar, I often worshipped beside her, remembering Jesus' death. I will never forget those times that shaped my faith and who I was becoming.

> *Care for the flock that God has entrusted to you. Watch over it willingly, not grudgingly—not for what you will get out of it, but because you are eager to serve God. Don't lord it over the people assigned to your care, but lead them by your own good example. And when the Great Shepherd appears, you will receive a crown of never-ending glory and honor.* (1 Peter 5:2-4 NLT)

So much more can be said about my mom's role in my life as I entered my adult years. She and my dad both walked me down the aisle at my wedding, and she was there to support me when I brought home each of my three newborns. Every time we moved, she was the first to help pack the boxes and load the truck. And she gave the best hugs!

In 2006, my dad was diagnosed with a glioblastoma – an inoperable and treatment-resistant brain tumor. He died within five months of his diagnosis, causing my mom severe emotional distress, as you can imagine. The results of her heartache began to highlight that all was not okay in her brain. Her emerging illness was a slow fade but was very apparent to each of us; her seven children.

My dad had spent his last lucid months setting things up financially for my mom and ensuring every part of the house was in working order. So surprisingly, just months after his passing, God sent my mom the beautiful gift of a new husband. Ken stepped in and loved and cared for Mom in a way that awed us all. We called him her angel.

They grew their life together, traveling and enjoying the spoils of retirement. However, each time I saw Mom, I would notice her mannerisms slipping into unfamiliar territory. It was disconcerting, but it was something I had to surrender. Ken was now her partner in all ways, including, quite appropriately, as her healthcare surrogate. I cannot stress how much he loved her and carefully provided for her. Still, as her daughter, it was difficult to see years of her established personality morph into something unfamiliar.

One Christmas, I arrived at her home with my traditional Christmas fudge in hand—she was thrilled as she loved my fudge. Later, when I was putting together a cookie tray, I nonchalantly said, "I'm going to put some fudge on this tray."

She looked at me and got so angry as she began explaining through frustrated tears that she hadn't made fudge. I said, "No, it's okay. I brought fudge."

She replied, "Well, how was I supposed to know that? You could have told me."

On a later visit, she got super-stressed about my husband, me, and our children staying with her. She would never have told us she was stressed; she was so kind. But she must have taken me to the linen closet a half dozen times to show me where the towels were—she wanted everything to be perfect and was preparing over and over again for our visit—unable to sit and relax and enjoy the company. I knew as I left her house that we would not be able to spend more than an afternoon there again. It was just too much for her.

I was losing my mom to Alzheimer's, and I had no choice but to surrender.

Eventually, Mom and Ken moved to an assisted living community about three hours north of us. They lived in a little cottage in "independent living" and enjoyed dining at the restaurants in the community and being leaders for outings to cultural events in the area. Ken worked at Disney a couple of days a week, and Mom worked at the gift store in their community. She worked with a lady, also named Linda, whose mind was as sharp as a tack but whose body was no longer physically adept. They often joked that my mom, with her strong body, and the "other Linda," with her strong mind, made a whole.

Ken and Mom also regularly visited the memory care unit, sharing communion with the residents. Their community is designed with different areas so residents can move within the facility as they age and need additional care. The memory care unit is a locked and enclosed facility for those with advanced memory issues who need full-time medical care. Visiting and serving the residents in the memory care unit was Ken's purposeful plan. He wanted my mom to be comfortable with the staff and layout of the facility, knowing that it would likely be her future home.

I regularly drove the three hours north to see Mom and Ken, but our visits got shorter and shorter as her illness worsened. At times she was an amazing hostess, wanting to know my name, where I was from, and if I had a family. Her gracious personality shined through her foggy memory as she repeatedly offered me coffee and granola bars—her favorite snack—not remembering that we had just eaten together at a restaurant. As she got tired, though, she became increasingly annoyed and agitated, and I knew it was time to leave and drive the three hours home.

For a while, my husband and I were intent on making sure Ken took regular breaks from being a full-time caregiver. My husband would take Ken golfing while Mom, the kids, and I would hang out, go shopping, or get our nails done. But more frequently, these outings ended with her in tears of frustration. Her "Kenny" had become the only person she was familiar with and trusted. And without being able to remember from one minute to the next where he was, she was left feeling abandoned and frightened whenever he was not with her.

At this point, I began replaying the mantra "safe and happy" in my mind. It's hard when your own mom doesn't recognize you and even harder when it is clear that your very presence agitates her. I increasingly had to surrender my needs and desires and focus on her well-being.

> Since God chose you to be the holy people he loves, you must clothe yourselves with tenderhearted mercy, kindness, humility, gentleness, and patience. (Colossians 3:12 NLT)

While my goal for Mom was to be as safe and happy as possible, her husband, Ken, worked diligently and lovingly to keep her active. Some days they would go to the grocery store, where he would have her walk all the aisles, telling her that he was looking for a specific product. Often they would take short trips so they could walk in different surroundings—their favorite destination by far was Disney World. Mom loved just walking—that is certainly a love I inherited from her! So it was devastating when her hip became so sore that it was difficult for her to walk and the doctor suggested she have a hip replacement.

They went ahead with the surgery, hoping to keep her physical quality of life intact, but there were complications. She had side effects from the anesthesia and trauma that made her enter an almost psychotic state, fearing that people were out to get her. The recovery period was also difficult. She couldn't understand simple instructions like walking with a walker or laying a specific way to avoid putting pressure on her healing hip. My brothers and sisters and I took turns staying with them in their small cottage, which was grueling and certainly irritated her, but was necessary for her and Ken's well-being. It can be difficult to persevere and surrender our own sense of joy as we strive to help others.

As the years went by, Mom's memory continued to get worse, and Ken learned to keep her on a strict schedule. He wisely kept track of when she was tired or hungry, knowing those conditions would add to her confusion. Steadily though, her days of happy confusion morphed into days of frustrated anger.

In January 2020, Ken and Mom spent a few days at a Disney hotel. While Ken was resting, Mom left the room. The Disney staff was wonderful in helping track her down, and thankfully, she was unharmed. They returned home the next day, but she continued to "wander," leaving the house regularly. Ken called me and asked me to come to help him—something he had never done before. I stayed for several nights, and in that time, we went through idea after idea, trying to quell the situation. The doctor prescribed different medications, but those were not immediately helpful. We put an alarm on the door, but that didn't stop her from walking out or aid in her return. The fact that she was in danger each time she left the house was scary, but the reason for her wandering was heartbreaking.

Each time, she explained she was looking for her mom. She was trying to find her way back to her childhood home.

I told her I had spoken to her mother and everything was fine. She looked at me in disbelief and asked how I knew Molly. Then I would give her a made-up story, using details about my grandmother that no stranger would know. Eventually, after returning to her home and sitting for a moment, the same ordeal would begin again.

I lay on the couch at night, just steps from the bedroom. For short periods there would be peace in the small cottage. But then my mom would awaken, angry and scared, and often yelling about "who the man was in her bed."

After a few days, Ken and I knew. My mom's condition had advanced to the point where she could no longer live at home.

> We are pressed on every side by troubles, but we are not crushed. We are perplexed, but not driven to despair. We are hunted down, but never abandoned by God. We get knocked down, but we are not destroyed. (2 Corinthians 4:8-9 NLT)

This was a devastating time, but God clearly went before us. We took Mom to her next scheduled appointment. The doctor, without hesitation, prescribed that she be moved immediately to a memory care facility. And there was a spot available in the facility where Mom and Ken had spent years serving. The next days were a whirlwind as we met with doctors and administrators. It was a beautiful facility with many daily activities and a caring staff who all knew her and had watched her disease progress. The love was palpable. And yet, our held-back tears and distress were agonizing.

As we left her in her new home, my mind went back to when I was little—the nights when my mom was so tired, but I wasn't ready to leave her for the day. She lay in bed while I sat in the doorway, waiting for her to fall asleep. But this time, she looked at me forlornly, trying to follow as I walked out the door that locked behind me.

She was safe. But would she be happy?

Nearly three years have passed since that day. COVID lockdown was excruciating as no one was allowed in or out of the facility—something we couldn't have imagined in our wildest dreams. For a while, I attempted calling her regularly, but she didn't know who I was, nor could she understand the concept of the telephone. Eventually, I realized the calls, what the world told me a "good daughter" should do, were causing more angst than joy on both sides. Later, the facility offered 15-minute "window visits." She would sit on one side of the window, and her visitors would sit on the other, connected by telephone. These, however, were impossible, too, as she would get angry that she couldn't come outside and then walk away exasperated.

She was not eating well, so they eventually allowed Ken to come in daily for lunch as an "essential caregiver." Since they offered him that option, he has rarely missed a day. He always arrives with a smile on his face, ready to help her eat. She no longer knows who he is, but she knows she likes him.

The facility has since re-opened for visits. For a period, Mom's face would light up when I walked in. Somehow she thought I was her childhood friend, Joyce. I played the part. It made her smile.

At this point, she is peaceful. Her medication keeps her calm, and she can safely wander about the facility as she likes. It is a bit of a joke because the nurses never know what bed Linda will end up in! I think of her as Goldilocks—always looking for the safe, comfortable spot.

Losing a loved one to Alzheimer's means grieving them over and over again. It means surrendering to a situation we cannot, on this side of heaven, understand.

Throughout this ordeal, one of the most impactful things someone told me was that she was praying that my mom was spending each day in the heavenlies. Isn't that beautiful? So now I choose to believe my mom has one foot on earth and one foot in heaven. I believe that when she was searching for her mom, it was because she had recently seen her. And I believe Mom thought I was her friend Joyce because they had, in fact, spent time together.

We serve a good God who loves us more than we can possibly imagine. Because of that, I know there are blessings in Alzheimer's hidden under the horrors so visible to our worldly eyes. Through my pain, God graciously gives me glimpses of His provision. For example, I see peace emanating from my mom at this point. Deservedly, after years of caring for seven children and being the family matriarch even through her husband's death, she now floats peacefully through her days without a care. And recently, when one of my sisters passed away after a long illness, I was struck by the thought that our loving God spared my mom the pain of losing her daughter. In fact, I believe that my mom now visits with my sister regularly.

Still, continually surrendering my mom to her "safe and happy" place is a battle I've fought daily for years now. And sometimes, resting in God's love, care, and provision seems like a cop-out, a poor excuse for doing little. It is in our nature to want to DO things for the ones we love. And I'm my grandmother's and mother's daughter, so doing is in my DNA! I yearn to care for my mom and make her smile and laugh, but my job now is to surrender her to God and fully trust His care. And though I don't understand, I know I can walk by faith, trusting Him who loves my mom even more than I do!

> *We have come into an intimate experience with God's love, and we trust in the love he has for us. God is love! Those who are living in love are living in God, and God lives through them. By living in God, love has been brought to its full expression in us.* (1 John 4:16-17 TPT)

Surrender Your Emotions

By Julie T. Jenkins

"Handle with care."

Have you ever received a gift stamped with the instruction, "Handle with care"? If you have, you may have experienced thrill and excitement as you wondered what was inside, but perhaps you also felt a bit of uneasy trepidation not knowing exactly *how* to handle the contents. Could the wrong action cause the gift inside to break? Or, in the wrong conditions, could the gift become dangerous?

Emotions are a gift from God we are to handle with care. When treated thoughtlessly, our emotions can break us or become dangerous. But when we handle them carefully and surrender them back to God, He will use them for His glory and honor and our growth.

Exodus 34:6-7 is God's proclamation of Himself as he passed before Moses. *"The Lord, the Lord, the compassionate and gracious God, slow to anger, abounding in love and faithfulness, maintaining love to thousands, and forgiving wickedness, rebellion and sin."* (NIV)

In this verse, we see that our God is FULL of emotions, including compassion, anger, and love. Additionally, the Bible reveals that God experiences satisfaction (Genesis 1:31), delight (Deuteronomy 30:9), joy (Zephaniah 3:17), hate (Proverbs 6:16), jealousy (Joshua 24:19), and grief (Genesis 6:6). And who can forget the sadness Jesus felt as He comforted Mary and Martha upon the death of their brother Lazarus (John 11:35)?

There is no doubt that God is emotional. And being made in His image, emotions and all, is His gift to us.

It can be easy to understand why God would give us the emotions of joy, peace, and love. Those are the "good" emotions, right? We can easily appreciate a gift that makes us feel good! But what about those more "challenging" gifts that make us struggle? How can anger, frustration, grief, and sadness be considered gifts from a God who loves us?

The simple answer is that each emotion, when handled with care, can lead us closer to God and allow us to showcase His glory. But when we react to our feelings rather than surrender them, we can easily fall away from God and obscure His glory from those around us.

Let's look at anger, for instance. In Matthew 21, we witness Jesus enter the temple, where the atmosphere had changed from one of worship to corruptive commerce wrought with greed. Jesus emotionally reclaimed God's rightful place in the temple, making way for the return of a worshipful environment. And yet, in other instances, even despite being beaten and betrayed, Jesus reacted peacefully and calmly, seemingly turning away from His human emotions.

By carefully surrendering His emotions to God in each situation, Jesus was able to yield to God's desires rather than His own flesh. And though the response was very different in each circumstance, both resulted in glorifying God.

So, when our emotions are threatening to drive us out of control, how do we surrender them to God?

The first step is to recognize how we feel. We are made in God's image, and our emotions are part of that image. And yet we will be better equipped to address our emotions when we first process them.

The second step is to speak to God about how we are feeling. God wants you to come to Him when you are excited, anxious, scared, angry, joyful, or sad. He recognizes that we need Him, and He is our ever-present help.

> *When he saw the crowds, he had compassion on them, because they were harassed and helpless, like sheep without a shepherd.* (Matthew 9:36 NIV)

The third step is to ask God for His wisdom. The Holy Spirit is always with us, guiding us and leading us. Yes, even when it comes to handling our emotions!

> *For the Lord gives wisdom; from his mouth come knowledge and understanding.* (Proverbs 2:6 NIV)

Once you quiet yourself, process your feelings and share them with God, and ask Him for His wisdom and guidance, there is still one more step.

Surrender in obedience.

This can be the most difficult part of the process. We may need to power through this step again and again—denying our own self as we rely on the Holy Spirit's power. Sometimes, we are to harness our emotions and use them to take action. But sometimes God asks us to turn away from our emotions and trust His handling of the situation as we allow His glory to shine through us. Whichever way God leads, as we follow His will, we will be transformed to reflect His image more clearly and develop a closer walk with Him as we rely on His power and strength.

We, as Christians, have the opportunity to show others God's heart. But to do that, we must surrender our feelings to God and allow Him to align our hearts with His. When we put our spirit in tandem with God's Spirit and surrender our emotions to Him, we create an atmosphere for God's will to be done on earth. And isn't that our great prayer?

> *Our Father in heaven...your kingdom come, your will be done, on earth as it is in heaven.* (Matthew 6:9-10 NIV)

Let's commit to surrendering to God's will as we handle our emotions with care.

. . . .

Raven Judkins

Raven Judkins graduated from Liberty University in 2020, dually endorsed in Elementary Education and Special Education. She is currently a Special Education High School Teacher in Virginia.

Raven also serves at her church, leading high school girls, and is extremely passionate about leading and teaching women of all ages about the Word of God and how to experience intimacy with Christ. She loves to travel and looks forward to pursuing ministry opportunities that will allow her to travel and speak at different churches in the future.

Her favorite Bible verse is Isaiah 43:18-19 which has become an anchor and reminder that God is always doing something new in and through us and that the best is yet to come.

If you enjoy this chapter and are desiring to learn more about how to live out being single and surrendered, check out her upcoming book, *Single Isn't A Bad Word*. Raven will take you on a deeper dive into the gift of singleness and how to experience contentment, enjoyment, and fullness in your season.

Single and Surrendered

By Raven Judkins

When I was a little girl, I just assumed that marriage was a given; that one day, I would innately meet the man of my dreams, we would get married, bring some beautiful babies into the world, and then live this incredibly happy and fun life. But then adulthood came and continued, and I still had no husband. As the years went on, I looked for excuses as to why I was not in a relationship—I was too young, still dealing with my trauma, I wasn't ready, or there weren't any guys I could even remotely see myself with. Eventually, I ran out of reasons and thought my only option was to "come to terms" with being single.

In this coming-to-terms phase, I conditioned myself to think and convince others of my contentment and security with being single. I often said things like, "I am a strong, independent woman," and that would typically shove enough *wow* in someone else's face to cause any conversation about my singleness to end abruptly.

But in complete and brutal honesty, I was trying to come up with anything that would speak louder than my very real fears and insecurities. In those temporary moments, you could say that using those strong words worked, but masking my present insecurities with petty phrases was not sustainable— or even reasonable. And thus, I continued to battle with whether or not it was possible to actually be content and confident as a single woman who single-handedly desired to be married.

I graduated from college when the world was fresh into a global pandemic. This time was difficult for many people for many different reasons, but one of the hardest things I faced was *my reality*. Although I had graduated, making it, in my mind, the opportune time to get married, I had zero prospects. And because of the pandemic, I couldn't even go anywhere in order to meet someone.

Fast forward a couple of months, the world began to slowly open up again. I thought for sure this was my chance. But then entered what I call "The Curse of the Wedding Band." Everywhere I went, all I could see was wedding band after wedding band. I mean, I went to every place humanly possible— the gym, church (including multiple different campuses), my small group, Target, coffee shops, out to lunch or dinner with friends, *everywhere*. And seemingly every guy I found myself attracted to or enjoying the company of already had a ring finger that was occupied. It was so difficult to constantly be in places where I felt like I was the only person who didn't get picked for a team.

Now I know God is good and His timing is perfect and all that jazz, but MAN! Can a single girl catch a break and not be constantly reminded that there are approximately a *ton* of married people, and I am not one of them?!

Through the frustration, I realized that my outlook on singleness needed a new foundation. I could no longer look at my singleness as a trade-in for anything I had done or a result of the person I was. What I mean is that I had to let go of this idea that being single was due to my past sins or even my personality. I had to sit down with the Lord and let Him pour His truth over my singleness.

Notice that I did not say that I needed to understand my *identity* in my singleness because my identity is consistent with who I am in Christ and not my present or ever-changing relationship status—something I am sure of and grateful for. But in *this* season, I needed to appreciate the value of being single and what it meant for me.

Praise God! When I quieted myself enough to hear to His heart, He revealed *His* truth to me that singleness is a gift. A gift, in the midst of uncertainty; a gift, even when it didn't feel good; a gift specifically for me, sent when I wanted something else; a gift presented personally to me from God Himself. That certainly means something.

Perhaps you can relate to my struggle in this area and have found yourself crying out to God, asking Him to bring you the desires of your heart. If you can, I encourage you to dive into this scandalous awakening with me— often, we are not okay with our singleness because our *focus* is entirely on us. And yet, in every season, God's design is that our focus should not be on ourselves but on His Kingdom.

I love what Proverbs 4:25 says: *Look straight ahead, and fix your eyes on what lies before you.* (NLT) We have to make the bold and sometimes uncomfortable choice to look ahead and fix our eyes on what God has in store, not what we want Him to have in store. His Kingdom is forever, while our desires are for now. So, we must fix our eyes on what we *know* is ahead: the presentation and promotion of the gospel worldwide and God's expectation that we each be a part of that.

I recognize that this could be quite a difficult concept to reflect on, especially if you are in a place of desiring and believing for a relationship that will lead to marriage. But know that no one can help you navigate through this better than God Himself. He may even lead you to sift through the same question as He did for me - *Am I furthering the Kingdom of God more in my singleness right now than I would be in a relationship?*

To get to the bottom of this question, I first had to be brutally honest with myself and surrender fully to God. Most importantly, I needed to be willing to accept and be okay with whatever His most authentic and purest answer was. Navigating to that place took a lot of time in prayer, establishing what

I now have as a solid relationship with Jesus and genuine contentment and joy in my singleness. Prayer is the ultimate game changer in any season of life. The consistent discipline of prayer allows your spirit to align with God's Spirit and learn to embrace, rather than fight, His gifts for you.

I found it was often easy to feel defeated when I didn't know what God was up to. But when I learned to surrender all of my expectations, desired outcomes, and best-laid plans—even in a very slowly-but-surely kind of way—I was then able to rest in the VICTORY He had waiting for me all along. Because even my emotional battles belong to God, and we know He always wins. I had to learn what surrendering truly meant overall in my life and, specifically, in this season.

Surrendering is letting go of what I want so that I can hold onto what God wants for me.

Specifically for me in this season, surrendering means learning to pray *into* all the possibilities and opportunities God has set before me in my singleness, instead of praying my way *out* of my singleness.

There is so much power in the way we view our seasons and circumstances - because *how* we view them will ultimately affect our attitude *as* we go through them. Because of this, I often remind myself, and others I disciple or walk through difficult seasons or circumstances with, how important it is to write things down. As a teacher, this is something I drill into my students' heads as well, because when we write stuff down, we are not only more likely to remember it, but we also have a place to come back to when doubt and fear and compromise come creeping in!

Things I have penned, rather than just thought about, always seem to have had a greater impact on my life. I love that even scripture encourages us to write things down. Habakkuk 2:2 records the Lord's words and encourages us to: *"Write the vision and make it plain on tablets, that he may run who reads it."* (NKJV) Visions the Lord has given me, prayers or praises I have brought before Him, and letters to friends in hopes of reconciling or digging deeper into that friendship are all things that I have physically written down. And I am better for it because I did. So I encourage you to write down whatever you need to surrender before the Lord and keep returning to that. Then watch how the Lord radically transforms your posture.

There are two major realities that I stand by when it comes to surrender and singleness: *miracles happen when we surrender,* and *surrender is the nucleus of contentment.*

Something shifted in the atmosphere of my heart when I surrendered my earthly desires for God's heavenly-timed plans. And this is because part of knowing God's heart is completely surrendering yours to Him. And as I've done this, I've realized that I could never be truly content, come whatever season or situation, without surrendering. Surrender and contentment co-exist; they form this beautiful team that allows us to experience *fullness* in any season, and for me, specifically in my season of singleness.

To dig just a little bit deeper, surrendering looks like laying down my desires before Jesus and trusting that He will be gentle and generous with them. It does *not* and did not mean that my desire for marriage is absent. I have the desire for marriage, sex, and children—a hefty desire—and I do not think it a bad one at that (if anything, it is a God-given one). But how I *handle* my desire shows whether or not I am truly surrendered and presenting myself to God as an approved worker who is not ashamed and rightly handles the Word of God, as 2 Timothy says.

I want to share with you some things I learned along my journey of trying to find out how to surrender what I want for what God wants more.

Five Myths I Had To Surrender in My Singleness

1. There is something wrong with or missing in my relationship with Jesus.

2. I'm not ready for a relationship.

3. I'm not desirable.

4. I am single as a consequence of my past, personality, or weight/body image.

5. God is unaware of or does not care about my desire for marriage and sex.

You may notice that several of these myths could have underlying truths to them. But the reality is that none of these statements are completely accurate or a cause for my singleness. If they were, then my singleness would, in fact, be a matter of contingency and could no longer be considered a gift. So be careful if/when you consider your own "reasons why I am single." Make sure that you are holding them up to the Word of God and not basing it on your ideals or justifications. Make sure you surrender your myths, too.

My heart in writing through my experiences is that any single woman who reads this chapter will understand how to take practical steps to surrender her own desires, plans, ideas, and failed and future relationships to the Lord. I want you to know that nothing is wasted when we surrender our longings to a King who first wants us to long for Him. I want you to fully embrace that surrendering means accepting where God has you, understanding that your current circumstance may be the only position where you can be both relatable and available in order to advance the gospel.

I mentioned above that nothing is wasted when we surrender, and I'd like to add that nothing is worth having without surrender. Because of this, a big prayer of mine that is on repeat is, "Lord, help me be faithful in the now, so I am fit for what's next." This prayer reminds me to cherish what

I have *now* more than striving for what I want *next*. Because although God has a great future for me, I can trust He also has a great present for me. So let me ask you, don't you think you need to first be a good steward of what God has given you right now before you are ready to receive what He has for you next?

Surrender isn't weakness—it's obedience, and obedience takes an incredible amount of strength. So, sweet Jesus, I choose to surrender. I choose surrender over sadness and anger. I resign my ideals of how it should all work out. I transfer my rights of trying to hold on so tightly to what I want with my timeline. I relinquish control of my future plans and desires over to you. I wave my white flag and choose to stop fighting these plans you have tailored uniquely for me.

I was at dinner one night with a friend who asked me, "How are you so okay with being single?"

While I absolutely loved that question (because it gave me an opportunity to talk about something I am extremely passionate about!), I also recognized that my window of opportunity to share without "over-Christianizing" was very small. So I am going to tell you the same thing I told her—

"I want first to clarify that I have a strong desire for companionship and to be married. But to answer your question – I trust that God wants more for me than I want for me. So if I am single, there's a reason for it. I know God wants to do incredible things in, for, and through me during this time. He wants to develop something in me that perhaps He could not if I was preoccupied with a romantic relationship. And even if all that is squabble, I lean on the Word of God, which says that singleness is a gift."

Let me tell you, it isn't easy, and it certainly isn't a one-and-done type of thing where I woke up one day and decided to surrender my desires and just *be content*. This place I am at and my posture towards singleness are ONLY because of my developed relationship with Jesus. Other relationships can certainly be additions, but there's no substitute for intimacy with Him, and that's the kicker, my friend.

But the question that the Lord stirred in my heart was an even greater one: *Would I be so okay with being single forever?* And that question, well, I wasn't as eager to answer. I have a vision and desire to be a wife and a mom, but if God asked me to surrender that completely, would I still be in a place of genuine contentment? Does this newly posed question pose a threat to my contentment? Does it change everything? Or nothing?

While this question did not wreck my world, it definitely shook things up. It truly humbled me and is now a frequent prayer of mine. Singleness is not a curse or a punishment; it is a thoughtful gift from God. So in this season, I find hope in verses like Psalm 116:10, which says, *I trusted in the LORD when I said, "I am greatly afflicted."* (NIV) This verse tells me that I have the freedom and permission in Christ to have my faith bucket filled up while also giving some stage time to my feelings about my situation. When I feel overwhelmed, frustrated, let down, confused, or even straight-up mad because I am single and not sure what the "Big Guy" is up to, that is okay. A part of journeying through faith is being honest with yourself and God about your feelings. He can and will help you to navigate them.

There are so many phrases that can apply to singleness: 'making lemonade out of lemons,' 'not crying over spilled milk,' and 'if it ain't broke, don't fix it.' But there is a phrase that I coined that I hope can be an anchor for you. 'You can either pout about it or make purpose out of it.' What I mean is, instead of spending your precious time and energy (which already has such limited capacity in this needy world), consistently complaining or being sad and frustrated about your singleness, you could be purposeful. In this season, I choose to be purposeful as I lead youth group girls at my church; love on my niece and nephews; travel this beautiful world made by our beautiful God; invest in the spiritual, emotional, and financial areas of my life; and take time to learn to be a better steward of everything given to me.

So with this, I challenge you, whatever season you are in, to live purposefully, too. Live like you've been gifted, making decisions that impact the Kingdom of God for the better. Because you *are* gifted, and God is calling you to live each day for the glory of His Kingdom.

Surrender Your Loneliness

By Kimberly Ann Hobbs

Loneliness is heavy. It makes you feel disconnected and isolated. It can seem like the world and its people lack the desire to be around you, and life just has no meaning. Everyone struggles with loneliness at some point in their life. If this happens to be one of those times for you, please take heart and understand that Jesus Christ is your friend and comforter.

God wants to have a presence in your life. He designed us that way. *For the sake of his great name the LORD will not reject his people, because the LORD was pleased to make you his own.* (1 Samuel 12:22 NIV) God made us His very own so we would not need to be alone.

If you are feeling lonely right now, please pray this prayer:

> *God, You know how I am feeling, and I surrender this feeling of loneliness to you. I need to feel your presence all around me. Please help me with every step of faith I take to believe you will never leave me. Your Word says in Psalm 34:18 that you are close to the brokenhearted and those crushed in spirit. I pray that you turn my sadness to joy, and please turn my loneliness to hope with your presence. In Jesus' name, Amen.*

Begin with baby steps as you ask God to be with you each day. Giant steps can sometimes be difficult for us when trudging through the valley of loneliness. Just practice spending time in God's presence. Ask Him to sit with you. Faith becomes more difficult during the times when we are isolated, but talking aloud to God and surrendering your feelings of loneliness will help. These steps to staying in God's presence may be easier for some than others, but power through, because God wants to spend time with you. When it

Surrendered: Yielded With Purpose

comes down to it, sooner or later, there will be things we cannot do alone. I often catch myself and need to stop impressions of knowledge of my own accord or faking strength to endure difficult situations, and I humble myself to the One who never leaves my side. It is difficult to do, and it is called faith.

God has prepared a path for me, for you, for each of us. It is our choice to follow or not follow, to have faith and remain in God's presence or do it on our own and be alone. We need to be active in this world; this is true, but instead of doing it alone, ask God for His presence wherever you go and whatever you do; that is where you will find continued peace and safety. Remembering to stay in the presence of God, who loves you, will prove to be most beneficial to you.

> *You make known to me the path of life; in your presence there is fullness of joy; at your right hand are pleasures for evermore.* (Psalm 16:11 ESV)

Nothing can harm you when you are safe in the dwelling of our Savior. You are not alone, no! You are never alone when your source of comfort is with you. May you fully understand what Moses says of God in His Word—*"He will neither fail you nor abandon you."* (Deuteronomy 31:8 NLT) Fully surrender your loneliness and fully trust what God can do when He is near.

. . . .

Tina Kadolph

Tina Kadolph is the co-founder and president of Love Missions Global, a 501c3 non-profit organization dedicated to the abolishment of modern-day slavery globally.

She is an entrepreneur and co-owner of Palate Coffee Roastery in Sanford, Florida. Tina's safehouse is a safe haven for children brought out of the sex trade in South America. She has a Life Center, "The Bridge," in Sanford where she helps survivors bridge from pain to purpose, giving survivors a second chance at life.

Tina has traveled the United States and internationally, using her God story to teach the basics of human trafficking with an emphasis on prevention. She has been trained in suicide prevention and is certified as a Life Recovery Trauma Specialist. She is currently working on her mental health coaching certification.

Tina was nominated Hero of the Year by Spectrum TV. She was interviewed by CNN as an influencer, encourager, and inspiration. Tina's goal is to use her pain to protect, educate, and prevent human trafficking so that others never have to go through what she has endured.

When Surrender Is Complicated

By Tina Kadolph

Surrendering to God isn't always easy. I've seen people say they have surrendered this or that to God but really have not. If we are honest, the true struggle with surrender is a battle between our heart, our mind, and God.

> *"For my thoughts are not your thoughts, neither are your ways my ways," declares the Lord.* (Isaiah 55:8-9 NIV)

It's easy to say you have surrendered to God. Surrendering the little things can be easier than the big things. Like, where should I go to school? Or should we get married this year or wait until we save up money and pay off our debts? These can feel like big decisions in the moment, and we can pray about them and then come to the conclusion that we need to surrender them to God. We can then easily say, "Lord, I give this to you. Whatever you want me to do, I am ready, Lord. Your will, not mine. I will surrender my desires, my wants, to you." I've prayed these prayers many times. And I've felt peace, felt good about my decision to lay it at the feet of Jesus and release it all to him.

But what if God asks you to surrender your pain, your hurt, your anger, and the person who abused and tortured you physically and mentally? How easy is that surrender? Let's be honest here. It is not easy at all. It sometimes becomes a difficult challenge.

It took time for me to understand what this kind of surrender meant. I had held on to my emotions and feelings for so long that I didn't know how I could live without them. When you don't realize these feelings or emotions have become who you are, how do you give them up? How do you hand over all the brokenness, all the parts of you that you had to use for survival to keep you alive during the worst part of your abuse? As an adult, the stronghold of painful emotions can be difficult to recognize, especially if you have lived with them for a long time. How do you surrender to God that which you are not even aware of? How do you let go and tear down those walls around your broken and damaged heart, allowing Jesus in and permitting the real healing and true surrender to begin?

When God told me to forgive my mom, who had abused me and sold me into trafficking, I argued with Him. "You can't expect me to forgive that lady. You know, Lord, more than anyone, what she did to me." But yes, that's exactly what He wanted me to do.

Even though I walk through the darkest valley, I will fear no evil, for you are with me; your rod and your staff they comfort me. (Psalm 23:4 NIV)

Going through such abuse as a child, I had to find ways to cope, so my mind blocked out a lot of memories. Your mind can do that to help you survive the trauma. So, in my 30s, little pieces of memory began to pop up. I didn't know how to deal with what was happening, so I tried to push those thoughts away. The flashbacks were horrendous, however, and I'd wake up screaming. As the memories showed up more and more, I reacted by not eating, becoming anorexic. This wasn't the first time I'd used this coping mechanism—I had learned in my teenage years that during times of trauma, not eating made me feel like I had control over something in my life. But at this later stage of my life, though I felt like things were out of control, they weren't. I just didn't know how to handle the past that was haunting me. Later, in therapy, I discovered the trigger for this flood of memories was the age of my daughters, which was nearly the same age I was when my abuse started. My unknown fear was that I couldn't protect my girls. So, I did not eat for over 40 days, trying to kill myself in such a tortuous way—starvation. Of course, I didn't logically realize that's what I was doing. I couldn't control my thoughts or memories, but I could control my food intake. I thought starving myself gave me control. But instead, I was losing control of everything in my life, and I didn't even realize what I was doing to myself.

After 40-plus days of not eating, I was so weak that I had to be rushed to the hospital. I couldn't stand in my own strength and weighed only 70 pounds. Some of my organs were getting ready to shut down. I was bones with skin. My doctor told me I was close to death.

After being stabilized in the emergency room, I was put in a mental hospital. God moved mountains to get me there. I didn't want to be there and was very angry because all I wanted was to die. I felt there was no hope for me. I was at my lowest point.

I share all this to show you how hard it was to surrender my pain, anger, and bitterness towards my mom and the men who abused me. I thought my pain was buried so deep it would never be uncovered. I thought that even God couldn't see the things that were deeply hidden inside of me. But it was time to bring what was hidden in the darkness and attempting to destroy me into the light.

> *He reveals the deep things of darkness and brings utter darkness into the light. (Job 12:22 NIV)*

The thing with trauma is that it eventually comes out. And in case you didn't know, nothing is hidden from God. God knew I needed to deal with my abuse so I could be wholly His. What I didn't know at that time was that He had a big plan for my life. I had to get to the root and pull out all the brokenness and pain so I could be restored, or I'd never be able to help anyone else.

So, my stay in the hospital was beneficial and exactly where I needed to be at that time. I wouldn't be here today if I had not gone; I know the enemy would have won. I was there for three months, and during that time, they helped me realize and understand my mom was a prostitute. Having been brought up in that environment, I thought mine was a normal way of life. I didn't realize my mom was a prostitute. Then the psychiatrist helped me understand what had happened to me. The only name for it at that time was child prostitution. My mom had sold me to men. Today we call it human trafficking. Let me tell you that description, child prostitution, made me feel like I was less of a person. It made me feel like I was a bad person. And I didn't want anyone to know what had happened to me. That was part of the hopelessness I felt. I still hate that description as it makes a child feel like they did something wrong or as if they don't have worth.

The only person who knew about my past was my husband. And he only knew what I remembered. There was so much of my memory that was blocked. In the hospital, they gave me tools to help when those horrific memories came back. This helped me work through my trauma in a healthy way. They also put me on medication for depression and anxiety and showed me that food was not my enemy. In my twisted, traumatized brain, I thought food was like poison. Food was the thing trying to kill me.

They also told me I needed to confront my mom and tell her how I felt—and then forgive her. They told me what she had done was horribly wrong, and they hoped she would apologize, which would begin my healing. Unfortunately, this was not a Christian hospital, so God was not part of the therapy. So, I did confront my mom, but she did not say she was sorry.

Instead, she said she didn't want to talk about it. I continued to tell her things I remembered, and she was dead silent. I didn't understand why she wouldn't respond. Eventually, she hung up. This set me back and hurt me even more. I needed her to respond because, in my head, I thought she would apologize, and then she would become the mom I always dreamed of and still believed I needed.

I thought my abuser could become the mom I always dreamed of. But again, I was looking for help and healing in the wrong places.

> God is our refuge and strength, a very present help in trouble. (Psalm 46:1 NIV)

Years passed from this time in my life. I was a healthier person coming out of the hospital. I dumped all the meds they had given me because, for me, they were not working. I had attempted suicide several times throughout my life, but that was the last time. So, I know my stay in the hospital was what I needed, even though, at the time, I didn't think it was. Ultimately, however, it was Jesus who healed me.

Over time, I got closer and closer to my Savior, became a leader in the church, and started my mission journey. Then I found out my mom was diagnosed with lung cancer.

Our relationship had continued to be unhealthy, and the more I tried to show her Christ's love, the further away she became. Looking back, I believe that seeing me reminded my mom of what she had done. She was drowning in guilt and shame. If only she would allow Jesus into her life, she could be set free from the bondage she was living in.

My mom was getting ready to have half of one of her lungs removed. She lived in California and I lived in Florida. I was as far away from her as I could be and still live in the United States. I was praying for her surgery and her salvation when I heard God say, "Go, help her."

I thought, *I'm sure I did not just hear that.* And I continued throughout my day.

Later again, I heard God say, "Go, help her." This time I knew it was GOD.

I argued, "Lord please send me anywhere but there. You know I'd go to the ends of the earth for you, but please don't send me there. I'll go to the desert of Ethiopia to share your Gospel, but please don't send me to her."

Then His voice was so clear. He said, "I need you to surrender to me. Your mom needs Jesus as much as the Ethiopians."

Wow, big stab to my heart. Still, I'd rather go anywhere on the earth but there. But, of course, He was right. She did need Jesus.

God wanted me to go, so I did. Reluctantly, fearfully, and apprehensively. But I went.

I did my best to be kind and loving to her. I wish I could say that my time there was amazing and she accepted Jesus and our relationship completely changed. But she was like a venomous snake who attacked me at every angle. I was so confused. *Why did God want me here? Why did I have to go through abuse from her again? Why?*

I'd go into my room, read my Bible, and pray—looking for the why.

She would ask, "What are you doing in the room all the time?"

I'd tell her, "Reading my Bible and praying." I'd let her know I was praying for her and her recovery.

She'd roll her eyes and let me know what I was doing was useless.

> *"But to you who are listening I say: Love your enemies, do good to those who hate you, bless those who curse you, pray for those who mistreat you."* (Luke 6:27-28 NIV)

I stayed a week taking care of her and trying my best to be like Jesus as she continued to attack me. It was one of the hardest things I've done. So many times, I wanted to run out of that house and never come back. But I was being obedient to God, so I stayed. One very hard day, when I felt like I couldn't handle the abuse anymore, I called a friend to pray for me. She said some wise words to me. She said, "Don't take what your mom is doing or saying personally. It's the demonic spirits living in her that are attacking the Holy Spirit that is living in you."

That made so much sense to me. Like I described earlier, her attacks were like a venomous snake.

That advice helped me make it through the whole week and not let the enemy win. After that, when the attacks came, I saw the enemy, not my mom.

When it was time for me to go, I felt God wanted me to leave my Bible there. It was my favorite Bible—one in which I'd written notes and had taken on many mission trips. There were so many special memories in that Bible. I didn't believe she was going to want it.

Nevertheless, as I was packing up my suitcase, I went to her and said, "Mom, do you want my Bible?"

She just looked at me.

I continued, "Mom, if you don't want it, just say so because I love this Bible. It's the Bible I take everywhere with me. I don't want to give it up, but if you want it, I'll give it to you.

She looked me in the eyes and said, "You can leave it."

I was so happy and surprised that she accepted it. I prayed she would read it, and God would touch her heart through His Word.

For the word of God is alive and active. Sharper than any double-edged sword, it penetrates even to dividing soul and spirit, joints and marrow; it judges the thoughts and attitude of the heart. (Hebrews 4:12 NIV)

I thought my mission was to bring my mom to Christ. But my mission wasn't about my mom at all. It was about me and God. He needed me to hand over to Him my mom, my anger, my bitterness, and my little-girl-Tina who was still longing for the mom she would never get and the apology that would never come. God wanted me to surrender to Him every broken piece of my heart connected to my mom and her abuse. He wanted to heal me, and that healing would not come from my mom or a hospital or medications or anything else. It could only come from me handing everything over to Him—completely— surrendering every part of me to Jesus. That could only happen with me doing the things I didn't want to do and letting Him fill all the holes in my heart.

When my mom passed away, things hadn't changed in our relationship. We never became close. I don't know if she accepted Christ, it didn't seem that she did, but I may be surprised when I get to heaven. I know that everyone in my family gave her the Gospel, so she had many opportunities. When she passed, I had complete peace and felt a freedom I'd never felt before. God had my life and my heart, and I had already surrendered her to Him. I know I needed to go through the time with my mom so my healing could happen. And because of my own healing, I was able to help other survivors who would one day need help walking the journey through surrender with Jesus like I did. I now know what that looks like. We don't all need to go to our abuser as I did, but Jesus knew what I needed. I can be very hardheaded. It was the only way for me to let go and let Jesus do His work in me.

> *Take delight in the Lord, and he will give you the desires of your heart.* (Psalm 37:4 NIV)

The sweet, beautiful ending to this story is that after my mom passed away, my stepdad moved in with my step-sister and brother-in-law, who are incredible Christians. Now my stepdad goes to church, sings praises to God, and prays. At 90 years old, he is a kind, loving, and praying man. These character traits were not seen while my mom was alive. He has sent me cards calling me his daughter that have brought me to tears. God is so loving and caring that after we have surrendered it all. He then gives us a blessing we didn't realize we needed.

Psalm 23 NIV

The Lord is my shepherd, I lack nothing.
   He makes me lie down in green pastures,
he leads me beside quiet waters,
   he refreshes my soul.
He guides me along the right paths
   for his name's sake.
Even though I walk
   through the darkest valley,
I will fear no evil,
   for you are with me;
your rod and your staff,
   they comfort me.
You prepare a table before me
   in the presence of my enemies.
You anoint my head with oil;
   my cup overflows.
Surely your goodness and love will follow me
   all the days of my life,
and I will dwell in the house of the Lord
   forever

Surrender Your Enemies

By Kimberly Ann Hobbs

Can you think of individuals you do not feel like loving but whom you could try to will good words? They may not necessarily be an enemy, but you do not like them for whatever reason. Maybe someone wronged you or a family member, and they ended up on your "hate list." Or possibly not as severe as "hate," but they antagonize you, or you just cannot stand being around them. God says, *"You shall not take vengeance, nor bear any grudge against the children of your people, but you shall love your neighbor as yourself: I am the Lord."* (Leviticus 19:18 NKJV)

Loving your neighbor was the basic expectation—the minimum standard, but Jesus asks for much more. He commands His people to love their enemies. What does it mean to love them? Jesus told us His famous parable of the Good Samaritan and clearly commanded us to "love your neighbor," which means to love all people everywhere. Jesus extended the rule of love to everyone.

"There Is a saying, 'love your friends and hate your enemies.' But I say: love your enemies! Pray for those who persecute you!" (Matthew 5:43-44 TLB)

It can be easy for us to love those who love us, but it is much more difficult to love those who do not like us. It is easy for us to pray for people we love but not for those who cause problems in our life. God loves His enemies by acting for their good. Love is an action word. We need to be aware of those who are difficult for us to love and set our concentration on showing them love, but how do we do this? Surrender your enemies to God.

When you surrender your enemy to God, you open the door to allow God to work in your heart and produce love that only He can—in places where it is otherwise beyond difficult for us to grow love. After you surrender those you find challenging to love, you can start moving in faith by praying for them. You might even choose to show them an act of kindness that involves doing something for them that would make them happy. Keep in mind that when God commands us to love our enemies, it is not about you. It is about what Jesus calls us to do. If this is speaking to your heart, if God is bringing someone to mind as you read, I want to encourage you to pray and release your grief by surrendering that person to God at this very moment.

Remember, God proves His love for us in that while we were still sinners, Christ died for us. What a victory we could have if we could jump this hurdle of surrendering to God our ill feelings for others. In some instances, this may be an Olympic-sized hurdle. But you are an overcomer. You can do ALL THINGS through Christ, who gives you strength.

Stepping out in faith and doing what you think is impossible will prove rewarding when God shows you victory through Him. Doing something so difficult can only be accomplished with God's help. That is why we need to surrender to Him first and then pray through every word and every action we take to show love to our enemy. The evil one does not want this. He wants to keep you stuck in a frenzy of gossip, hatred, and discord, causing anxiety and added suffering to your life.

Let us remember that Jesus is not asking us to *feel love* but to *act in love* toward everyone, including our enemies.

. . . .

Carol Ann Whipkey

Carol Ann Whipkey is a published author in four books. She is a Christ follower, and much of her retired time is devoted to serving in the Women World Leaders ministry as a writer and encourager through her uplifting, joyful spirit, guidance, and love for writing.

Carol has enjoyed her career as a beauty consultant and worked in an accounting position at UPS until retirement.

She is an artist trained by the world-renowned wood carver Joe Leanord, whose work is in the New York Museum of Art and Disney in Paris and the USA. As a hobby, Carol spends much of her time carving horses, birds, and other commissioned work that comes her way.

Carol lives in her own park-like setting on 52 acres in Thompson, Ohio, with her husband, Mel. She is the mother of 4, which includes her first-born child Kimberly Hobbs of Women World Leaders, and is the grandmother of 6 and great-grandmother of 7.

A Changed Heart

By Carol Ann Whipkey

Putting trust in God is the way forward in life. The Bible is clear that we should trust Him, and the story God gave me to share is one of hope that anchors me. I hope it will encourage you that, through our surrender, God can change even the hardest heart. Surrendering your will as you trust God for His brings lasting happiness.

It was a whirlwind relationship when I met the father of my four children, who wined and dined me and took me to the best places. He married me, treated me like a princess, and gave me everything I wanted. We were happy. We had some problems but always resolved them quickly, mainly because he gave in to me.

After having our second child, I became pregnant again, although I did not want to be. The pregnancy led me to meet Jesus personally. God started changing my life the moment He came into my heart. My third child was born, and then the fourth. Mike, my husband, was so thrilled. He loved his children with a fatherly love that the good Lord put into his being. Mike was not religious, but he knew there was a God. At first, I would invite him to church, and he would pass. I never insisted on him going, but with love, I would always ask. Finally, one day he decided to go with us. After a time,

God spoke to his heart, and Mike accepted Christ as his Savior. Many God stories happened after Mike met Jesus, and I must share one.

Mike always worked to ensure that the children and I would be cared for if something were to happen to him. He wanted us to have money and have the house paid off, so he went to three different doctors to be evaluated just to get insurance coverage. He finished the process with all three doctors and passed with flying colors. Three months later, God took him home after a massive heart attack.

At Mike's funeral, God gave me a vision. Mike was standing in front of me, telling me that he was with God and I should be happy and go on with my life!

Facing life as a widow, I had everything paid off and had money in the bank. But I was alone to finish raising our four young children, the youngest of whom was just six years old.

> I'm sleepless, shivering in the cold, forlorn and friendless, like a lonely bird on the rooftop. (Psalm 102:7 TPT)

> To the fatherless he is a father. To the widow he is a champion friend. To the lonely he gives a family. (Psalm 68:5 TPT)

One day, a friend asked me to attend a Parents Without Partners (PWP) meeting with her. I went and joined. It was a very nice group of people, and a few men asked me out. They were OK, but I kept hearing God's voice telling me not to be unequally yoked with any of these men. So I decided not to go to the meetings anymore.

Not having anyone but the kids to share my days with, I was not doing well. One night, my girlfriend called and asked me to go to the PWP dance. I told her I did not care for the type of men we were meeting and did not want to go anymore. That night, I woke up and cried out to God, telling Him I needed someone to share my life with. I prayed He would send someone to me. As the sun came up, I asked Him to direct my path. Soon after, the phone rang. It was my girlfriend, asking, "What if we went to a different chapter of the PWP? Maybe we'd meet a different crowd of people?" She convinced me to go. Evening came, and with it came a terrible rainstorm; the streets were flooding. I knew I would be crazy to go, but something inside was pushing me, so we went to the PWP dance anyway.

When we arrived at our destination, only one person was at the door. Then we entered the room, which was empty except for two men sitting at a table far across the way. Something strong came over me. I grabbed my friend's hand, pulled her across the room, plunked myself down next to the man I was drawn to, and said, "Hi, my name is Carol. What's yours?" It was totally unlike me to be so forward.

We began talking. As the evening progressed, the room filled, the band played, and we continued talking. I was not paying attention to anything else. I was solely focused on the person who sparked my interest. After a few hours of telling each other about our lives, I remembered something my mom had told me. She said, "If you want to know anything about a man, look at his hands." So I did. His hands were very clean and smooth, and his nails were manicured. I asked him what he did. He said he was a brain surgeon. I really believed him, but then he laughed and told me he was a machinist.

He asked me what I did, and I told him, then added, "I do not know how you will feel about this, but I am a born-again Christian."

With a big smile, he said, "I am too."

From that moment, I felt God lead me to him. When the event ended, he asked for my phone number, and we parted. My friend and I talked about him all the way home. I felt like a kid again, having a guy paying attention to me.

I arrived home to no kids as they were away at my mom's for the weekend. I got ready for bed, my head spinning with excitement. After getting in bed, my phone rang. It was him. We talked long into the night, asking and telling each other everything. We had so many things in common.

The next day was Mother's Day, and I had to pick up my children. But before I left, my doorbell rang—and it was him. In his hands was a beautiful bouquet of flowers. He said, "Every mother deserves flowers on Mother's Day." Now I was certain he was a God-send! From that day forward, I would have another whirlwind relationship. We got married only two months later, and our life together began.

I had three boys at home; my daughter had moved to her own home by then. He had two little girls from his previous marriage and was paying child support. He moved into my home, and we rented out his. Months went by, and he was not happy living in my house. I did not want to live in his, so we decided to buy a home together. We found a place to purchase, put mine up for sale, and sold it quickly. With the money, we bought our new house in the country! However, it was a long distance from where I worked, so I would need to commute.

Moving day came, and so did his children. They wanted to live with us, and I agreed. I opened my heart to them. My husband received custody, and we became like *The Brady Bunch*. Everyone had chores in the home. But when his kids did not want to do them, they would call their mom, and she would tell them they did not have to. So, the problems started.

The younger child would write notes to her father about things, and he would come to me and ask me if they were true. Then, he would try to correct me instead of the children, and it got rough. We would argue about what was written until, one day, I found one of the notes. It upset me so much that I left. I took my children, packed our bags, and went to see our pastor, who had become a very good family friend. I asked him what I should do. He gave me this advice: When you come to a fork in the road, you can go one way or the other, but whatever way you go, go with prayer; it will be the right way.

> *Then you will discover all that is just, proper, and fair, and be empowered to make the right decisions as you walk into your destiny.* (Proverbs 2:9 TPT)

I came to that fork in the road and decided to go to my daughter's home and stay for two weeks. My husband called me every day and asked me to come back home. He said he would send his children back to their mothers. My heart bled because I grew to love them, but I understood they had a mom, and it was not their fault that their parents were no longer together.

I went back home, and things were good again, but my husband was different to me. I did not know if he resented me because the girls were now gone. We went to a picnic at the church campground, and I am guessing he did not like something I did because he took the car and left me there with my kids. I thought he would come back, but he did not. We had to get a ride home from a friend. I made excuses to my friends but really did not understand why he left. When I asked him later, he just said, "You know why." No, I did not.

Time went by, and we had little arguments. Then one day, we were to meet at a department store at 5:00. I was ten minutes late because traffic was heavy from my 65-mile, one-way commute from work. I pulled into the parking lot with a big smile, happy to see him. He waved at me from his car and left! I was devastated. Again, I asked him why he would do that, and again all he said was, "You know why." No, I didn't.

It seemed every time we had words or problems he would give me the silent treatment. I spent many nights crying to the Lord and asking God, "WHY?"

I would read the Bible seeking answers but still did not know what I was not doing right in my marriage. I was always trying to please my husband and examining myself in the process.

Years passed, and the children grew older. We now had just two of my boys living with us because my oldest son wanted to live with my mom. I often thought my husband resented me because I had my kids and his kids were not with him. I prayed for all of us to be together as one happy family again. It never happened.

We eventually changed churches because our pastor friend moved, and we could not get comfortable with the new one. So we joined a church closer to where we lived with a spirit-filled pastor. We both liked him. At church one Sunday just before Christmas, the message was about the joy we should have in Christ.

"Do not grieve, for the joy of the Lord is your strength." (Nehemiah 8:10 NIV)

We came home from church, had supper, and everything seemed fine. I went to our family room to do my craft painting while my son slept on the couch. Then my husband came in with harsh words to me about my son sleeping, so my young son got up and left. The mother-bear syndrome kicked in, and we began to argue. I was in a defensive mode but still tried to talk about the joy message we had just heard. That did not go over well. Although he never got physical, and I have somewhat of a temper, when he started toward me, I felt he was going to use force. I picked up a little screwdriver that I kept in my paint basket to open my paints and held it up to him. He was taunting me. The screwdriver nicked him. He then said I stabbed him, so he was going to call 911. I said, "Don't bother; I'll call for you." And I did. I was completely unaware that if there is a domestic issue, somebody is going to jail. Guess what? I was the one going to jail.

The police came, put us in separate rooms, and we each had to write our version. Then they told me I was going to jail. I felt BETRAYED! Immediately my husband tried to get me out of going, but they would not let it go because of the screwdriver. I never felt so betrayed in my life. After everything I'd been through in my life, this happens to me? "Why, Lord? Why? I prayed you would send me a man who would love me and love my children, and what did I get but all this agony and pain? Now, the most devastating thing is, I am the one going to jail? Why, Lord, why? I believed you!"

The officer did not handcuff me—probably because I was a basket case. But, he put me into the back seat, locked the doors, and went inside the house to talk to my husband. I sat in the backseat crying and asking God what and why He was doing this. The answer was not coming.

I was taken to jail, where officers took my shoes off (because they had shoelaces) and gave me slippers. They put me in a holding cell all alone. I was still crying out to God, sick to my stomach. I cried and cried, asking Jesus if this is how He felt when He was betrayed and taken to jail. It was the worst feeling I HAVE EVER FELT! They fingerprinted me, leaving me humiliated. Then they brought me back to my cell, where I was completely alone. All I could think about was Jesus and why this was happening to me. Later my son came to bail me out. I was not allowed to go home, so I went to my daughter's house, where I would spend weeks on my own, sleeping on an air mattress.

That same night when the boys heard what had happened to me, they went to our house to give my husband a piece of their mind about what he had done to their mother. That is when something happened. I was not there to see or hear, but when the boys came back crying, they testified that the Holy Spirit was there and my husband was changed. I was not having any of it! They could say what they wanted, but I was broken!

This is where my surrender began.

Everything was stripped from me. I had nothing left but to surrender to God. "I SURRENDER, LORD. Do what you will to me or to whomever, but please show me what I should do."

I had to appear before the judge for sentencing, but he expunged the case because I spent due time away from my husband and home. The alone period gave me a lot of time to think about the reasons God dealt with both of us the way He did. I spent most of my time reading the Bible, praying, and journaling. I wrote the title, "Diary To God; The Worst Years Of My Life, Yet The Best."

While I was reading my Bible, I turned to Joel 2:25 and read what the Lord said. He said He would give me back what the swarming locust had stolen. It spoke volumes to me. I told the Lord I heard Him, but I was still hurt to the core.

Weeks went by. I spoke with my husband a few times. He wanted me to come home, but I still could not. He kept telling me he was sorry, but how many times had he done this before and was always sorry afterward? I just could not trust him anymore, but I did trust God.

February came, and my husband called me once again, asking me to come home for Valentine's Day. I finally agreed. I went home for just a visit! We sat on the couch, talking about everything. He told me what happened the night the boys came to vindicate me. He told me exactly what the boys had told me—that the Holy Spirit was there, and they were all changed. I still was not having it. But as we sat on the sofa together, I began to see a different person appear before my eyes. He was a gentler man whose eyes and heart were full of love. His face appeared changed, softened. Then my own heart started to change. It was like a brightness appeared, and I was overwhelmed with the love I had for my husband. I prayed in that moment and asked the Lord what I should do. My surrender to God was coming through. I had fought with my own control until now, but I honestly wanted God to take over.

God spoke to me in a voice only I could hear. "Carol, do you trust me?"

"Yes, Lord, I trust you."

He said it again. Then again. "Carol, do you trust me?"

"Yes, Lord, I trust you."

"Then you should go home," He said.

Meanwhile, my husband had been talking to me. But I didn't even know what he was saying because God had my attention. Then my husband asked me again to please come home.

I looked at him in that moment and said, "Yes, I will come home."

My heart opened, empty of the resentment and hurt I felt toward him, overflowing with love. This was a true miracle for me to agree to return home because that had not been my intention. But I had to go through this experience to be able to totally surrender my heart to God and understand His plan for me. My husband and I are supposed to be together for the rest of our lives.

God straightened us both out in so many ways after that incident. Yes, we still have little glitches, but our love has grown deeper and deeper every day through all these years. We enjoy sharing life together, being together, and doing everything together. I feel blessed beyond measure to share my life with him.

I realize now that in my early adult life, I was like a child, wanting and getting everything my way. I played the game until I realized God wanted my attention. And He opened a door to direct me through so I could come fully surrendering my will to His.

If you want to be happy and fulfilled, surrender to the One who loves you. God will change your heart if it needs changing. We must trust Him with every ounce of our being. Trust and obey God, for there is no other way.

Trust in the Lord with all your heart and lean not on your own understanding; in all your ways submit to him, and he will make your paths straight. (Proverbs 3:5-6 NIV)

Surrender Your Plans

By Julie T. Jenkins

Planning and preparing are not bad. In fact, the Bible instructs us to be careful not to be caught off guard.

Jesus cautioned His listeners to plan for their lives to change when they followed Him. *"Suppose one of you wants to build a tower. Won't you first sit down and estimate the cost to see if you have enough money to complete it? For if you lay the foundation and are not able to finish it, everyone who sees it will ridicule you, saying, 'This person began to build and wasn't able to finish.'"* (Luke 14:28-30 NIV)

Proverbs 15:22 advises us to seek the counsel of others when we are planning, so our plans won't go awry. *Plans fail for lack of counsel, but with many advisers they succeed.* (NIV)

And the Parable of the Ten Virgins, told in Matthew 25, gives us the lesson to be prepared and *keep watch, because you do not know the day or the hour.* (Matthew 25:13 NIV)

So, if we can surmise that planning is, in fact, good, why are we talking about "surrendering" our plans?

We should first recognize that many of the Bible's teachings about planning are actually direct references to our necessary preparation for the sudden return of Jesus. This is stressed over and over because it is a topic of insurmountable importance yet can be difficult to comprehend. After all, how many thousands of people waited for Jesus' return only to die before He came back? Though we *believe* with all our hearts that Jesus *will* return, history can make it easy for us to *think* His return won't come in our lifetime. And it may not! But we must always be prepared.

Surrendered: Yielded With Purpose

However, common sense, daily living, and experience tell us that planning in life is more than planning for Jesus' return. We have events, retirement, and even unexpected catastrophes we will soar through more successfully when we prepare in advance.

The key to planning God's way is to first, wisely and purposefully formulate each step needed to accomplish your God-given directive. And then, as you take each step in faith, recognize that our God is wiser and infinitely more mindful than we are, and He may guide you to make a sudden turn at any given point.

In other words, seek the Lord's plan in total submission and be ready to surrender your own plan at any moment.

> *In their hearts humans plan their course, but the Lord establishes their steps.* (Proverbs 16:9 NIV)

> *Commit to the Lord whatever you do, and he will establish your plans.* (Proverbs 16:3 NIV)

I love that we have a God who will never leave or forsake us but will guide us every step of the way!

In 2019, we at Women World Leaders were planning our first big event. We had the venue, the program, the speakers, the advertising fliers, and we were in the middle of selling tickets when a telephone call came that forced us to change *all* our plans. The venue cancelled. And we were crushed. But, as a ministry, we cried out to God, surrendering our plans. And we committed to His plans, and we walked (and worked!) in faith, knowing that He would provide. And He did! In miraculous ways! (You can read the full story in *Victories: Claiming Freedom in Christ.*[1])

Even when God clearly shows us our destination and calling and we prayerfully plan each step, circumstances may necessitate a new path. Sometimes, like with our event, we simply won't have a choice but to surrender, but sometimes, we are to surrender by faith in response to a directive we hear from God. In those times, we should go to God in prayer, search for clarification in the Bible, and ask trusted Christian friends or advisers to pray and seek God's will with us. And then, we are to courageously surrender our plans for His in total faith, knowing, as Psalm 20:6-9 teaches, we have a God we can count on who will lead us to victory.

> Now this I know:
>   The Lord gives victory to his anointed.
> He answers him from his heavenly sanctuary
>   with the victorious power of his right hand.
> Some trust in chariots and some in horses,
>   but we trust in the name of the Lord our God.
> They are brought to their knees and fall,
>   but we rise up and stand firm.
> Lord, give victory to the king!
>   Answer us when we call! (Psalm 20:6-9 NIV)

. . . .

---

1   Hobbs, Kimberly Ann and Jenkins, Julie T. *Victories: Claiming Freedom in Christ.* World Publishing and Productions, 2021.

Justina R. Page

Justina R. Page is an international speaker and natural storyteller who speaks with a bold and refreshing honesty. She's the author of the award-winning book, *The Circle of Fire,* which tells the story of how her life was changed forever when fire swept through her home, causing the loss of her 22-month-old twin son, Amos; severe, lasting injuries to her other twin son, Benjamin; and her own devastating experience of third-degree burns covering 55 percent of her body. She's also the author of 16 other literary works.

Justina now inspires audiences with a powerful message of hope and triumph. She's the Founder & Executive Director of The Amos House of Faith, a nonprofit organization established to provide post-burn support to families affected by burn trauma. She's a voice-over actor, children's audio producer, and an actress in the award-winning, faith-based movie *We Are Stronger* and the inspirational TV series *Breaking Strongholds.* She resides in Richmond, Texas, with her husband of 35 years, Pastor James Page. She believes that with God, all things are possible!

It's Not About You

By Justina R. Page

I met my husband, James Page Jr., many moons ago on the college campus of The University of Missouri – at Rolla. We were both Electrical Engineering majors. He was one of the favored Bible Study teachers on campus who taught at our Agape Fellowship meetings. James had grown up in a faith-based home and was solid in his faith and love for Jesus. I didn't even know the name of Jesus when I hit the college scene until someone who witnessed to me shared His glorious light. After becoming a Christian, I was hungry for the Word, and James was excited about teaching, so it wasn't long before we became best friends. To my great delight, love replaced friendship for us, and he asked me to be the mother of his children. We were married three months later - a handpicked, God-ordained union, full of hope and expectation of God's power working in our lives.

> *Whoso findeth a wife findeth a good thing, and obtaineth favour of the Lord.* (Proverbs 18:22 KJV)

James was a Shell Scholar who had obtained a full-ride scholarship to college and a summer internship with Shell Oil in Houston, TX. After he graduated, we moved to Houston, and family life began. I'd always dreamed of having a daughter. I envisioned us wearing matching outfits, doing each other's hair, and my daughter confiding in me. So, we got busy. We weren't interested in having a James Page III, so we agreed that if we had a boy, we would give him James' first name for a middle name. Baby #1 – boy Jonathon James Page. Baby #2 – boy Joseph James Page. Baby #3 – boy Caleb James Page. I had to keep trying for that girl, so Baby # 4 – boy Daniel James Page.

Now I was nervous. I was also stubborn, so I tried for that girl one more time. Baby #5 & #6 TWINS -2 boys, Amos Beniah & Benjamin Josiah! I finally got the Lord's message. I settled into my role as a boy mom. Loving every minute of it. I felt I was at the apex of my destiny. I was a happily married homeschool mom and youth group leader at my church. We ministered, traveled, and enjoyed the life God had graciously granted us!

Many people saw me as a woman of faith, a great prayer warrior, and they came to me often for support and encouragement. I was happy, faithful, and full of joy. But why wouldn't I be? My life was stable and blessed. I wondered how I would respond if something tragic happened to my family or me. I remember staring out my living room bay window, asking God this question: "Would I be able to stand?" I wanted to know what I was made of in the deep recesses of my heart. *Search me, O God, and know my heart: try me, and know my thoughts: And see if there be any wicked way in me and lead me in the way everlasting.* (Psalm 139:23-24 KJV)

Two weeks later, at the crack of dawn on March 7, 1999, something went terribly wrong.

I awoke to explosions, smoke, and darkness. Oh, my God! The house was on fire.

Our family was jolted from our peaceful bliss and thrown into chaos in a home totally engulfed with flames. The sound of appliances exploding was deafening. The heat and stench had thrown us into confusion and shock.

James began frantically jumping in and out of windows, desperate to save our young children and me. The three oldest boys grabbed their younger autistic brother and waited at a pre-designated point for their father.

I was the first to be dropped from a window, but I was hysterical. I re-entered the inferno, determined to reach my twenty-two-month-old twin boys. I was pinned by a large, burning oak bookshelf that fell on me. I was trapped, burning, and unable to speak above a whisper. My husband saw me under the bookshelf and shoved me out our bedroom window again.

I crawled from the window to the front lawn, leaving pieces of burned flesh as I went. My hands were so badly injured that I could no longer use them to support myself. I shouted from the edge of the street, where a neighbor steadied me by pressing her head to mine.

"I have six sons! Get my babies!"

But the count of sons who made it out never reached six.

The house collapsed before James was able to get our son Amos out. He died in the fire.

Amos' twin, Benjamin, and I were severely injured.

I drifted in and out of oblivion. The paramedics tried their best to rouse me. "Breathe," one of them said. "Please breathe, baby!"

I saw tears falling down his face. That can't be good, I thought. And I heard panic in his voice.

Then I heard another voice, an unearthly voice, the cry of a fearful, wild animal. But it wasn't an animal; it was Benjamin's voice.

I could not bear the thought of Benjamin feeling the horrific pain I was experiencing.

I passed out, succumbing to utter darkness.

My eyes slowly opened, and they were as heavy as lead. I awoke from a six-week coma, intubated, disoriented, and in excruciating pain. It was insanely hard to focus. *What is that odd, overwhelming smell? Why can't I breathe? What is this large obstruction down my throat?* Suddenly, I felt like I was losing my grasp on life; I felt the eerie nearness of death. I fought for life. *Why am I tied down? Where in the world am I? Where is my family—my husband and my sons?*

I plummeted into a full-blown panic attack. *The fire! Who lived? Who died? Do I have a home?* The pain was severe; it hurt to think. I wanted to talk, but I was unable to. I had lost the ability to do anything on my own. I was dependent on everyone for everything. My orderly world was out of control, and I was not in command of anything.

The intensive care unit nurse must have notified my husband that I was awake because I heard footsteps approaching the door. I was unable to turn my head toward him, but I knew it was him. I was very familiar with his presence.

I felt love and concern flowing from him before he even touched me. He was cautious and gentle. The depth of his love uplifted my spirit. We looked into each other's eyes, determined to be strong. For a fleeting moment, everything was okay.

James began to speak, but I could not hear him. My thoughts and faith were battling each other as my strong façade faded. I was tumbling, out of control again. James could not see the sudden withdrawal of courage because the retreat took place inside me. I knew he would have saved me from this freefall if he had known it was happening, but the descent was concealed.

It was easy to predict who my next visitor would be. I would have been shocked to see anyone else but my pastor, Bishop A. Jones, and his loving wife, Norma J. Jones, who were the essence of love and faith. They entered the room with my husband and his cousin, Minister Richardson. I saw determination on my pastor's face.

There was something they needed to tell me. My senses instantly awakened. *What is it?* Anything could have happened while I was comatose. I knew bad news was coming. My heart began to beat in an irregular pattern. I felt like I was going to faint. I wanted to escape the news, whatever it was, but I was cornered. I silently prayed, *Lord, please help; give me strength. I can't—*

My prayer was interrupted by my pastor's voice. I tuned in fully, accustomed to intently listening when he spoke. He made eye contact. There was no turning back.

My heart was breaking into a million pieces as he spoke. I wanted to scream, lash out, stomp, and break something—anything but just lie there. But I couldn't move. I had to take the beating of the news like a slave tied to a whipping pole; the words were like lashes striking my spirit.

I was still intubated, so I could not even vocalize my hurt and pain. All I could do was let the tears flow and nod to acknowledge that I had heard what he said.

There was a devastating fire.

We lost our home and everything we own.

Joseph and Jonathon were treated for smoke inhalation and released the next day.

Caleb and Daniel suffered first and second-degree burns and were released the following week.

Benjamin suffered second and third-degree burns on his face and upper extremities. He was in the pediatric unit and was also intubated. He had been in the hospital as long as I had.

And then he told me.

Amos was gone.

My baby, my son, my precious child, was no more.

I went numb. I was in shock. My heart had tried to notify me about Amos's death, but I ignored the signal. Hearing someone else vocalize it made it all too real. Destiny had not brought good news.

The confirmation of Amos' death rocked me. I felt myself entering a strange place. I saw a morbid image: my husband burying Benjamin and me. I imagined him going into a depression and the children being left all alone.

That last image jolted my motherly instincts. I would fight to the death for my children. I was sure of it. I had already proven my protective nature by running through fire to save them. They would not be left alone if I could help it. A lifeline had been thrown to me that I had not anticipated.

I had something to live for. I had five surviving children and a devoted husband. Yes, I had lost control, and yes, my world had been horribly disrupted, and yes, my health was hanging by a thread. Even so, I had something powerful left: I had a mind and a will. I couldn't move or talk, but I could desire to do so. I would fight.

Even though I could not summon my will at that moment, I would not starve my desire. I would do one more thing. I would surrender. Humble myself and pray. Angry, fearful, confused, and hurt, I would still pray. I would surrender myself and talk to the one to whom I had entrusted my soul. Jesus was the only one I had ever talked to with my mouth closed and my voice silent anyway.

> *Then Job arose, and rent his mantle, and shaved his head, and fell down upon the ground, and worshipped, And said, Naked came I out of my mother's womb, and naked shall I return thither: the Lord gave, and the Lord hath taken away; blessed be the name of the Lord. (Job 1:20-21 KJV)*

A year later, I could finally walk, use my hands again, and return to some semblance of normalcy, but the questions remained. The despair, fear, and sorrow had dissipated, but the why's haunted me. They kept me from being fully surrendered to my Savior. Finally, one day while sitting in my car, I had a life-changing interaction with God that led me to the ultimate road of surrender to His will.

"Why?" I asked as tears fell heavily down my face. "WHY did you take my child?"

His response was powerful: "THIS IS NOT ABOUT YOU."

Those words stopped me in my tracks. The Lord went on to say, "I am the Son; it's my will that must be done."

We must surrender to His will. If God allowed it, He has a purpose for it.

In that moment, I began to understand that God does not revolve around our will; He doesn't surrender to us. We are the children of God, and we revolve around His will. He makes all things (good, bad, ugly, painful,..etc.) work together to fulfill HIS purpose.

And we know that all things work together for good to them that love God, to them who are the called according to his purpose. (Romans 8:28 KJV)

We must trust God's character even when we can't see His plan. I had to surrender to the divine plan He had and trust His timing, knowing that He is good and the plans He has for me are good as well. When we surrender, His wonderful plan for our life has time to blossom.

He hath made every thing beautiful in his time: also he hath set the world in their heart, so that no man can find out the work that God maketh from the beginning to the end. (Ecclesiastes 3:11 KJV)

When we surrender our hearts to Jesus, He gives us a hope with a solid foundation. Hope is the heartbeat of survival. We can survive and do anything when our hope is in the Lord. As we move forward on our Christian journey, we must keep hope alive.

And hope maketh not ashamed; because the love of God is shed abroad in our hearts by the Holy Ghost which is given unto us. (Romans 5:5 KJV)

There are many types of fires that we experience in our life: financial, health, relationships, and otherwise. God is able to handle them all. He will not waste an ounce of our experiences, so I don't fear anymore. Fear is no more than faith in reverse. I've learned that the only way to overcome pain is to walk through it. So I keep my hope in God. Hope is the heartbeat of survival. I stay honest with God because I realize that He is not afraid of my true emotions. Victory looks different for all of us. Triumph does not have a universal measure. It is tailor-made to fit the person obtaining it. My surrendered life has opened many doors for some of the most amazing blessings and ministries: I am currently an author, speaker, actress, podcast host, and nonprofit founder. All for His glory and His purposes. I am so grateful that God brought me to a place of total surrender to Him. I relinquished control of my life and have willingly given it over to the Lord. He has never failed me. He did it for me, and He will do it for you, if you trust Him.

Trust in the Lord with all thine heart; and lean not unto thine own understanding. In all thy ways acknowledge him, and he shall direct thy paths. (Proverbs 3:5-6 KJV)

Surrender Your Heartbreaks

By Kimberly Ann Hobbs

We are thrown curveballs in our life all too often, which seem to carry tremendous pain when they hit us head-on. How do we cope with such heartbreaks in our life? God's Word is a source that can bind up your wounds and heal your hurts. By regularly implementing God's Word with His infinite wisdom provided within, He will help you through your hurts.

Surrender your heartbreaks to God. Recite this scripture back to Him: *The law of the Lord is perfect, refreshing the soul. The statutes of the Lord are trustworthy, making wise the simple.* (Psalm 19:7 NIV)

When you surrender all your past mistakes and heartbreak, releasing them to God in full surrender, God's Word will guide you forward. The application of His Word will begin to alleviate the hurt we often bring upon ourselves by not living in pure and holy ways.

> *The precepts of the Lord are right, giving joy to the heart. The commands of the Lord are radiant, giving light to the eyes.* (Psalm 19:8 NIV)

God clearly tells us that by obeying His words, joy will be restored, replacing the hurt. However, we will not know how to free ourselves of this pain unless we study God's Word to find out.

> *Jesus said, "If you hold to my teaching, you are really my disciples. Then you will know the truth, and the truth will set you free."* (John 8:31-32 NIV)

Surrendered: Yielded With Purpose

If you are wounded with heartbreak, please understand that your weakness is where God's power will be revealed in you. I have learned that I can minister out of my brokenness. It brings on tremendous healing whenever I surrender my heartbreak to God. While surrendering my greatest heartbreak of all, I was able to begin a ministry with God's help. We can encourage others through what we have experienced because it is through our vulnerability that Christ shines most brightly.

There is a world out there that is looking for smiles through tears. There is a need for men and women who know the heart of God to reach out and show a spirit of forgiveness, caring, healing, restoration, and even sympathy. Surrendering your own heartbreak is a way you can offer help and healing to another.

Do not remain stagnant in your struggles of heartbreak. Surrender them to God so you can be a vessel used by God today. Smile through your tears and allow God to use your pain with a purpose, and embrace someone else who needs your experience to encourage them.

Helping others in their lives allows us to turn our brokenness into glorifying God. He will give you smiles through your tears, and your ability to be used will bring everlasting joy in your healing process.

. . . .

Kayla Follin

 Kayla Follin is an entrepreneur and creative spirit who aims to serve God through every facet of her life. She is a best-selling contributing author of *Victories: Claiming Freedom in Christ* and *Embrace the Journey: Your Path to Spiritual Growth.* Kayla received a degree in Graphic Design and Photography from Liberty University and now works as a freelance graphic designer and wedding photographer.

Kayla has a heart for ministry. She is the graphic designer for Women World Leaders, designing *Voice of Truth* magazine and other published material for World Publishing and Productions – including the book you are holding! She is also the graphic designer for Lionheart Ministry, which provides biblically based children's books to families around the world. She also enjoys equipping children to use their creative abilities to glorify Christ by teaching graphic design and photography.

Kayla is from Virginia, USA, and resides in Southwest Florida. She loves to travel and enjoy the outdoors. Her favorite place to be is in His creation, and where she feels closest to God. Alongside her best friend, Lindsey Sullivan, Kayla cohosts *A Kindred Narrative* podcast, sharing insightful advice for young Christian women.

Healing the Hurt Places

Surrendering Friendships to God

By Kayla Follin

As a young woman in my early twenties who had recently finished college and moved to a new state, the loss of friendships stung my heart and soul again. I'd been in this place before and knew the familiar pain well. Unfortunately, the memories of once glorious friendships replayed in my head like a movie I watched over and over again. *What went wrong? Why does this keep happening to me?* I began to question whether I was worthy of being in close friendship with anyone.

This deep-rooted pain is a sore in my identity. My first lost friendship was in elementary school. I can still recall the feelings of dismay watching the neighborhood girls blatantly ignoring me when I asked if I could join their playtime. Many have similar stories. Feelings of being rejected often start when we are young—just children. How can innocent children hurt people the way we all have? Even in the most irreproachable time of our lives, we can create wounds in others that sting for years and sometimes decades to come.

Fast forward to my senior year of high school. After a few more cycles of sorrow and healing, that sore was opened once again. This time it was more like a dagger that was stabbed into a wound that had just scabbed over. I had a perfect friend group! Honestly, it was everything I had dreamed of having in a group of friends. We had a special connection, shared interests and experiences, loads of inside jokes, and nights where we would stay up all night laughing. I had been in close friendship with some of the girls for almost six years! It felt perfect. We were starting our senior year full of ambition and excitement, looking forward to all the football games, school dances, and senior award ceremonies. All the hard work I put in to make sure I was a good friend was paying off. I had always made it an utmost priority to be a loyal and caring friend who was always there. Looking back, I probably poured myself out a little too much. Anyway, I'm sure we all remember high school and its ability to make people feel small. Some aim to be in the "popular" crowd; others to lay low and just survive. But I longed to create lifelong memories with friends who would go through every stage of life by my side. I thought, *This is it! These are my people.*

Until, one day early in our first semester of senior year, my sweet little boat of friendship didn't just hit an iceberg; it completely capsized and sank to the bottom of the ocean. (Titanic, is that you?) I was absolutely crushed. I lost every single one of my friends in a rather painful way. There was no big explosion of drama—there were no words at all. Suddenly, there was just silence. I'll save you all the details of the scandal, but I'll just say my friends rejected me due to something I had no control over. One person, one little ripple, had created a tidal wave that wiped out everyone I thought I knew and trusted. I searched for closure, and it wasn't until I approached the situation face to face that I received a reason for the breaking off. Again, my wound of rejection was torn open—even wider this time.

I persisted, knowing the Lord wouldn't allow something to happen that would destroy me. (Hebrews 13:6) Certainly, He had a plan for that time, even if I couldn't see it then—which I definitely couldn't. Nevertheless, I trusted that He would reveal more and more as time went on. And He did! I spent those lonely months digging deeper into my relationship with Him. I look back now on that time and remember how sweet those sorrowful moments with Him were. I had no one to fill my time with besides Him, and my friendship with Him grew.

Still, I longed deeply for intimate friendships with other girls who loved the Lord just as much as I did. And through a chain of acquaintances, I became part of a small group of girls who met every Friday to study God's Word. What an answer to prayer they were! As I reflect on that time, I realize that I had actually grown up with these girls. They were a part of my softball team and in my classes, but I had never gotten to know them as I was too caught up in the group I thought was perfect. God's timing and direction were flawless, as we all had been through similar situations. We were each starting fresh and needed friends who were longing after Christ just as much as we were. Oh, how I wish the story ended there—that from then on, I walked in perfect friendship with each of those girls. But, after having made some beautiful memories together, we all went to different colleges. Although I stayed connected with two girls, I had to start fresh once again as a freshman in college.

Now, I had some big expectations for college. In this technological age, my generation grew up constantly bombarded with movies and TV shows based on the college friend group that remained intact indefinitely. Friends who would get married, be in each other's weddings, have babies who became best friends, and then retire together, reliving their college days. My yearning for and determination to find the perfect group began to take over again. I made a few really close friends (praise God!), but we weren't a group. Instead, I had individual friendships with God-loving girls who were so kind and encouraging. We built each other up and supported one another through those crazy college years of figuring ourselves out.

Still, I couldn't help but feel like something was missing. I kept seeking and searching for that "group" feeling. All over social media, I saw these huge friend groups who seemed to have it all together, even going on adventures and trips together frequently. Why couldn't I have that? I let jealousy trickle into my soul. I started to pray for more, asking the Lord to fulfill that desire for me. I was unsatisfied with what He had given me already.

.

It wasn't until my junior year of college when I heard God say, "Why are you asking for more when I've given you everything you need?" The Lord gently reminded me He had blessed me with wonderful women to stand beside me, and I needed to tend to the gardens He had already placed in my possession. I didn't need to seek out more. I had everything that He wanted to give me and knew I needed. My story and friendships didn't need to look like everyone else's seemingly "perfect" ones on social media. Because, as it turns out, I was comparing what I had to a false image of what others had. Through talking with a classmate who seemingly had what I longed for, I realized that the big, fun group was actually filled with toxicity. This led me to a game-changing mindset. I surrendered my desires for friendship and placed them in God's hands, accepting what He had already so graciously given me. *For you need endurance, so that after you have done God's will, you may receive what was promised.* (Hebrews 10:36 CSB)

What a breakthrough that was! I started to pour into and invest more into the people in my life. I became intentional, focusing on being the friend who would help others become more like Christ. *As iron sharpens iron, so one person sharpens another.* (Proverbs 27:17 NIV) Those friends walked with me through some really hard times. They were there when my life seemingly fell apart (see my chapter in *Embrace the Journey*), and we made so many memories together that I will cherish for the rest of my life. That little perspective shift the Lord so graciously taught me changed everything. My circumstances remained the same, but I saw things differently as I turned to and appreciated the blessings I had already received from the Lord.

Again, I wish this was the end of the story! I wish that breakthrough was all the learning I needed and that those friends were still currently walking through life with me. Don't get me wrong, most of them are. But there was one who tore open that freshly healed wound once again. This time, it became so vast and ached daily. It still aches. We were roommates, but gradually we lived in the same house and barely talked. Resentment grew inside me. It was like someone turned off the light of our friendship. I thought I created an open environment for conversations, but because of our past hurts, it was difficult to discuss even small offenses. That friendship dragged on with something missing. I moved out after graduation, thinking maybe we weren't fit to live together and our relationship would grow stronger when we were no longer roommates. But I know now we had become different people, growing in separate directions in those last few months of living together. Honestly, I thought that was the only issue and our friendship had just run its course. However, I discovered months later she had some very hurtful things to say to me. The wound I had spent almost ten months patching up was ripped open through her cruel words.

I convinced myself that I forgave her for the hurt and rejection, but suddenly, those feelings of rejection came flooding back. I had only shoved those feelings down where I couldn't see them—like old T-shirts buried in the back of the closet. Then God gave me a lesson in forgiveness that changed my life. I met Dana Louise Cryer.

Dana was abducted and sexually abused for years as a young girl. We sat in a circle of support and Christian sisterhood as she replayed some of the darkest memories of her childhood. Someone asked how she could forgive her perpetrator for hurting her the way he did, and she responded with, "How could I not forgive him when Christ forgave me?" She said the Bible says unforgiveness stands between us and the Lord and can put a block between Him and our prayers. *And whenever you stand praying, if you have anything against anyone, forgive him, so that your Father in heaven will also forgive you your wrongdoing.* (Mark 11:25 CSB) I was convicted. It was quiet, and, as a spirit-filled woman, she looked at me and asked what I was feeling. I'm sure she could see the Holy Spirit working in my heart. I was tearful and admitted that I needed to forgive.

From that moment, it's been a daily decision to release my former roommate into forgiveness. Not only to forgive *her*—but to forgive every person and situation that has dug this wound so deeply over the years. I still feel like I'm in the grieving process. Memories will flash back, and I must surrender to the Lord that it is better to be in His will than mine. Still, it's never easy to lose someone you love. When we think of grieving, we often think of death. But the grief of losing someone dear can be even more painful when they continue their lives without you and you without them.

As a generation so affected and influenced by social media, it can be hard to see friendship and life as it truly is. Social media is a curated highlight reel of everyone's lives. It's easy to get stuck in the trap of wanting what others *seem* to have without appreciating what the Lord so graciously gifts us. We think we know what we need better than He does. But that is the biggest lie from the enemy!

Perhaps the worst part is that the enemy harnessed my sensitive friendship wound to create stings of rejection and unworthiness in my identity. I wondered what was wrong with me or my personality because of the frequency with which loss of friendship had struck me. I began believing that surely it must be my own flaw causing my friends to up and leave repeatedly. I wondered if the hurtful words others said about me were valid. I considered that no one would choose me as their close friend. Satan was using some of his greatest tactics against me.

I am not naïve enough to say I don't carry any blame for the loss of my friendships. But I have intentionally asked for forgiveness for whatever I have done to hurt anyone, and I know that my heart's desire has always been to be a loving, kind, generous, and Christ-like friend. The Lord knows my heart; at the end of my life, He is the only one I'll have to stand in judgment before. And I have come to fully understand that Christ is the one who determines my identity—and He says I am chosen. *Blessed is the God and Father of our Lord Jesus Christ, who has blessed us with every spiritual blessing in the heavens in Christ. For he chose us in him, before the foundation of the world, to be holy and blameless in love before him.* (Ephesians 1:3-4 CSB) He says that I am worthy. *But you were washed, you were sanctified, you were justified in the name of the Lord Jesus Christ and by the Spirit of our God.* (1 Corinthians 6:11 CSB) He says I am made in His image and created for a purpose. *So God created man in his own image; he created him in the image of God; he created them male and female.* (Genesis 1:27 CSB)

After all my cycles of friendship and losing people I cared deeply about, I've learned what the Lord says about being a good friend. As Christians, it is vital to choose the right friends—those who love the Lord deeply and seek after His face (see Proverbs 13:20). But, as good as it is to choose people who have a relationship with Christ, we must also face the reality that we are all sinners who will hurt each other. We must recognize that just because a friend loves the Lord doesn't mean we will never hurt them or be hurt by them. However, it is essential to operate with humility and open hands to the Lord, following the guidelines He gives us in scripture.

To have good godly friends is to be a good godly friend. We must walk in the example given in Colossians 3:12-13 (CSB), *Therefore, as God's chosen ones, holy and dearly loved, put on compassion, kindness, humility, gentleness, and patience, bearing with one another and forgiving one another if anyone has a grievance against another. Just as the Lord has forgiven you, so you are also to forgive.* One of my favorite pictures of friendship in the Bible is in Exodus 17, specifically verses 12-14, where Aaron and Hur hold up Moses' arms when he is so tired that He can no longer hold them up himself. Let us stand beside our sisters and hold up their arms when they are in the thick of battle.

When we find ourselves in conflict, we must leave all selfishness at the altar. The Word gives us a godly way to resolve conflict in Matthew 18:15-20. It may be hard to follow through with this example of conflict resolution. If you're anything like me, you might want to pretend like nothing happened or shove it to the back of the closet. But the Lord calls us to walk in truth, forgiveness, and love, which is impossible in our relationships without addressing those who have sinned against us. To protect our relationships, we must address sin so it cannot grow into resentment and unforgiveness.

We see in God's Word that everything has a season. Ecclesiastes 3:1 (ESV) states, *For everything there is a season, and a time for every matter under heaven.* This applies to the season of friendship. The likelihood we will end our lives with the friends we began with is slim. God brings people into our lives in His good timing and for His good purposes. If you are suffering the loss of a close friend, know that God is in total control. Perhaps He removed that friendship because its purpose was fulfilled or even as a means of protection. Whatever the cause, you can surrender to His good and perfect plan. We shouldn't hold on to things by our own power alone. Instead, we must trust God. Sometimes a loss is required for us to grow. He is our vinedresser: sometimes pain is part of His glorious pruning to our souls. I am the true vine, and my Father is the vinedresser. *Every branch in me that does not bear fruit he takes away, and every branch that does bear fruit he prunes, that it may bear more fruit.* (John 15:1-2 ESV)

We must always remember that the Lord is our ultimate friend! Proverbs 18:24 (CSB) says, *One with many friends may be harmed, but there is a friend who stays closer than a brother.* There may be times when you find yourself lonely and without companions. I pray that if you do, you can reflect on this verse and know it is better to have one friend in Jesus than many friends that will not make you more like Christ. Use this time of loneliness to get to know Jesus as your friend!

The best way to find the tribe that will hold up your arms, as Aaron and Hur did for Moses, is to pray that God will bring those people into your life. God does not call us to go through life alone and without community. He designed us for community! So don't be afraid to pray and ask Him how you can be a godly friend, where you need to grow, how you need to be intentional, who you need to forgive, and for His provision for those deep-rooted friendships to grow in your life. Pray that He will lead you and show you others who are yearning to know Him as much as you are. Anything done in our own power and not surrendered to Christ is futile and will pass away. But things done in the sovereign power of our God and have His ultimate blessing will last.

The glorious part of this story is that through these hurts and painful times, God has healed those wounded parts of me that go way back to that first memory in elementary school. God used all my experiences and heart-wrenching times to help me understand godly friendship and teach me that striving for perfect friendships was not His will for me. He taught me that I don't have to give every part of myself to force a relationship. The friendships that I now walk with each day have brought healing to those wounds. You see, when you walk surrendered to God, He uses His ordained friendships to rewrite your broken places. When your identity is found in Him and not who you are friends with, there is room for Him to show you His kindness through the blessing of truly perfect friendships—because our only hope at perfection resides in our relationship with Him.

Surrender Your Relationships

By Kimberly Ann Hobbs

We all make choices about who will and who will not be in our lives. And our relationships will always include a variety of people. Some can be husband/wife relationships, some can be boyfriend/girlfriend relationships, some may be friends, while others can be family. Some relationships are old, while some are brand new and developing. We can be assured that God cares deeply about those who are part of our lives in relationship with us and those who are left out. So how do we choose who stays in and who goes?

People are a huge part of the lifestyle my husband and I wish to live. Together, we have developed relationships that have grown over the years, and we also regularly establish new friendships with people God brings into our lives. Despite the tenor and time of our relationships, God asks us to show love to everyone. Therefore, we try very hard to accommodate the relationships we have established and the ones yet to come, maintaining them by making room in our hearts and lives.

There are always people we should make room for whom God will bring to us unexpectedly. For example,

- The new neighbors who are moving in across the street

- One who may have different political leanings than you

- The couple who stepped in front of you with their kids while you were waiting in line at the grocery store

- The family member you do not know very well because other family has alienated them

Surrendering relationships—those you hold dear, those that come out of the blue, and those yet to come—means placing them before God. Living in God's Kingdom involves loving God's people, because relationships are important to God. Loving others and inviting and including people in your life reflects the heart of your King, your Savior, your Creator God, who helps develop healthy relationships.

Not always are people beautiful; it is especially hit-and-miss when people do not have a personal relationship with Jesus. People can be quite ugly on the inside, but God still calls us to surrender even those ugly relationships over to Him. Our own sin has made us unclean, like a leper, and He did not cast us out, right? Instead, God calls us His daughters. That signifies a relationship. We were foreigners, yet He made us citizens. He established a relationship with us to be close to us.

Jesus made room for all types of people: neighbors, the poor, His betrayers, strangers, children, and more. He gave of Himself, offering Himself to others and the Father.

Surrendering our relationships to God is a selfless act. It takes the focus off you and places it on someone else despite their needs, wants, or situation. Make room in your heart for the relationships you are in and those God prompts you to develop. Why? Because God in His Word shows us the example we should follow.

We love because he first loved us. (1 John 4:19 ESV)

Asking for God's help in relationships—whether they are new or old, with the Lord's people or strangers, with those who may need your time or a good listener or a moment of care— shows that you can surrender your own needs and actively help others. God works in ways we can't always understand, and if you let Him, He will work through you to reach another through a relationship. You just have to have a heart willing to say, "Yes, Lord."

. . . .

Anita Setran

Anita Setran serves as the Executive Director for Prayer Stations, Inc. Their focus is prayer evangelism, meeting people's felt needs through prayer and their eternal need through Jesus. Anita was previously the Director for YWAM Metro, Inc. in New York, overseeing operations and training missionaries to serve around the world.

She is a certified life coach, licensed finance coach, a speaker, and an author.

Anita is also the co-founder of Frontline Community Care Network, which started as a result of their family's COVID-19 journey. FLCCN seeks to educate and empower others to serve their families and communities in health and wellness. Learn more at www.frontlineccn.com.

Anita grew up in a missionary family, traveling the world. She and her husband, Ron, have been married for 30 years and have three grown children, one daughter-in-law, and will soon welcome their first grandbaby. Their youngest daughter has Down Syndrome and has encountered several medical hurdles, which they have faced together.

Learn more about her ministry or contact Anita at www.sparknewlife.com or www.prayerstations.org

Spark New Life

By Anita Setran

The world grappled with the COVID-19 pandemic beginning in 2020. My family spent the first 18 months mainly on the fringe, spending some time researching, reading, and (let's be honest) stocking up on essential oils, supplements, vitamins, and, yes, toilet paper. Although the world seemed gripped with fear of the unknown, we, as a family, knew God was in control.

In July of 2021, our 21-year-old daughter tested positive for COVID-19. Our primary care physician prescribed Karissa the necessary medication, and she got through it like a champ. Then, four weeks later, our youngest daughter, Kiersten, came down with symptoms that led us to believe she had an intestinal issue. However, she, too, tested positive for COVID-19. Our precious girl has Down Syndrome; therefore, keeping Kiersten in quarantine was more difficult. And my husband, Ron, and I became ill in no time. Soon after, our oldest son Caleb also tested positive.

Unfortunately, COVID-19 had become a family affair.

We took the same medications Karissa had, and, at first, it seemed that Ron was kicking the illness much better than I was. The doctor even told us he was "out of the woods." Our bedroom had become quarantine central, and Caleb and Kiersten healed quickly. After that, however, Ron and I both went downhill.

By August 31st, we were both coughing incessantly, experiencing extreme weakness, and had COVID-19 brain fog creeping in. With our breathing labored, we were grateful to have my mom's oxygen machine for extra support. The doctor prescribed me an additional dose of medication that, unfortunately, Ron did not receive. Finally, we decided to go to an emergency room for fluids and an overall assessment, where we learned things were becoming much worse.

When we arrived at the emergency room, we were both brought into a shared room in wheelchairs. Our lungs felt like we were being hugged so tightly that we couldn't inhale. I could see that Ron was definitely NOT out of the woods. In fact, he seemed a little too deep in the woods, even having a difficult time breathing in the required mask. He removed it constantly to gasp for breath and could barely talk. Adding to our quandary, the doctor was rude, uncaring, and judgemental. Not at all what we expected or needed.

In our world, fear had become what fueled every decision, overcame common sense, and separated families. Fear seemed to grip many of the hospital staff. Without Jesus, I can understand that. The Bible says, *"Peace I leave with you; my peace I give to you. Not as the world gives do I give to you. Let not your hearts be troubled, neither let them be afraid."* (John 14:27 NIV)

The hospital staff started intravenous (IV) fluids on me, then took blood and did a chest X-Ray on both of us. It was then that we learned that Ron had the beginning stages of COVID-19 Pneumonia. Within minutes of Ron's diagnosis, they unhooked my IV, got a wheelchair for Ron, and quickly escorted us to the street, where we had to wait for Karissa to return to the hospital to pick us up. It was so hot, and the sun of south Florida beat down on us, stealing any ounce of fight we had left.

Over the next 48 hours, I helplessly watched as Ron became worse. He was dependent upon the oxygen machine. Without it, his oxygen saturation fell well under 90. At the same time, I was showing slight signs of improvement.

The night of September 1st, we both turned a corner. Me for the better and Ron for the worse. His coughing was severe, and he couldn't catch his breath. I had fallen asleep, and he didn't want to disturb me, so he wheeled the oxygen machine out of the room, sat down at his computer, and wrote a letter to the kids. He felt that his body was failing with every passing hour, so he wanted to write to them about how much he loved them and encourage them never to let go of Jesus. (This letter remained unknown to us until several days later when Karissa went onto his computer to look up information regarding COVID-19 management. At that point, Ron was already in the COVID Intensive Care Unit – the COVID ICU. Reading the messages that he had left behind brought us to tears.)

I remember waking up on September 2nd thinking, "I slept." It was the first night I had only woken a few times since falling ill. I felt that my body was finally fighting back against this awful sickness. But that hope was quickly overshadowed when I realized how much Ron was suffering. While my body was strengthening, his body was weakening. I didn't know what to do. Karissa helped me pack a small bag, and we tried to get the oxygen machine to work in our car. It was a 25-minute drive to the hospital, and we knew Ron couldn't go a minute without it.

I sat down at my desk, head in my hands, and prayed that God would tell me exactly what we should do. In Psalm 4:1, David cried out to the Lord, *Answer me when I call to you, my righteous God. Give me relief from my distress; have mercy on me and hear my prayer.* (NIV)

At that very moment, Karissa came running out to me with the digital thermometer—BRIGHT RED—and reading 105.1. That was it; I had my answer. While Karissa covered Ron in ice packs and cold compresses, I immediately called for an ambulance. They arrived in record time and quickly strapped Ron into the gurney. He was whisked into the ambulance before I had time to kiss him goodbye.

As I stood alone in our driveway watching the ambulance pull away, I tried to make sense of it all. The only thing I was sure of was that God was still God, He was still sovereign, and we were dearly loved by Him. I surrendered my husband and best friend to Jesus, trusting He would heal and protect him. I later learned that in those crucial moments in the ambulance, Ron nearly died. When God spoke, thankfully, we listened.

Once Ron arrived at the hospital, we immediately had many critical health decisions. It was the beginning of our crash course on making sense of the hospital's protocol.

My daily prayer was, "Lord, we trust You, You are the great physician, and You know exactly what Ron's body needs. So please, Lord, if there is anything detrimental to Ron's health and healing, would You remove it and fill his veins with the medicine from heaven that will heal him and restore every inch of his body?"

Ron was quickly rushed through the system, from the emergency room to a COVID unit, and within 24 hours, they had him in the COVID ICU. Each day grew harder, and the news grimmer. Although I had begun to heal, my body began failing again. The stress was palpable; all I could do was pray and trust God. In the four years leading up to our COVID-19 event, God gave us many promises of what the future held. So I knew in my heart that God still had more for us to do here on earth. Hope was present. Although dim at times, it was all we had.

Friends in the medical field were preparing me for the worst. They, too, trusted God but told me that based on his vital signs and markers, Ron's future, without a miracle, did not look good. Ron wasn't expected to live.

By September 4th, my health had deteriorated. I was also within minutes of being rushed to the hospital via ambulance. Those moments will forever be imprinted in my memory. I called my parents, fearing that this might be it for both Ron and me. I struggled for breath to tell my dad where my life insurance and important papers were. The line went silent. I asked if he could hear me; it wasn't like him not to respond.

My mom's soft voice came on the line, "Honey, Dad hears you. He just isn't able to respond right now."

Finally, I heard his broken response, "Everything is going to be alright—I hear you, and God hears you."

I hung up the phone, tears streaming down my face, and called out to God for wisdom, grace, and to spare Ron and me and not allow us to leave our children or parents behind. I knew we had to fight, but how could I when I could barely breathe or even stand? *What am I supposed to do?*

Right then, my sister called. "Anita, don't leave—I'm coming!"

It was a brave move. My sister, Rebecca, is a survivor herself. Having been misdiagnosed for 17 years with Late Stage Chronic Neurological Lyme Disease, she spent the last 12 years since her diagnosis fighting to live. As a family, we had fought with her and done everything we could to save her, serve her family, and see her body restored. Now she was equipped and ready to fight for me.

Rebecca arrived, bringing her entire arsenal of wellness supplies. She stayed with me for two days and became my drill sergeant. She prepared small healthy meals and put me on a regimen of supplements, essential oils, treatments, hydration, and, of course, my medications. It was exactly what I needed to begin to heal, yet again.

The next day, September 5th, was our 29th wedding anniversary. I was out of danger, but the news on Ron continued to get worse. His blood gas levels were bottoming out, daily X-rays showed his lungs continuing to fill with fluid, and breathing was nearly impossible. He was on 40 liters of pure oxygen and had graduated from the cannula (the small tube placed just below the nose) to a full mask. He was introduced to the Bi-pap machine, which blew oxygen straight into his mouth—they compare it to driving down the highway at high speeds with your mouth wide open! Ron called it a torture device. Thankfully, although brain fog was still a significant issue, his fight was returning, and he absolutely refused the Bi-pap. It was, after all, the final stage before being put on a ventilator—something we were adamant would never happen.

That afternoon, Karissa walked into my room with a dozen red roses. I thanked her, and she quickly corrected me and said, "You need to thank Dad—they are from him."

Once again, tears rolled down my cheeks. Although my husband lay dying in the hospital, he refused to allow our anniversary to pass without demonstrating his love for me.

How grateful I was during those difficult days for Karissa. She never left my side and slept in my bed every night after Ron went to the hospital.

September 6th was no better, but it wasn't worse, which is saying something because until then, the news had only gotten worse every day. We kept trusting God and praying for a miracle—that's all we could do. Right?

During those days, when hope seemed grim and Ron lay gasping for every breath, he felt a nudge from God to work in full-time ministry, by my side. At that moment, he dedicated his remaining years to full-time service. A life surrendered even amid an unknown future.

September 7th was our day of reckoning! Once again, all of Ron's numbers were bad but holding. His X-ray looked white as snow, which was not at all good. His blood gas level was 43 when it should have been in the 80s or 90s.

I had a telehealth appointment scheduled with our primary care physician, but I actually met with the nurse practitioner, who was very kind and prescribed more medicine.

That morning I prayed, "Something has to change today."

Both Ron and I had plateaued, each at our own levels. We weren't healing, and we weren't getting worse.

It was decided that I would benefit from some vitamin infusions. So, my daughter-in-law, Diana, drove me. On our way, I received a text from a Christian friend who lived nearby. She had been reading my daily Facebook posts and had been praying for us. Her text read, "Are you ready to do something crazy?" Everything inside of me yelled back, "Yes!" But my body said, "How?" I couldn't respond. I was too weak, and my brain fog was too thick.

When we finally arrived at the IV center, I felt my body begin to strengthen with each drop that entered my bloodstream.

On our way home, Diana stopped to pick up the medicine prescribed earlier that morning. As I waited in the car, the Holy Spirit told me to call my friend. I began to dial but immediately put the phone down, feeling weak, tired, and nervous. Then the Holy Spirit spoke a second time. "Anita, pick up your phone right now and make the call!" I heard Him loud and clear.

I knew I only had a few minutes before Diana returned. After that, I would not be alone again as my three older kids were not leaving my bedside. So, I picked up the phone and called. At that very moment, my friend was on the phone with the nurse she wanted me to speak to, so she merged the call.

I sat and listened to this amazing Christian nurse give me strong and direct advice on what I needed to do to save Ron. There was something I could do after all, and now I knew what it was, but how could I pull it off? I was so weak I could barely sit up or walk, let alone drive my car. I was going to need some help, and I wasn't sure my kids were ready for "crazy."

I texted Rebecca, "I'm ready to go rogue. Are you with me?"

Her answer was loud and clear—she was in!

Upon arriving home, Caleb, Karissa, and Diana were all in the room with me. I prayed, asking the Lord to help me convey what I was about to do and that they would be on board. As I began to share, our primary care doctor called my cell, checking up on me as my chart had crossed his desk that morning. I told him that Ron was in the COVID ICU, and things didn't look good.

I told him that I had several calls with the ICU doctor, requesting various medications and vitamins but was refused; he said he would see what he could do. He knew the head ICU doctor, having worked with him previously for 17 years, and he agreed that Ron needed that regimen of medicines, but he worried things had already progressed too far. I told him that people all over the world were praying, and he replied, "Good, keep everyone praying. I will call now."

I called my parents. Over speakerphone, with my kids present, we stormed heaven on Ron's behalf. Suddenly, in the midst of praying, my doctor called back.

I took the call; my heart beat quickly as I waited to hear what he would say,

"Anita, I begged on my knees. I pleaded with the doctor to allow the medication." There was a pause—it felt like a lifetime, and then he continued, "He will allow one dose of the medication we requested, but you must get it and bring it to the hospital—they will not supply it."

That was it! That's all I needed! Something happened in that instant—it was real, tangible, and the answer to our prayer! I knew God was moving and that He would bring healing. Sometimes He allows us to be part of the plan. Isn't that awesome!!?? We surrendered, and God had a purpose in all of this!

Rebecca put the word out, and people responded—we got the medicine we needed!

My strength was returning, and this news energized me! I collected the dose of medication that was given to me earlier that day. Then the kids and I got in the car, drove to the next county where a kind Christian friend gave us her extra dose, and we headed to the hospital. We texted Ron, "We are coming, and we have what you need!"

Earlier that day, we learned that the COVID ICU was on the ground floor; although we were not permitted to visit Ron, we would be able to see him through his window. The kids ran around the hospital, searching for his room. Upon finding it, they drove me as close as we could get. Finally, we rounded the corner, and that moment I saw my love after so many days apart, not knowing if I would ever see him again, was filled with pure happiness and tears. I held the medicine to the window and proclaimed, "We have it!"

We delivered the medicine and said our goodbyes with a deep hope that God was in control and He would be glorified.

Ron took the medication at 11 pm, and we prayed! Like clockwork, they checked Ron's blood gas level at 4 am, just 5 hours after taking the medication. His blood gas number jumped from 43 to 93!!! Within three days, Ron was released from the ICU. And four days later, we were reunited with tears and a long embrace at the hospital's main entrance! God had answered ALL of our prayers, and His purpose for our lives would be fulfilled!

COVID-19 has attacked the world, but we can all be assured that God is still in control. My family was blessed to come through this disease, but I know that many others have a different ending to their story. No matter the outcome, we can all trust that our God is good, in control, and cares for each of us in the hardships and the joys.

It's been almost a year since Ron's healing, and God has opened incredible doors! We now serve in full-time ministry together, and He has allowed us to coach others through their COVID-19 journeys! We serve a God of love, redemption, and healing! He has a purpose for us all, even in the midst of the unknown—never give up hope!

Surrender Your Prayer Life

By Kimberly Ann Hobbs

Can anyone say that they spend enough time communicating with God each day? Daily prayer is a necessity in a life surrendered to God. We must find quiet time to be alone with Him, to communicate with Him effectively so that He can hear us and we can hear Him. The scriptures teach us that God not only desires to hear from His children, but He also wants us to approach Him with a clean and surrendered heart as we pray.

I read a verse in Proverbs that prompted me to share about surrendering our prayer life to God. He got my attention in His Word when He said, *Anyone who turns his ear away from hearing the law—even his prayer is detestable.* (Proverbs 28:9 CSB)

How could this be? Could there be times when my prayers don't please God? Yes. Our prayer life is not strong when we have unresolved issues in our lives concerning sin. When we continually pray while knowing we have unconfessed sin in our life (deliberate sin we don't want to get rid of), the consequence of our disobedience could mean that our prayers go unanswered. I looked up the word detestable; it means revolting, loathsome. I don't believe any of us would want God to view our prayers or prayer life as being such. For me to grow in God, I need to keep asking Him what He wants me to do and then respond. If I don't ask Him, I may not know His desires. And even if I feel I'm doing right, I must ask Him to show me where in my life I might be displeasing to Him. We can't receive all God has for us if we aren't living in obedience.

If we want a strong prayer life with God, we must surrender our prayer life to Him and learn to pray in a way that is pleasing to Him. We can't communicate properly with God if He doesn't hear us because we are separated by sin.

I encourage you to make confession and repentance a part of your prayer life and surrender your prayer life completely to Him for His glory. I believe we all want our prayers to be heard. God instructs us in His scriptures very clearly how to pray to Him. Repentance and forgiveness are important parts of a surrendered prayer life.

"Pray like this: 'Our Father, dwelling in the heavenly realms, may the glory of your name be the center on which our lives turn. Manifest your kingdom realm and cause your every purpose to be fulfilled on earth, just as it is fulfilled in heaven. We acknowledge you as our Provider of all we need each day. Forgive us the wrongs we have done as we ourselves release forgiveness to those who have wronged us. Rescue us every time we face tribulation and set us free from evil. For you are the King who rules with power and glory forever. Amen.'" (Matthew 6:9-13 TPT)

A surrendered prayer life is essential for every believer to communicate with their Creator. God is a forgiving Father who loves us and keeps no records of wrongs. He wants to hear from us continually, and we want to make certain He hears us. So as you surrender your prayer life to God, thank Him for the instruction He gives in scripture, teaching us how to pray. Study the passage in Matthew, paying attention to the many examples of ways to pray to the Father that Jesus showed us. Rest knowing that when you ask Him to forgive you, completely repenting of any disobedience to Him, He will forgive you. Then move on to a healthy and essential part of your life—communication with your Heavenly Father.

He has removed our sins as far from us as the east is from the west. (Psalm 103:12 NLT)

· ·

Ellie McGraw

Ellie McGraw is a dynamic, fiery, passionate, prophetic voice who loves the presence of God!

From the early age of 9 years old, Ellie heard the voice of God audibly. Since then, she has had many interactions with the Holy Spirit as He speaks to her through various avenues. Because of the freedom she herself has received, Ellie loves to see the body of Christ set free, healed, and delivered. She has a passion for equipping leaders and raising up champions through giving sound biblical keys to the Kingdom of God.

Ellie has spoken in many churches in various nations and has served on numerous teams. Since the year 2000, she has had a counseling, healing, and deliverance ministry called FREEDOM TO SOAR. She leads many different kinds of groups—healing, prophetic, and prayer groups—and leads intercession on a 24-hour prayer line called The Canadian Firewall. Ellie is a mother to 4 children, grandmother to 11 grandchildren, and resides in beautiful Okanagan Valley in Kelowna, British Columbia, with her husband.

Let Go And Let God

By Ellie McGraw

Over and over, my husband's words ripped into my soul; expletives and derogatory words.

His lies echoed in my mind. "You have no value. You are unworthy. You don't measure up. You are nothing. It's your fault." Shame and condemnation covered me like a blanket. The world was closing in on me as I struggled to survive the hands around my throat as he choked me from behind. Fear paralyzed me. His hands, like claws of death, would not let go, trying to make me submit. The cussing was deafening. Ripping at those fingers as they tightened around my throat, I tried to loosen his grip. Hands that once touched me with love, cherishing, caressing me. No, these hands were cruel and torturous. His words pierced me, twisting my mind as he squeezed the life out of my body and assaulted my already deeply wounded spirit.

What brought us to this verbal assault, this emotional and physical abuse after 15 years of being together? How did we get this way? He had been the love of my life.

I looked over at my two girls, Rachel and Enya, aged 4 and 5 years, staring with shock at the nightmare in the kitchen. Their eyes were wide with disbelief and fear. Mommy and Daddy in such turmoil!

I wished I could loose this grip so I could explain, so I could grab them and run. I struggled, kicking at his feet and legs, to no avail. All the while, the devil whispered lies in my ears. "See, you are exactly what you are being called. You are no good. No one could love you. You deserve this. You are going to die." In the spirit realm, I could hear the sneering, the laughing. I believed it all.

What triggered this outburst? I knew that Holy Spirit in me was confronting the demons that, at this moment, controlled him and hated me.

Thinking my children would soon be without me, I whispered a silent prayer to God, "Oh Lord Jesus, please look after them."

My youngest daughter, Rachel, was standing just a little behind the older one, Enya. Rachel's beautiful big brown eyes were sad and in tears. It was like my eyes were saying goodbye to them as my body became limp and my last breath exhaled. I gave into death, forced upon me by the grip on my neck.

Suddenly, Enya's piercing shrill scream rent the atmosphere. "Daddy, stop!! Stop! Stop!!"

Immediately the grip loosened.

LIFE began to pour back into me. Amid the sputtering and the coughing, I came to with just enough air to regain my balance. Still gasping, I struggled to stand. Then, grabbed the kids, including my 3-year-old step-granddaughter Lily, who was staying with us.

I yelled to the dog, "Lassie, come!" We ran into the dark night. I quickly shoved them into the car and prayed to God that my older Volvo station wagon would start so I could speed out of there and not look back.

Where to go? My best friend had told me that we were always welcome at their house. Her kids were all grown, and she and her husband lived not far from us. Over the years, they had become a calming, gentle Grandpa Heinzel and Grandma Gerta to the kids. So, I arrived with three little girls under seven and a dog in tow.

Years earlier, I had made a vow that if anything like this assault happened again, I would report it to the police. Now, at my dear friend's home, I called the police and reported the crime. The marks were evident on my neck. The scratches and bruises on my throat, face, and arms were fresh. The picture of assault was clear.

But I wondered where God was. Why did my husband hate me so much? Was it God who used my daughter's voice to speak to the demonic entity that had been controlling my husband? Was I really that horrible of a person? My identity had been thrashed a thousand times over in the past.

I was a child of the King, a daughter of the Most High, a priest in the order of Melchizedek, called, appointed, chosen, the bride of Christ. Really? Then why was I being treated with such cruelty? Words were my first love language, so words cut deeply. I grappled with lies battling truth, praying truth would win out.

I lay on the bed, sobbing as I thought about the children because, if the truth be known, I wasn't sure I was making the right decision. Confusion, wounding, fear, regret, loss, betrayal, and guilt all blurred together. My heart felt ripped apart as I sought to make sense of my life. My gut twisted into a huge knot. I pulled myself into a fetal position and rocked back and forth, soothing myself. My mind whirled a million miles per hour as I sought a way out of this mess. For now, I would pray to God that I could sleep. I prayed He would collect my tears and keep them so He could one day pour them out for a restoration harvest.

Gerta and Heinzel would be my support through this turmoil. Mom, who was ever the reassurance of love, stood by me, as did my sister and two brothers. The church I attended also cared for me. I would make it, although that night, I had no answers, only questions. Still, I was blessed in the midst of crisis. They could have all turned away.

The next few days were a blur. Traumatized, I made decisions focused on survival, with no clue how I would support us. One regret I will carry for the rest of my life was calling my stepdaughter Carla to come to pick up Lily. I knew that was the worst place for that girl to go because her mom was an escort—a lady of the night.

The day Carla came to pick up Lily, I cried. Guilt, shame, condemnation, and failure—all accusations from the devil. I was worried for Lily. How would she survive this? I cried out in prayer to my Lord, who sees all things and knows all things. I felt like this sweet, innocent, little blue-eyed, blonde 3-year-old was going into the "lion's den."

But God graciously reminded me, "Don't worry, Ellie. Just like I closed the mouths of the lions for Daniel, I can also close the mouths of the lions for Lily. No one will ruin her. Give her to Me".

In great reluctance, I surrendered her to Carla. And to God.

As the days went by, reality sank in that I had left my beautiful home in the forest with the treehouse and the crystal clear swimming pool in the backyard. Gone was the safe, secure neighbourhood and the little girls who used to come to play with my daughters at our home. Where would we live? I was homeless with no money, two kids, a dog, and an old station wagon.

But God began to show me He is a husband to His bride, and He cares.

I learned that surrendering my brokenness to our beautiful Creator would give me peace, true freedom, and lasting contentment. 'Let Go and Let God' became my new motto as God showed me Bible verses to cling to and live by.

Call unto Me, and I will answer you and show you great and mighty things, which you do not know. (Jeremiah 33:3 NKJV)

I am the Good Shepherd, I know My sheep, and I am known by My own. (John 10:14 NKJV)

> *I will instruct you and teach you in the way you should go; I will guide you with My eye.* (Psalm 32:8 NKJV)

> *Trust in the Lord with all your heart, And do not lean on your own understanding, In all your ways acknowledge Him, And He shall direct your paths.* (Proverbs 3:5-6 NKJV)

I surrendered my home and let go of the rights that I thought I had. Each moment I chose to believe that God is who He says He is - my Provider, Shepherd, and Healer. I hid in His love banner over me! I prayed that one day He would bring my (ex) husband and me to reconciliation.

Unfortunately, that wasn't the extent of my trials. A month later, I received a phone call. My brother-in-law spoke in a monotone voice, "I'm sorry, Ellie, but your father had a heart attack and has passed away!"

What! No! Not my father, who loved me so dearly, talked to me about everything, taught me the value of work and family, and had stood firmly by me with so much love as I struggled through the many landmines of my life. Not my father, who I closely hung out with my whole childhood! "No!" my mind screamed. First, I was left without my husband, and now, a few weeks later, I was left without my father.

In February of 1993, at 33 years old, my whole world crashed down around me. I was broken, alone, orphaned, rejected, and abandoned.

God, are You here? Do You care? The questions rumbled around inside of the blackness that I felt. I no longer saw vibrant colors, only grey and black. The mountains in front of me stood like rock formations. Is this how one gets a Breaker Anointing? Do we have to face mountains?

Going through the motions, I packed up the kids, drove the 18 hours for my father's memorial, and tried to comfort Mom. My parents had been happily married for 44 years—going through thick and thin together, they trusted in their Rock, the Lord God Almighty. They showed me over the past 30 years how it looks to surrender to God, who loves and cares about every detail of our lives. Would He do that for me?

> *The Lord will perfect that which concerns me. Your mercy, O Lord, endures forever.* (Psalm 138:8 NKJV)

After the memorial, I left the girls with Mom and drove back to Kelowna, a glistening city in the beautiful, sunny Okanagan Valley, to find a job and a place to live. I would have to rely on government welfare for emergency funds to get me through. But being homeless with two kids to raise required me to let go of my pride and reach out for assistance.

Amidst the blackness, I once again surrendered to God. I embraced Him like never before through reading the Scriptures.

> *Your word is a lamp to my feet And a light unto my path.* (Psalm 119:105 NKJV)

The Lord is my Shepherd, I shall not want. (Psalm 23:1 NKJV) That means I won't lack anything. I can rest in His green pastures and drink deeply from His waters. He is my refuge and my shield.

> *Your ears shall hear a word behind you saying "This is the way, walk in it," Whenever you turn to the right hand or whenever you turn to the left.* (Isaiah 30:21 NKJV)

The strength of the Lord began coursing through me as I encouraged myself with the Word. I resolved to go forward in His strength.

I stopped at the cemetery beside Dad's freshly dug grave and told him, "Dad, please, I'm sorry. But I cannot mourn and grieve for you right now. I must survive. I will grieve at a later date when I feel safe again." I knew he understood.

I needed to find a new home for the girls and me.

But where would I live, and how would I survive? How would I provide for the girls' needs while I could hardly think straight? I grieved as I drove to Kelowna, wondering again why the kids had to leave their beautiful, quaint, safe neighbourhood where they knew all the children. Why, why, why? I questioned God, who said He loved me. But was He even listening?

He was there. He kissed my tears away. I could feel His tenderness as I surrendered to Him. Song of Songs, Isaiah, Psalms, Proverbs, and John became some of my favorite books of the Bible.

Still, I went back and forth between fear and faith. Could I truly trust God? He gave me grace! My own faith equaled .5%, and He supplied the other 95.5%. Lord, I need your sufficiency in my insufficiency. Give me grace and faith. Show me the way.

As long as I held tightly to the Bible, God did show me the way.

> *God told me He would provide the wisdom I would need. If any of you lacks wisdom, let him ask of God, who gives to all liberally and without reproach, and it will be given to him. (James 1:5 NKJV)*

> *God told me he would make a new path for me. Behold, I will do a new thing, Now it shall spring forth; Shall you not know it? I will even make a road in the wilderness And rivers in the desert. (Isaiah 43:19 NKJV)*

> *He told me He had a plan for my life. For I know the thoughts that I think toward you, says the Lord, thoughts of peace and not of evil, to give you a future and a hope. (Jeremiah 29:11 NKJV)*

I read the Bible daily. And my God never let me down.

Holy Spirit spoke to me, leading me through the governmental system, helping me find accommodations - a two-bedroom basement suite. It was much less than we were used to and looked cold and dumpy, but it was a roof over our heads. And I could afford it. God was making arrangements to manifest His glory.

A week later, I found work. That gave me just enough money and time to drive back to Mom's, again the 18-hour trip, so I could get my girls and bring them to their new home and new school. They, too, were beginning a new chapter.

Though my girls were also grieving, God took care of them too. Grandma Gerta became a gift to us as she supplied babysitting every now and then, baking bread with them and teaching them how to bake cookies. The RCMP (Royal Canadian Mounted Police) Crime unit provided a box filled with all kinds of Christmas gifts, goodies and candy when Christmas came along. A man came to stay over to take care of us when my ex-husband was on the rampage. Enya's grade 2 teacher gave us a monetary gift to supply piano lessons for both girls. She marked it from the Christmas Angel. There were so many miracles. Another man gave money when we prayed, asking Father God to supply money for ski lessons for my oldest daughter. That was a big lesson in faith for Enya. Other people would hand us $50 bills when I didn't know how I was going to make it. The girls made new friends who have stayed with them for all these years. On and on I could go retelling God's miraculous provision and care for us.

My ex-husband got out on bail and threatened to come after me and take the kids. I prayed for angelic assistance, and God responded. One day Grandma Gerta picked us up and helped us find places to hide, so my ex-husband could not take the kids. Or kill us. I was so petrified I didn't know what he would do.

Grandma Gerta was also God's mouthpiece, reminding me, when I got fearful about my girls' future, that God loves them and has a plan for their lives, too. She insisted that I should surrender my control of every aspect of their lives, which was difficult as these were my miracle children. Before they were born, I had been barren for ten years. I had miscarried four babies and gone through numerous surgeries and fertility drugs trying to conceive them. But despite this, I knew I had to trust God, the words of my godly friend, and, most importantly, the Bible.

Through my tears, I broke the stronghold of fear inside my heart. I decided to trust Jesus – even for the welfare of the children He had put in my care. Sobbing, I cried out, "Oh Jesus, I give You my girls to guard and protect, to keep safe. Oh, Jesus, I let them go. I surrender them to You! I believe I can trust YOU!"

I have seen God's miraculous ways as I have surrendered through the years. One example is the powerful gift of forgiveness. My ex-husband and

I reconciled to be good friends to this day, thus co-parenting the girls and giving them a stable foundation (in spite of the circumstances) to stand on in life. We have enjoyed being at their graduations, attending their weddings, sharing grandchildren and many birthdays and holiday celebrations together as a family.

Let go and let God is easier sometimes than others. Back when the incident occurred, I prayed to God to take care of my children, and He did—but I had to let Him. The girls have grown up and have children of their own. They are contributing members of society in their work, their homes, and the community, as they are used to bring joy to those they serve.

God has taken me to many nations as I share this story and many others that God has taught me in my life. I have become a speaker, a teacher, and, from time to time, a preacher. God continues to use me powerfully as I am a tool to counsel people, to bring them through healing and deliverance with my Freedom to Soar Ministries. Truly the motto: Let Go and Let God is a great way to live!

Surrender Your Dreams

By Julie T. Jenkins

"Follow your dreams."

If I were to cite a pinnacle catchphrase for how society teaches us to live today, "follow your dreams" just might be it. But what if we were to recognize that we may not completely understand the complexities of the dreams that reside in our own hearts? And what if we were to surrender our dreams and, instead, ask God to allow us to live out the dreams He has for us?

Imagine a fully packed stadium at a sporting event. Thousands of eyes are on the athletes, and every fan has an idea of what their favorite team must do to ensure a win. And yet, each set of eyes sees the unfolding events from a single angle. So the fans, and even the players, must trust the coach, who can see the big picture. Likewise, as individuals on this earth, it is impossible for us to fully and completely understand all the nuances of any situation. Only God can do that.

We have a limited view of life—even our own life. Therefore the dreams we hold in our hearts might be flawed or not yield the best results should they be realized. But although we can't fully trust our own dreams, we serve a God whose view and vision we can trust implicitly.

Praise God that He is omniscient (all-knowing) and omnipresent (present everywhere and at every time). He alone can see the whole picture. He knows every detail of every circumstance. He understands you better than you understand yourself. He sees how everything works together. And He is ready to download His dream for your life into your spirit.

Besides being omniscient and omnipresent, God is also omnipotent! That means that He has unlimited power. God is almighty, supreme, and able

Surrendered: Yielded With Purpose

to overcome. So not only will God's dreams be perfectly crafted for you, but when you cooperate with Him, you can trust that His plans for you will succeed.

> He who began a good work in you will carry it on to completion until the day of Christ Jesus. (Philippians 1:6 NIV)

God's biggest dreams for you are that you will become His child, grow closer to Him every day, and invite others to become followers of Jesus.

> I urge, then, first of all, that petitions, prayers, intercession and thanksgiving be made for all people—for kings and all those in authority, that we may live peaceful and quiet lives in all godliness and holiness. This is good, and pleases God our Savior, who wants all people to be saved and to come to a knowledge of the truth. (1 Timothy 2:1-4 NIV)

Please don't ever think that God's dream for you is boring—did I mention how creative our God is? He specializes in using your specific gifts and talents to glorify and reach the world for Him, and when you surrender to Him, our creator God will handcraft a dream for you that is better than you could ask or imagine.

Recently, I attended the Grand Ole Opry in Nashville, Tennessee. This is perhaps the most celebrated country-music stage in the world—a venue where every up-and-coming country musician dreams of performing. While there, I witnessed a young artist who grew up in Nashville welcomed to the stage for the first time. As he sang, his exuberance filled the air. The unique thing about this artist is that his joy didn't flow from performing country music; his exultation came from praising and worshipping God. Colton Dixon is a Christian musician, and he was performing his hit song *Build a*

Boat to a packed house from the most famous country stage. Colton followed God's dream for him as he sang unashamedly about his faith. And as he was being interviewed, this young artist gave the glory to God alone for making his dream come true. There were no altar calls at the Grand Ole Opry, but Colton Dixon undoubtedly made a difference for God's Kingdom that night as God fulfilled the dream He had prepared for that talented young artist.

When we focus our hearts on God, He will allow us to realize His dreams in the most amazing ways—and it will never be boring.

> *Make God the utmost delight and pleasure of your life, and he will provide for you what you desire most. Give God the right to direct your life, and as you trust him along the way you'll find he pulled it off perfectly!* (Psalm 37:4-5 TPT)

While society wants us to follow our dreams, we can only see the world from a single angle, so we must surrender those aspirations to our omniscient and omnipresent God, who can see the whole picture. God has a plan for us that fits into His Kingdom's vision, and our omnipotent creator has the power to make His dreams for us come to life in the most ingenious ways. So let's surrender our dreams to God and seek His heart, trusting the realization of His perfect glory.

Lindsey Sullivan

Lindsey Sullivan is a lover of Jesus Christ, a singer-songwriter, artist, and journalist. She graduated from Pepperdine University in 2021 and currently resides in Southwest Florida, where she serves as a worship leader and music teacher for the families of Lionheart Ministry. Lindsey's passion for truth, creativity, and inspiring others is the lifeblood of her work. She is the founder of Alabaster Heart, a ministry aiming to equip generations with worship and revival for the Lord's glory. Her heart's desire is to provide beautiful, fragrant music, products, and services that please the Lord and lead others to His presence. Lindsey is also a contributor for *Voice of Truth* magazine, a freelance copyeditor, and co-host of "A Kindred Narrative," a conversational podcast aiming to inspire young Christian women that she runs alongside her best friend, Kayla Follin.

When she is not serving in ministry or writing music, Lindsey enjoys exploring the natural beauty of South Florida, traveling, and making new connections.

To learn more about Lindsey and her ministry or to listen to her music, visit alabasterheart.co.

With All of the Broken That I Am

By Lindsey Sullivan

Where do you run to when you feel low, weak, or vulnerable? I'm embarrassed to admit I don't always turn to the Lord as my first course of action. In fact, there was a time in my life, not too long ago, when I openly talked about the Lord and even said I loved Him, though secretly, I was brushing years of pain under the rug, hiding my heart from Him, and numbing myself from His voice.

It was nearing the end of summer 2021, and I was a recent college graduate. Like many of my peers, I had moved back home with my newly acquired journalism degree to figure out what I should do with my life. Feeling confident about my decision as I needed the time and space to think deeply about my first big career move, I was honestly craving a restful season to recover from the fast-paced hustle of school life.

One summer afternoon, I was sitting on the back porch reading a book when I received a phone call that caused my heart to sink. It was my sister, who lives in Charleston, South Carolina, telling me that our mom had been staying with her for a few weeks. The backstory is that my parents split up when I was young, and "home" for me meant my dad's house in Virginia. Mom lived not too far in a town about 40 minutes away. So, you can imagine my shock when my sister told me that our mom had been several states away for weeks. During that phone call, my sister didn't spare my feelings — our mom was not doing well. In fact, her life was on the line. And though my sister had helped her condition to stabilize, my mom would have to come home soon. And if I wanted her to live, I would be responsible for caring for her.

A million thoughts raced through my mind. It was no secret; my mom's health was in peril because of her lifelong battle with substance abuse. I felt burdened in my heart for her and troubled with anger. I was angry because substance abuse is a terrible thing to witness up close. It robs people of true life, enjoyment, and dignity. I have watched my mom battle it for most of my life. And I won't lie, my relationship with her wasn't great before that phone call. I loved her and honored her as I knew how to, and she loved me the same, but our relationship was not what I wanted it to be. I never really knew which side of her I would get, which caused my heart to be distrustful and to form walls between us. As I listened to my sister on the phone, I felt the anger rise in my heart, but I quickly pushed it back down. This was no time to be angry. I needed to step up and be there for my mom. After all, she needed me. Giving in to my anger at this point would be plain selfish.

When I picked my mom up from the airport a few days later, I barely recognized the woman who got in my car. She was severely malnourished with swollen eyes and yellow skin, and her hair was tied back and knotted from weeks spent lying in bed. We exchanged a few words and then spent the remainder of the car ride in silence. Her body and soul were weak, so conversation was difficult for her. When we got home, I helped her bathe and brushed her hair. She couldn't stomach much food, so we skipped dinner, and I tucked her into bed.

A couple of weeks went by like this, and she seemed to be on the road to recovery when, one morning, I found her sick in the bathroom. We drove to the hospital and I checked her into the emergency room. We waited all day and night for a bed. When the doctor finally visited, his diagnosis was less

Surrendered: Yielded With Purpose

than encouraging: cirrhosis, he explained, is a condition in which the liver becomes scarred and permanently damaged and, in her case, could require a liver transplant. I sat at the foot of the hospital bed, muttering a less-than-eloquent prayer as I scrambled for the right words to console her, but all my words fell short. I felt totally inadequate to be in that room with her, and I desperately wished there was a magic prayer I could pray to heal her.

I would spend the next four months checking my mom in and out of hospitals, taking her to doctor appointments and a detox center, and attempting to find her a good rehabilitation facility. Traveling back and forth between my hometown and the town where my mom lived, I was carrying more weight than I could manage in my own strength.

Besides tending to my mom's physical and mental needs, and making sure she didn't fall into drinking again, I was still working, trying to save up to move out and start a life on my own. I was also helping my father with the home and caring for my little sister. All the while, I was ignoring my own needs and wearing a smile, attempting to be strong for my family. Somehow I managed this balance and gave the Lord what little I had left over. Some nights all I gave Him was a small prayer before falling asleep. Some days, taking a moment to worship Him gave me just enough strength to take the next step. But the truth is I was hiding my heart from the Lord. I didn't like the place I was in spiritually, but I knew that if I really turned to Him—if I surrendered my pride and revealed the emotions weighing down my soul—it would make a huge mess. And I couldn't afford to be a mess; there was too much at stake.

Around that same time, I began to open myself up to a romantic relationship. The Lord actually warned me not to get involved with this person because I was so emotionally vulnerable. But of course, I thought I knew better than the Lord and could handle it myself. Truth be told, my heart was desperate for affection—to be seen, understood, and loved. See, it wasn't just my relationship with my mom that was suffering, but also my relationship with my dad. We were both in a rough place, and neither of us knew how to support the other.

I felt like I was doing everything on my own, in my own strength, with no one to help or even see me in my struggle. So, I fell into the trap of expecting a new romance to provide what I wasn't receiving from my family.

I don't open myself up to relationships often. In fact, I never had in this way before. I knew there was a real chance I could get hurt, but I reasoned that I was already hurting, so I might as well let myself feel something good. I know I'm not the only one who has been there, surrounded by so much darkness and desperately searching for a fragment of light, a momentary glimpse of hope. My hope, however, was severely misplaced and led to great disappointment when the relationship ended quickly and without much closure. My heart was running out of the will to fight, and years of unresolved hurt in my heart led me toward a breaking point.

One night I sat on the bathroom floor. I was broken and alone, drunk in my attempt to numb myself, and horrified that I had let my wounds fester into such a mess. My tears grew into sobs, which eventually steadied into long gasps for air between whimpers. I felt like someone had taken the very breath out of my lungs, and there was a gaping hole in my chest. I knew God was with me, but honestly, I didn't want Him there. I didn't want Him to see me like that. How could He look at the awful mess I was and still love me? Yes, I was hurting due to the weight of life I was carrying, but the root of my pain was much deeper.

I was hurting because the little girl in me who felt abandoned by her mother years before was being exposed. The same little girl who took on the weight of helping her father care for a home and raise her little sister. That little girl was crying out, "This is too much!" And no amount of numbing could absolve me of that kind of pain. All those years of soothing my wounds with bandages and running away from problems had finally caught up with me. This was an infection I could no longer ignore. The Lord was bringing all my hurt to the light. I felt ashamed. I was asking God, *"How* could *I* love *You?"* I yearned to know and understand how, with all of my brokenness—the messy, dirty, unlovable pieces of me that I had concealed for so long—how could I, the girl whose heart was so broken that she turned everywhere but to her Savior to heal her, how could *that girl* love a perfect, Holy God? And why would He want me to? And how, *how* could He possibly choose to love me back? Surely there had to be some statute of limitations on His grace for us. And clearly, I had reached them.

You see, it's the enemy of our souls who wants us to hide in shame, conceal our pain and run anywhere but to our Lord. It's not unique to how he first deceived Adam in Genesis 3:9 (NIV). *"Where are you?"* The Lord calls out to Adam after he ate the fruit the Lord told him not to. The Lord wasn't confused about Adam's location. Of course, God knows everything; He is everywhere at all times. Instead, God was piercing Adam's heart with the question that he was too ashamed to face himself. Adam covered himself with leaves, and when he heard the Lord's voice, knowing he was apart from the Lord's presence, he answered, *"I heard you in the garden, and I was afraid because I was naked; so I hid."* (Genesis 3:10 NIV)

I am no different from Adam. I might not have covered myself in leaves, but I wrapped my heart wounds in spiritual bandages, believing that they would keep me from feeling the hurt and keep the Lord from seeing all of the broken I truly was. But a bandage can't fix deep wounds. Only the Lord can. All a bandage will do is keep you trapped in the cycle of hurt, preventing others from seeing your need and leading you back to the source of healing, Jesus Himself. And worse, with lack of attention and proper care, that wound will get infected and spread to other areas of your soul. Don't do what I did and try to stuff it all down. Don't hide where you are hurting and bleeding out in your heart. God already sees it anyway. Bring your hurt to Him. He is ready and able to take it. There is nothing too big, too messy, or too broken for Him.

I love what the author of Hebrews tells us. *For we have a magnificent King-Priest, Jesus Christ, the Son of God, who rose into the heavenly realm for us, and now sympathizes with us in our frailty. He understands humanity, for as a man, our magnificent King-Priest was tempted in every way just as we are, and conquered sin. So now we come freely and boldly to where grace is enthroned, to receive mercy's kiss and discover the grace we urgently need to strengthen us in our time of weakness.* (Hebrews 4:14-16 TPT)

That night, as I felt the unbearable weight of shame, hurt, and loneliness crashing in on my soul, I heard the voice of the Lord quicken my spirit — the same voice that called to the very first man Adam, thousands of years before me. It wasn't an audible voice but a still, quiet knowing in the deepest part of me, telling me He was near, and He was ready to take my pain as soon as I was ready to surrender it to Him. His voice didn't come from a place of shame or anger or disappointment, but instead it came from His pure love and concern for me. It was gentle and sweet, and that's how I knew it wasn't my own voice. I never spoke to myself that way. All I could ever seem to do was condemn myself by pointing out my inadequacies and failures. But His voice didn't condemn me; it called me higher, closer toward Him. I didn't know how to get myself out of the mess I was in, and clearly, what I was doing before wasn't working.

When I heard His voice, I felt the little girl in me who was holding on to all her hurt out of a need to protect herself finally let go. I surrendered to His voice and prayed a very simple prayer. I repented and asked for forgiveness. I asked Him to lead me as I surrendered to Him. It was not a beautiful prayer; I was still an awful mess, and my voice was hoarse from crying so much. But God saw my heart. He heard my surrender, even if it was my weakest yes.

I can't tell you that I woke up the next morning with all my problems solved, my relationships restored, and my heart completely healed. That was very much not the case. Instead, I was slightly hungover, still heartbroken, and feeling barely alive.

My circumstances hadn't changed, but I certainly did. I wasn't carrying the weight on my own anymore. Yes, I still had to walk out the process of healing from that day forward, but I no longer had to do it alone. It would be months after that prayer before my circumstances changed for the better. In fact, from the outside, it probably appeared that my life was only getting worse. My mom's health wasn't seeing any improvement, and my relationship with my father grew so unhealthy that I eventually had no choice but to move out. And because I had been working for my father's business, I suddenly found myself without a home or a job. But the Lord honored my surrender and provided for me, over and abundantly, through the love of friends and family.

What I couldn't see before, while I was wrapped up in all my striving to be enough in my own strength, is that God never asked me to be enough. In fact, apart from Him, I can do nothing. (John 15:5 NIV). What I missed while I was blinded by my own hurt is the whole point of the gospel; the beautiful invitation of grace, which is that we aren't enough on our own. People will hurt us, we will fail in our flesh, and we need a Savior and Lord to make things right. We need a Good Shepherd to mend our brokenness, to love us back into communion with Himself when we stray, and to lead us on the right path daily.

I wish I could tell you, almost a year after that prayer, that the Lord has redeemed all that was lost and that I have seen the complete resolution of all of the brokenness in my family. But I can't. I wish I could write that I have seen my mom's health fully restored and my relationships with my parents made new and whole. But I haven't yet. These are the promises I am still believing for. But I will say this—God has never once backed down from His word to love me and lead me.

God's grace is sufficient for me! (2 Corinthians 12:9) And His grace is sufficient for you, too. I don't know what the Lord is calling you to surrender. Maybe you have hidden wounds like me. Perhaps you're still believing for a miracle, a restored relationship, or a family member's salvation. Whatever it is that you need today, go to the Source. Let us daily surrender, with all of the broken that we are, to the Good Shepherd that He is. He is willing, ready, and able to lead us beside still waters, to restore our souls, and to lead us in the path of righteousness.

Psalm 23 (NKJV)

The Lord is my shepherd;
I shall not want.
He makes me to lie down in green pastures;
He leads me beside the still waters.
He restores my soul;
He leads me in the paths of righteousness
For His name's sake.
Yea, though I walk through the valley of the shadow of death,
I will fear no evil;
For You are with me;
Your rod and Your staff, they comfort me.
You prepare a table before me in the presence of my enemies;
You anoint my head with oil;
My cup runs over.
Surely goodness and mercy shall follow me
All the days of my life;
And I will dwell in the house of the Lord
Forever.

Surrendered: Yielded With Purpose

Surrender Your Judgments

By Julie T. Jenkins

When many non-Christians think about Christianity, the word "judgmental" often comes to mind.

Wouldn't it be great if the first word others identified with Christianity was "love"? That is what Jesus wanted.

Jesus taught, in no uncertain terms, *"Do not judge others, and you will not be judged."* (Matthew 7:1 NLT) And later, He told His disciples, *"I am giving you a new commandment: Love each other. Just as I have loved you, you should love each other. Your love for one another will prove to the world that you are my disciples."* (John 13:34-35 NLT)

As Christians, we are privileged. We have been given the truth of humanity and God in the Bible, and the Holy Spirit has revealed God's eternal mysteries to us. Oh, we surely don't understand or know all there is to know, but as we walk with God and seek His wisdom, we grow wiser each and every day. And there isn't anything the devil can do about that—because, as God's children, we are forever sealed into His presence. But that glorious fact doesn't stop the devil from diving into His bag of tricks to make our lives miserable and keep others from being drawn into God's presence.

Enter pride. And arrogance. And self-righteousness. All tools that are found in the devil's toolbox.

The devil loves to use those tools to twist our understanding of Jesus' teachings. If we let him have his way, we will no longer recognize Jesus' personal words of instruction to each of us as a means of becoming a better reflection of God's image. Instead, we will use Jesus' teachings as a filter through which to judge the actions of *others*.

For example, when we hear Jesus say *repent* (Matthew 4:17 NIV), the devil wants us to hear, "Make sure others repent."

Obey your leaders and submit to them (Hebrews 13:17 NASB) becomes twisted to "I am in authority, so others should obey me."

We misconstrue *let your light shine before others, that they may see your good deeds and glorify your Father in heaven* (Matthew 5:16 NIV) to "I need to shine my God-given light so everyone else can recognize what they are doing wrong."

And when we read, *People will be lovers of themselves, lovers of money, boastful, proud, abusive, disobedient to their parents, ungrateful, unholy, without love, unforgiving, slanderous, without self-control, brutal, not lovers of the good, treacherous, rash, conceited, lovers of pleasure rather than lovers of God—having a form of godliness but denying its power* (2 Timothy 3:2-5 NIV), instead of checking ourselves and our own actions, we quickly turn and point the finger at others.

God did not put us on this earth to judge and condemn each other, but to uphold, support, teach, guide, and love each other.

Be devoted to one another in love. Honor one another above yourselves. (Romans 12:10 NIV)

Do nothing out of selfish ambition or vain conceit. Rather, in humility value others above yourselves. (Philippians 2:3 NIV)

"Love your neighbor as yourself." (Matthew 22:39 NIV)

Scripture clearly states that we are to surrender any judgmental thoughts. Our sole job is to love others, and we are to leave judgment to the only One who can judge fairly and accurately: God the Father.

We learn in Ephesians 4 that, as Christians, we are called to a higher purpose. We were not only made in God's image, but we are to represent Jesus on earth, so we must always seek to leave our judgments behind and operate only in love.

> As a prisoner for the Lord, then, I urge you to live a life worthy of the calling you have received. Be completely humble and gentle; be patient, bearing with one another in love. Make every effort to keep the unity of the Spirit through the bond of peace...Do not let any unwholesome talk come out of your mouths, but only what is helpful for building others up according to their needs, that it may benefit those who listen. And do not grieve the Holy Spirit of God, with whom you were sealed for the day of redemption. Get rid of all bitterness, rage and anger, brawling and slander, along with every form of malice. Be kind and compassionate to one another, forgiving each other, just as in Christ God forgave you. (Ephesians 4:1-3, 29-32 NIV)

God has given us the gift of living joyfully and peacefully in love while surrendering our judgment of others to Him—the only qualified Judge.

. . . .

Tina Rains

Tina Rains, RN, is the mother of 7, Mimi to 7, and married to Monty.

Driven to help all women know they are a masterpiece and help them step into their calling and lead like Jesus, Tina founded Masterpiece Women and Masterpiece Women Podcasts - www.MasterpieceWomen.org. Masterpiece Women is a movement of women pursuing authentic community, personal and professional excellence, and local and global impact for good. The ministry is based on Ephesians 2:10, *For we are God's masterpiece. He has created us anew in Christ Jesus, so we can do the good things he planned for us long ago.* (NLT)

Tina is also helping launch an international health and wellness company focused on improved health, weight loss, and mindset. The first product is a revolutionary product that accelerates fat loss by working on the leptin levels in your body. As a nurse, Tina is committed to helping others get healthy physically, emotionally, and spiritually.

To learn more about Tina Rains, Masterpiece Women, leadership, or improving your health, visit www.TinaRains.com

Climb to Freedom

By Tina Rains

Each day is a climb.

Some days, the mountains we climb are immense: illness, financial struggle, marriage issues, divorce, children, infidelity, abuse, or other trauma. On other days our mountain can consist of the lies the enemy uses to control us.

I remember sitting on my comfortable leather couch overlooking our beautiful patio and tiki hut on the intercoastal waterway. Before me were our boats, jet skis, and other toys - the things I had worked so hard to obtain for my family to bring us fun. It was such a beautiful home, and I loved just sitting out there, watching the children play.

But as I sat there that day, I wondered how long it would be before I lost it all, and I asked myself, "How will I ever get past all this mess?" I felt so alone as I cried out to God and begged Him to change my situation, saying, "God, you have me highly mistaken for somebody else. I cannot handle one more thing." I was going through the biggest climb of my life. Or so, I thought at the time.

I was facing divorce and the loss of my home due to the divorce. Additionally, my staffing company was failing due to the recession, my best friend and business partner had married my ex-husband leading to tons of drama and pain, and a rebellious teenager wasn't making things easy. I was trying to balance the weight of it all on my shoulders. It was unbearable. So many days, I wanted to give up. I could not see the summit from the weight of the burdens. I soon discovered, however, that although the climb was tough, it was nothing for God. I just needed to surrender.

I struggled with surrender. Surrender is letting go of the controls. As a victim of sexual abuse, I felt the need to control my circumstances. How on earth could I trust anyone again to take the controls, let alone a God who had allowed all this pain to happen? I was still living as a victim. I didn't trust God, and I no longer trusted myself to control things. I had made a mess of our lives. The bad choices I made brought me to this point. I had chosen the wrong people to be in a relationship with, the wrong partners in business, and I made so many other mistakes it would take me days to share. I was losing everything I valued.

So how was doing it my way going for me? Not very well, to say the least. I had a choice, and I knew it. Do I give up on life or surrender to God? Do I choose to trust God? I knew God well enough to know I could surrender it all to Him if I truly trusted Him. But how could I do that? I recognized I could no longer navigate things on my own. I was drowning in self-pity, hopelessness, victimization, and pain. Something had to change – and that something was me.

It was that day that my surrendered climb towards Jesus began. It was the best choice I have ever made. I decided to truly follow Jesus, surrender my life to Him, and do the work it would take to know Him intimately, changing my life. I pulled out my Bible and began to read and pray as I continued to cry out to God. Right then, my transformation began. I began to stand on the verses I read that day: Proverbs 3:5-6, *Trust in the Lord with all your heart; do not depend on your own understanding. Seek his will in all you do, and he will show you which path to take.* (NLT) And Jeremiah 29:11-14, *"For I know the plans I have for you," says the Lord. "They are plans for good and not for disaster, to give you a future and a hope. In those days when you pray, I will listen. If you look for me wholeheartedly, you will find me. I will be found by you," says the Lord. "I will end your captivity and restore your fortunes. I will gather you out of the nations where I sent you and will bring you home again to your own land."* (NLT)

My climb had just begun.

No matter how large the mountain is, the answer is the same. We must surrender it and ourselves completely to God. I know all so well how difficult that can be. More times than not, it is a great struggle. I had huge mountains to climb. However, this time I had the best guide in the world.

First, I would deal with the trauma that had begun at an early age. At the age of 12, my life changed significantly. I discovered that it was not normal for a stepfather to do the things my stepfather did to me. My stepfather, who had sexually molested me for years, left my mother. This was a very painful time for her but a celebration for me. I suddenly had this new freedom. He was gone. I was so relieved and yet, so sad at the same time. I also had great shame and guilt as I blamed myself for him leaving my mother. I had told my stepfather that if he ever touched me again, I would throw him in jail. I felt so brave saying it to him. It had taken months for me to muster up the courage. I replayed in my head a thousand times how and when I would say it. Once I did, the threats came again, and I was scared. However, I look back and see that God gave me the courage to stand strong. Despite the threats, he left the next day.

Still, I questioned my actions as I watched my mother weeping in agony. Her heart was broken, and the reality of our financial state set in. My stepfather paid the bills but was behind on all of them. My mother did not work at the time, so she was trying to figure out how we would pay the overdue electric bill, buy groceries, and pay the mortgage. I asked myself, "Should I have given him the ultimatum? Or should I have just allowed it so my mother wouldn't be going through this?" I blamed myself for my mother's suffering. How could I have done this to her and our family?

My mother did not know what had transpired with my stepfather, and she was so devastated by his leaving that she accepted her friend Norma's invitation to church. That night my mother accepted Jesus as her Savior. The next night she took my brother and me to the church to attend a revival. And we both accepted Christ as our Savior as well. God changed our lives and home forever. I was very grateful and on fire for Jesus. I shared Him with anyone who would listen. That was until I went to high school. I didn't realize all the inner healing that my soul still needed. So much of the trauma I had experienced left me feeling vulnerable, insecure, and desperately seeking to feel loved and accepted by others. I took those void areas into my teens and adulthood.

Entering my adult years, I was still so wounded, and I had created more wounds and pain by the choices I continued to make in my brokenness. I married my high school boyfriend, who had been unfaithful to me many times. And I found myself pregnant with my first child at 19. She is and always has been such a gift from God. My daughter is living proof that what the enemy means for destruction, the Lord uses for good. The Lord even used her to show me His miraculous power. It would take a book of its own to share the incredible story of how Jesus literally brought her back from death when she was two months old.

Despite the miracles I saw in my life, I still made poor choices as an adult based on my pain, lack of self-worth, and shame. I also suffered from other abuse (both verbal and mental), infidelity, betrayal, divorce, and financial misconduct, which compounded an already broken vessel. So, guess what happened? I wasn't happy at home; raising children could not fill my void, so I went in search of something else that would. Despite my pain and trials, the Lord blessed me with the ability to make millions of dollars. At 25 years old, I started my first business with my best friend, who was also my matron of honor and, eventually, the stepmother to my children. Our business thrived. Within a few short years, we were making millions of dollars a year.

A few years into our organization's launch, however, she and I realized that we both had very different goals. So we split our company. She kept her portion, which began to fail miserably, and I kept mine which grew like wildfire. At the time we split, we each had one office. We determined that whatever we each made at our own branch, we would keep, manage, and do with it what we deemed appropriate. That didn't go so well in the long term. Eventually, we were in a massive lawsuit, which I had to drop when she married my ex-husband. It was too difficult for my children. I had put all my energy, heart, and hard work into building the businesses, and my offices flourished. Within a few short years, I had eight offices around the country. I was filling my void and brokenness with money and things. Yet it still wasn't enough.

Maybe you can relate. How many times do we reach for the next shiny object to fill the void within when coming back to our Savior is really what we need? I tried filling my emptiness with everything besides the only One who could quench my thirst and hunger. My whole being longed for the pain to go away. In Psalm 63:1 (NLT), King David cries out: *O God, you are my God; I earnestly search for you. My soul thirsts for you; my whole body longs for you in this parched and weary land where there is no water.* But unlike David, I had not been searching for the One I knew could fill my parched heart.

Then one day, I just couldn't go one more step on my own. I needed His water to survive. That day in my living room, I had had enough. The climb was too steep for me to go on alone. I feared I would jump off the cliff if I didn't do something soon. Although my mask covered it to most, my pain was great. I sat there and offered the little bit I had left to my Savior, and I begged Him to forgive me. I rededicated my life to Him, and I remember a peace that surpassed all understanding washed over me. I knew my life was finally going to change. Something was different. I made a choice; I was going to try it God's way.

That Sunday, I went back to church. And I started attending every time the doors were open; I was serving and growing. My time in church was now different than it had ever been before. Praise God. I dedicated my life to growing close to the Lord. I had a joy I had never experienced, even after years of counseling. I immersed myself in the Word of God and learned to know His voice. Wow! What a difference there was in my thinking, behavior, and choices. Many of the difficulties remained; however, I was no longer walking alone. For the first time in my life, I depended on God and not myself. Romans 8:28 (NLT) says, *And we know that God causes everything to work together for the good of those who love God and are called according to His purpose for them.* God has called us all for His purpose. I stood on that and many other verses for strength to get through the divorce, short-sale of my home, closing of my business, and being a single mother. God not only got me through it all, but I also thrived for the first time in my life. Our Lord is so gracious. He loves us so deeply.

During that season, the Lord used many programs and Bible studies to heal my wounds. Over the course of the next year, I began to serve as a leader in our singles ministry, lead Bible studies, and involve myself with Christian ministries in our community. Prayer, Bible study and worship became my priorities. Ladies, I'm not going to profess that I was perfect at that point because I will never be perfect until I reach heaven. I will also not claim that suddenly my life became easy. It didn't. If anything, my finances became worse and worse. I tried to get a job as a registered nurse to supplement my income (or lack thereof), but I had not practiced in many years, so that became almost impossible. There were months when I did not know how I would pay my electric bill. But I was blessed with some dear friends who helped me through the difficult times with sweet gifts.

By far, the greatest gift I received that season was accepting I was loved dearly by my Savior. It was finally real in my heart and my head. I am His masterpiece, just like Ephesians 2:10 says: *For we are God's masterpiece. He has created us anew in Christ Jesus, so we can do the good things he planned for us long ago.* (NLT) In that season of transformation, God renewed my mind and my vision for my future.

And in that season, the Lord called me on my first trip to India. I knew that I knew I was supposed to go. He confirmed it in multiple ways - in scripture and through several events. So, I obeyed, despite my complete lack of desire to go. On that trip, I shared my testimony for the first time publicly. That was a huge step of healing for me, and it was so powerful for others who had suffered just like I had.

Our stories have a purpose and can help so many. When was the last time you shared your story? A year or so after returning from India, I gave my testimony to hundreds of people at a fundraiser in my community. Since then, I have spoken to thousands of people around the world. I once again decided to say yes to God when He asked me to climb Mount Kilimanjaro to raise funds and awareness for projects all over the world addressing human trafficking and the oppression of women and children. This time my climb was truly physical. Was I scared? Absolutely. I had never been a hiker. To be candid, I preferred the Ritz Carlton. Wow, had God changed my heart. I even rode in coach rather than first class when I went to India. Growth. Ladies, it comes in many forms. I must laugh at myself. Feel free to laugh with me.

Our God is good and faithful. Proverbs 16:9 says, *A man's heart plans his way, but the Lord directs his steps.* (NKJV) That truth was playing out before my eyes in my own life. He was directing my steps and would be with me each step I took up Mt. Kilimanjaro. It was only because of Him that I was able to summit that mountain. It was just like the personal mountains I had climbed before. If He can take this mess, transform my life, and get me to the top of the mountain, then He can also change your life. Trust Him with every part of your life. He will get you to the summit.

I believe God does have a sense of humor. What happened next was incredible. He not only got me to the brutal 19,341 feet summit of my first

Mt. Kilimanjaro climb, but I was also asked to take the Director position of the entire ministry when I returned. I would donate all my personal belongings, rent a condo, become a missionary, and go on to lead the movement. I climbed Mt. Kilimanjaro again, Mt. Kala Patthar (18,519 feet and just above base camp Everest), the Alps, dozens of 14,000 ft-plus peaks in Colorado, and so many more mountains. God took this girl who was brokenhearted just a few years earlier and transformed her into a woman after His heart. Then, He gave me a burning passion to transform the lives of women all over the world.

I left that organization in 2017, and after, God ignited a new vision in me. *Masterpiece Women* was birthed from a desire that every woman would know that they are a masterpiece and be able to live out Ephesians 2:10. During my tenure at the mission organization, I met women from all over the world whose stories of brokenness were the same. Little did I know that God would use the pain I had lived through and the leadership skills I learned while building business to impact the Kingdom of God. Masterpiece Women provides tangible tools to become strong leaders and build organizations with biblical principles. We believe that all women are leaders. From the mom staying home raising her children to the woman who is a CEO, we are all leading. When a woman knows her value and has the tools she needs to thrive, it positively impacts individuals, families, communities, and the world.

God is calling you to step into your calling. Your first step is to surrender and then trust Him with each step of your climb. Let's go change the world, ladies! The view from the top of the mountain is remarkable!

Surrender Your Treasures

By Julie T. Jenkins

> "Do not store up for yourselves treasures on earth, where moths and vermin destroy, and where thieves break in and steal. But store up for yourselves treasures in heaven, where moths and vermin do not destroy, and where thieves do not break in and steal. For where your treasure is, there your heart will be also." (Matthew 6:19-21 NIV)

It can seem like money makes the world go around. It is tempting to judge ourselves and others by the car we drive, the house we live in, and the clothes we wear. It's tempting to consider ourselves "secure" when our bills are paid off and we have a hefty sum of money to fall back on. But Jesus tells us that all that is a façade, and we could, at any point, lose all our earthly treasures.

I live in South Florida, where we are always on guard for hurricanes. Depending on where you live, your home may be threatened regularly by wildfires, snowstorms, erosion, or even war. But here is something to consider: when and if we lose our homes and all our possessions, do we also lose our security?

Jesus warns that, in this world, our possessions can be destroyed or stolen, and we also know that things wear out. But we were not meant for this world or the things of this world. We are merely passing through. And our security certainly isn't held in or exemplified by our homes, clothing, cars, or bank accounts.

True security only lies in God Himself.

This is difficult for us to grasp as security is one of those things we cannot see, and we want to see it! We want to hold things and have tangible evidence that we will be okay. But security isn't tangible. We can only recognize security by faith.

When we give our lives to Jesus Christ, He assures us that He will take care of us.

> *But seek first his kingdom and his righteousness, and all these things will be given to you as well. Therefore do not worry about tomorrow, for tomorrow will worry about itself. Each day has enough trouble of its own.* (Matthew 6:33-34 NIV)

When we give our lives to Jesus Christ, He offers us innumerable opportunities to grow to be more like Him. One of the powers that God gifts us with is generosity. But to claim this gift, we must turn away from the power of possessions the world ingrains in us and seek to live our lives with open hands.

We can trust that God, in His mysterious and miraculous ways, will enable and guide us to responsibly provide and care for those we love AND give generously to those in need. It is not an either/or proposition.

> *Whoever sows sparingly will also reap sparingly, and whoever sows generously will also reap generously. Each of you should give what you have decided in your heart to give, not reluctantly or under compulsion, for God loves a cheerful giver. And God is able to bless you abundantly, so that in all things at all times, having all that you need, you will abound in every good work.* (2 Corinthians 9:6-8 NIV)

But in this process of providing and giving, God just may call you to let go of your own treasures and possessions and bank accounts as you allow Him to grow your faith in your one true provider—because God wants us to recognize that our only security is in Him.

As Christians, we trust God with our salvation. We trust Him with our eternity. We know that when we die a physical death on this earth, the best is yet to come. And yet, we often have a difficult time trusting our all-sufficient God with our today and tomorrow. That is all part of our growth process. Do you want to look more like God? He is calling you to look to Him for your security. Don't just give God your heart; give Him your treasures and finances as well. He's the best financial guide you will ever find!

. . . .

Kelly Williams Hale

Kelly Williams Hale is an entrepreneur, speaker, and mentor. As an intimacy and empowerment coach, Kelly guides women on their journey to embrace their uniqueness, cultivate confidence and own their personal power. She's passionate about helping women claim their calling and discover the destiny God has for them!

Kelly has been featured on *The Kingdom View* show on the NOW Network and is a best-selling author as well as a contributing author to the *Voice of Truth* magazine. She hosts a monthly podcast with Women World Leaders and is a sought-after speaker. Kelly provides monthly training and encouragement in her *Sisters who Shine* Facebook community.

She is happily married (third time's a charm!), a mom of three—all born about a decade apart—delivering her youngest when she was 44 years old! Kelly is living proof that past mistakes don't define future success.

Kelly loves sushi, music, and Taco Tuesdays. She can often be found dancing to anything by the band *For King & Country*.

God's Plan, Not Mine

By Kelly Williams Hale

Looking at my phone, I saw that I had missed a call from my mom and two calls from my brother, Tim. Heart in my throat, I called Tim back.

When he answered, I could tell he had been crying.

"Oh, Tim, is it Dad?" I asked. My dad had been in the hospital for a week with some health issues.

"No, not Dad. It's Scott." My heart began racing.

"He died this morning, Kelly. Car accident, on his way to work."

My whole world tilted. Scott was a cop and the middle boy of my three brothers. The one sibling everyone loved and who connected us all.

What do you do when you suddenly realize this is not how the story is supposed to end? Scott was only 46. I cried out to God, "Why, Lord? Is this really happening?"

In that moment, I had no other choice than to surrender to God's plan. Not mine.

Surrender.

Such a powerful word. It brings to mind images of white flags and defeat. For me, the idea of surrendering always felt like giving up. Like I've lost control, and there's no point in continuing.

The world tells us that surrendering is weak.

Yet God calls us to surrender to Him. The surrendering He requires has paradoxically provided me with MORE strength.

> Trust in the Lord with all your heart; do not depend on your own understanding. Seek his will in all you do, and he will show you which path to take. (Proverbs 3:5-6 NLT)

I certainly didn't understand how it was for the best that Scott had to leave so soon—and so suddenly.

I never had a chance to say goodbye.

Scott surprised the whole family when he announced he wanted to be a cop. He was 33 years old and, prior to that time, had several different jobs but never found "his thing." Ironically, he was the sibling who got into trouble with the law! I believe he struggled with insecurities and doubt (like we all do) and felt like he had to prove himself. He was often the one who started the trouble, but he would also stand up to bullies, protecting someone who was being mistreated.

Scott played hard and loved harder. He knew the Lord but struggled with the same challenges many of us do: finding our place in the world, knowing what we should do with our life, determining what we want, and knowing God's plan.

After graduating from the Police Academy, he took a position with our hometown police department. It soon became clear that this was his calling. He loved catching the bad guys and worked as a Brooksville, Florida, cop for nearly ten years before he was let go.

Talk about surrender! He was devastated.

He had found his calling, but it was pulled out from under his feet like a rug, and he found himself falling and didn't know where he would land.

I've learned that God often allows obstacles and adversity in our lives to see how we will navigate the disappointment. Will we lean on Him and surrender to what is in that moment? Or will we—like the Israelites who experienced God's mercy yet still complained about not having choice food—look at our trials from a purely self-centered point of view? (Numbers 11:4)

We WILL experience times in our lives when everything we hoped for or dreamed of vanishes, disappearing like mist in the morning. These moments are when we get to exercise our faith muscles.

Now faith is the substance of things hoped for, the evidence of things not seen. (Hebrews 11:1 KJV)

When we can't see what's ahead of us, we must trust the One who does. God sees the big picture, and while we may feel like He's forgotten us, He is always working. For us.

Meanwhile, the moment we get tired in the waiting, God's Spirit is right alongside helping us along. If we don't know how or what to pray, it doesn't matter. He does our praying in and for us, making prayer out of our wordless sighs, our aching groans. He knows us far better than we know ourselves, knows our pregnant condition, and keeps us present before God. That's why we can be so sure that every detail in our lives of love for God is worked into something good. (Romans 8:26-28 MSG)

I'm sure Scott struggled with understanding how God would work this situation into something good. But I also know that the Lord pursues us. And He uses difficult circumstances to get our attention.

When we hit rock bottom, the only way out is up, and reaching for the Lord's hand allows Him to pull us out of the pit.

During this time in his life, Scott began to really lean into his faith, even though he had some misgivings. He knew Jesus. He loved God.

When God first called me to ministry, I also had some trepidation. *Really, God? Me?* I had recently gone through a second divorce and was a single mama with two kids. But I clearly heard God's voice telling me to share His message of grace and hope with women who felt discarded and hopeless.

I, too, was faced with an opportunity to lean into my faith. After learning that my husband was unfaithful, my dream of "forever after" was shattered. I had to surrender my plan and the expectations of how I thought my life would be. But when I leaned into trusting the Lord and believing what He says, I could clearly see He had a plan.

> *"For I know the plans I have for you," declares the Lord, "plans to prosper you and not to harm you, plans to give you hope and a future." (Jeremiah 29:11 NIV)*

Too often we say we trust God—and I believe we really want to. But as soon as things get uncomfortable, unpredictable, or scary, we're quick to grab the reins and hold on tight. We decide to surrender our problems, issues, and challenges, but then we snatch them right back.

We feel like there is safety in control. OUR control.

True surrender says, "You take it, God. I trust you."

It's really quite freeing to be okay with what IS right now.

No striving for tomorrow.

No longing for yesterday.

Just today.

> *This is the day the Lord has made. We will rejoice and be glad in it.*
> (Psalm 118:24 NLT)

It was a beautiful thing to witness Scott's relationship with Jesus strengthen. On the day of his accident, I went with my daughter and my brother Jamie to Scott's home. There we saw an open Bible by his chair. And the book *Jesus Calling* by Sarah Young... in his bathroom! It makes my heart happy that he started (or ended!) his day with God's Word.

I visit my family often, and when I went home to visit, Scott would typically go to church with me and my mom. When my mom struggled with a situation or had a concern, Scott would tell her, "Just pray, Mom."

Since that tragic morning, a million "what ifs" have played over and over in my head, like a song on repeat. But no amount of wishful thinking, pleading with the Lord, or rehashing the woulda, coulda, shoulda was going to bring back my brother. His time on earth was done.

> *You saw me before I was born. Every day of my life was recorded in your book. Every moment was laid out before a single day had passed.* (Psalm 139:16 NLT)

God knows our start date, and He knows our expiration date. It's what we do with the time in between that He leaves up to us—the dash.

After Scott lost his job at the Brooksville Police Department, he spent a few years working for a friend, installing air conditioning units for commercial buildings. He didn't love it. But he never complained. Well, "NEVER" may be an overstatement!

But he still had hope. And faith. He was keeping his eye out for openings with other police departments and submitted his resume to several of them. They all came back with, "No, sorry – we're not hiring." Or, "You failed the background check." (Remember his history with the law I mentioned?)

Until.

An opening came up for a position in Taylor County, Florida, where his son Tommy lived.

I was home visiting one weekend when Scott told me about the opportunity. If he was hired, though, it would require him to move two hours away. I forgot to mention that for most of Scott's life, he lived next door to my parent's house, where we all grew up. However, if he took this position, he would have to say goodbye to not only the convenience of home (Mom would often do his laundry and feed him!) but also the comfort and support of our family and his friends.

If you've ever started a new job, you know it can be intimidating to meet new people, learn new processes, and basically start over.

He was hesitant and shared his concern. Where would he live? What if the people were jerks? Like any other business, the police department is filled with PEOPLE! Making new friends and working with new co-workers can certainly instill anxiety.

"Scott, the first step is to at least take the interview," I advised. "Then, when they fall in love with you—because I know they will—YOU get to decide if YOU like THEM."

Well, Scott aced the interview, and they hired him on the spot. Even better, HE liked the folks he met. It was the perfect job for him. Taylor County encompasses several small coastal towns, including Steinhatchee, where Scott made his new home. His son, Tommy, lived close by, which allowed them to spend a lot of time together. And because Scott was older and joined the department with previous experience, he was a mentor to some of the younger deputies. It didn't take long for him to make friends at the office and the businesses he would frequent while patrolling Steinhatchee and the city of Perry, Florida.

On the morning of October 31, 2016, Scott was in his cruiser driving to work. He received a call from dispatch that required his attention. He was on the job. It was Halloween, and the girls at the office were excitedly looking forward to showing him their costumes. They knew Scott would be the one to appreciate them. Scott looked for any opportunity to tease and have fun. He had only been a Taylor County Sheriff's Deputy for about 18 months but quickly became a fixture in the community.

He would never make it to the office.

He was traveling north on US 19 and hit a logging truck from behind. Once his vehicle was loose from hitting the hanging logs, he veered to the left and came to a stop on the southbound shoulder. We don't know if Scott was trying to pass the logging truck or if the logging truck was stopped. It's still unclear.

What we do know is we lost a good one that tragic Halloween day.

I've often said to leave it to Scott to go on April Fool's Day or Halloween. That's who he was—the kid who loved the holidays, pulling pranks, and making people laugh. He was one hundred percent genuine, the real deal, and people felt it.

In law enforcement, it's not difficult to gain a few enemies. But Scott had that special something that even when he was arresting someone, he was endearing.

It became clear to me that Scott's life—and career—ended exactly where he was supposed to be. See, God knew all along what was best for Scott. Scott knew that God knew too! He loved his job, he loved being close to his son, and he had made some very close friends. He would come back home to attend church with Mom every chance he had, thinking nothing of driving two hours each way to spend the weekends with family (and probably get his laundry done!). Scott also loved music. Rascal Flatts—a country band—was his favorite. He also loved contemporary Christian artist Lauren Daigle. We would both belt out her hit song, *Trust in You*, during worship at my mom's church.

And he did.
Scott trusted the Lord.

He surrendered to God's plan for him and, despite all the obstacles, never lost his faith.

> *Take delight in the Lord, and he will give you your heart's desires.*
> (Psalm 37: 4 NLT)

Scott spent his dash doing what he loved and was called to do. And while I've cried countless tears and think of all the moments he's missing, I can't help but be extremely thankful for the time we had with him.

There's peace available when we choose to focus on gratitude.

My nephew Tommy was just 22 years old when he lost his dad. Soon after Scott's accident, he was contacted by Concerns of Police Survivors (C.O.P.S.), a non-profit organization that supports the families of fallen law enforcement. There are local chapters across the country, and we were connected to the one in Jacksonville, Florida.

Every year, C.O.P.S. hosts an annual Christmas party, inviting families to connect with other families as they honor their fallen officers. That first year,

Tommy and I went and were given an ornament with Scott's name on it to hang from the Christmas tree positioned in the corner.

It's difficult to describe how incredibly emotional it is to be in a room of 100+ people who know exactly how you're feeling. Like Scott, their loved ones had chosen a profession where they put their life on the line each day. And just like Scott, their officer ultimately lost their life upholding the oath to serve and protect. They all had ornaments on that tree.

The room of survivors was varied. One woman lost her son back in 1987. Several police officers in uniform were there to honor their partners killed in the line of duty. There were widows and widowers. And there were children—little kids doing arts and crafts, enchanted by the clown creating animals out of balloons.

Several of them had lost their dads.
Like Tommy.

After the luncheon, we decided to take a drive. We began talking about the event, how nice everyone was, and also how sad it was that we all lost someone we loved. Tommy was quiet. And then said, "At least I had 22 years with him."

There it was.
Gratitude.

Tommy was on the path to peace. He was now in a position of trusting God, surrendering to what was – in that moment. No amount of wishing, begging, or praying would change the fact that Scott was gone. Walking this road with my nephew has been heartbreaking, for sure. They were just getting to the place of true friendship, as adult children tend to do with their parents. Tommy has chosen to be thankful for the time he had with his dad. He's grateful for the many years with him. And for the many, many memories.

Deciding to trust God can often feel like a complicated equation: surrender, plus obedience, minus holding on, divided by doubt and fear. The calculation may not be simple math, but one plus One can equal peace. Us + God = Peace.

> *Let the peace of Christ rule in your hearts, since as members of one body you were called to peace. And be thankful. (Colossians 3:15 NIV)*

God cares about us. Our pain. Our sorrow. We have a partner in Jesus, guided by the Holy Spirit, to co-create a life worth living.

> *Humble yourselves, therefore, under God's mighty hand, that he may lift you up in due time. Cast all your anxiety on him because he cares for you. (1 Peter 5:6-7 NIV)*

> *He heals the brokenhearted and binds up their wounds. (Psalm 147:3 NIV)*

Losing my brother that morning in 2016 changed everything. For me, my family, and so many others. God created us to glorify Him. And Scott did.

The Bible tells us to *Work willingly at whatever you do, as though you were working for the Lord rather than for people.* (Colossians 3:23 NLT)

He did.

Over the years, God has given me many opportunities to surrender my life to His will, but this was by far the most difficult. And not difficult in the sense of obedience, but difficult because I just missed my brother.

The online resource, *Macmillan Dictionary*, offers this definition of surrender: "to say that you have been defeated and will stop fighting."

The amazing truth of God's Word is that we are never defeated. Jesus' death on the cross gave us victory. Victory over the sinful nature that we were born with. And victory over any obstacle or situation that can knock us off course.

When we stop fighting against our circumstances and lean into God, He will fight for us. Raising our white flag of surrender is not a sign of defeat but rather a battle cry of freedom.

> For you have been called to live in freedom, my brothers, and sisters. But don't use your freedom to satisfy your sinful nature. Instead, use your freedom to serve one another in love. (Galatians 5:13 NLT)

Scott wasn't perfect. Nobody is. But he loved the Lord, and he was a good cop.

I've learned that surrendering our plans to what God has for our lives will always be the better route. We may take a few detours (or many!), but trusting Him will lead us to our ultimate destination: Eternity with our Heavenly Father.

Do I wish I had more time with Scott?

Yes, I do.

But knowing he's in heaven this very minute, hanging out with Jesus, makes my heart so happy.

He's the lucky one.

Surrender Your Defeat

By Julie T. Jenkins

> *We are hard pressed on every side, but not crushed; perplexed, but not in despair; persecuted, but not abandoned; struck down, but not destroyed. We always carry around in our body the death of Jesus, so that the life of Jesus may also be revealed in our body. For we who are alive are always being given over to death for Jesus' sake, so that his life may also be revealed in our mortal body. So then, death is at work in us, but life is at work in you.* (2 Corinthians 4:8-12 NIV)

Our God can take what feels like defeat and turn it upside down into victory.

Oh, this life is not easy! Many think that when they come to know Christ, they will land in a bed of roses and lavender. And we may—but roses have thorns and lavender can cause a headache! Don't get me wrong—giving your life to Jesus is the most amazing thing you will ever do. When you give your life over to the pursuit of God, He will infuse you with the power to overcome the enemy. He will gift you with the strength to face the struggles of life. And He will grant you peace and joy and love like you have never experienced before. But the path will not always be easy. At times, you may be pushed to the brink, where all you can do is hold on and cry out to God.

But do you know what? When you do cry out to God, surrendering your defeat to Him, He will always be there! Because when you live your life for Christ, you will never be alone again. And even though the world and all its forces may come against you, you will never be conquered—because our God turns defeat into victory!

Our lives are full of sin, but when we surrender, Jesus forgives that sin, claiming victory for us. We once were separated from God, but Jesus granted us eternity with Him, overcoming death. And though we, as Christians, still have evil slung at our door, God holds the key to that door that protects us from evil. Only with His permission can evil and pain reach us, but when they do, God will be there to turn what looks like defeat into victory for Him.

Just ask Job. Job suffered in this life more than most of us can imagine. He fell from prosperity to poverty, and along the way, he lost his children and his health. And God allowed all this to happen because He had a greater victory in store for Job. Job triumphantly recognized and proclaimed that although he was utterly defeated, by the world's standards, He still wore the victor's crown—because he had God. And God was all he needed.

> *"I know that my redeemer lives, and that in the end he will stand on the earth. And after my skin has been destroyed, yet in my flesh I will see God; I myself will see him with my own eyes."* (Job 19:25-27 NIV)

When we give our lives to Christ, God claims us as His own and will never let us go. *"The Lord himself goes before you and will be with you; he will never leave you nor forsake you. Do not be afraid; do not be discouraged."* (Deuteronomy 31:8 NIV)

Jesus warned us of the rocky road ahead, not to discourage us but to prepare us and give us hope. *"I have told you these things, so that in me you may have peace. In this world you will have trouble. But take heart! I have overcome the world."* (John 16:33 NIV)

As Christians, we can walk through whatever trials and pain come our way, trusting that our God is with us and has amazing things in store. So when you feel defeated by the world, surrender to God, remembering that in His eyes, you are not defeated at all. You are simply on your way to the victory God has planned for you!

Stacy L. Thomas

Stacy L. Thomas is an author, speaker, WWL leader, and a past ministry leader at Panama City Beach, Florida, Celebrate Recovery. In addition, she has practiced as an occupational therapist for 28 years and currently serves in a Level 3 Neonatal Intensive Care Unit (NICU).

Stacy is a thankful follower of Jesus Christ who has a wonderful husband, three successful adult children, one beautiful daughter-in-law, a spirited pound puppy, and two grand puppies. She enjoys everything outdoors, including hiking, boating, scuba diving, and gardening. While continuing her own recovery journey, Stacy has developed a passion for helping others experience Jesus in their everyday lives as they imperfectly journey into His perfection. She believes we are all sinners on the road to recovery until we pass through the heavenly gates.

Currently, Stacy is trusting God for complete healing from Chronic Lyme Disease. She is learning the discipline of completely surrendering to God to live in her divine purpose. Stacy's deepest desire is to love others right where they are, be a light in others' darkness, and live out humility in service to God and others.

Love Letters on the Lanai

By Stacy L. Thomas

"I'm divorcing you."

I grappled with those words as they pummeled my ears. The exact words that had often surfaced in the recess of my mind in moments of discontent and anger now, coming from my husband's mouth, caused me devastation and hurt. How many times in the past had I wanted to scream that sentence out loud? As the proverbial fence rider, I sat stunned, though not really surprised that we had arrived at this place.

Our marriage had been challenging since Day One. We blended our family fairly immediately after we each divorced our first spouse. He came with a three-year-old son, and I had a two-year-old son and a one-year-old daughter. We enjoyed the refreshing newness of our relationship and the mutual understanding of single parenting, but we were both haunted by past hurts. Frequently, our innate fight-or-flight responses dominated our conflicts. We loved very deeply and fought to the very core. Unfortunately, we fought against each other instead of the true enemy.

I sat on the shower floor while hot water pelted my overwhelming numbness. Attempting to find comfort, I folded my legs to my chest and hugged them. The events from the night before replayed in my mind. Words and actions fueled by discontentment, anger, and resentment.

Why didn't you just keep your mouth shut?

With no apparent answer, self-pity emerged. After two failed marriages, I began to believe that my fate was to be alone.

Alone.

A state that I had spent my entire adult life avoiding. Control and manipulation had become my greatest allies while I maneuvered into relational connection at all costs. My heavy head now hung low with the weight of self-disappointment while the ache of rejection filled the caverns of my heart. Belligerent lack of self-control and pride launched devastating blows to our fragile marriage. It had been less than 24 hours since our misunderstanding. However, it felt like an eternity.

We both said terrible things.

Surely we would forgive each other once again.

Once again.

How many times had it been?

For 12 years, we had been on this roller coaster ride. Twisting turns of jealousy fueled by insecurity, pride, wrong thinking, and unresolved resentments. So many times, we had created division. Multiple separations resulted in one parent moving with their biologicals in tow. All three children suffered repetitive abandonment by their respective stepparent, only to be followed up several months later with reconciliation. The children's sense of security degraded with each irrational move.

Oh! The kids! Where were they?

As the fog lifted, I remembered that my children were at their dad's home, safe from this chaos, if only for the moment. My bonus son, exposed to our explosion, was whisked away in the dark of the night by his father. Ultimately, we had added more injury to each child's already wounded soul.

The natural-colored porcelain tiles seemed to close in on my spa-like surroundings while no comfort or rejuvenation penetrated my soul. I silently prayed that I would wake from this horrible dream. With my eyes tightly shut, I imagined my husband offering his gorgeous smile and a hot cup of coffee as the bright morning sun shone through our oversized jacuzzi window. I opened my eyes. Unfortunately, nobody was there. I could blame my husband for this state of affairs, but I knew I needed to look at the current condition of my own heart.

I had spent the last year attending Celebrate Recovery®, where I completed a step study. This ministry is not just for traditional addicts. It addresses any hurt, habit, or hang-up that prevents God's peace and an individual's movement into their divine purpose. Our gender-based small group faithfully met weekly to share lesson answers, pray, and fellowship as the Holy Spirit led us on the road to recovery. It required me to stop hiding the issues and become vulnerable to admit my mistakes and imperfections. I found renewal in my spirit as the Lord helped me to reconcile the anger associated with my father's death. I learned to find serenity in certain areas of my life. However, I did not fully grasp Jesus' sacrifice on the cross. Instead, I continued to live my life, surrendering only to the limits of my humanity while codependency, a recently identified issue in my life, continued to silently influence my responses toward others.

The hot water from the shower began to cool, as did my anguish. The Holy Spirit reminded me of my recent progress. I repositioned myself on my knees and prayed.

Jesus, thank you for your sacrifice on the cross. Thank you for never leaving my side, even when my choices made you sad or mad. Thank you for this past year at Celebrate Recovery and the truths you brought to light. Thank you for loving me so much that you would not allow me to stay in the darkness. Lord, search my heart and find all remaining filth hidden within its deepest crevices. Reveal all denial and entirely remove any pride. Help me to let go and let you. Help me accept my circumstances while I wait. God, I need your grace. Please forgive me for my selfishness. I'm sorry.

Jesus is and always was THE answer.

I was, and always had been, powerless. Yet, I had denied my part, God's love, and His help. It was time for me to get off the fence and surrender my will for His.

Surrender.

Surrender was a foreign concept and one that my mind perceived as a weakness. Still, I recognized its necessity to navigate my current situation. Surrender to my Creator, the author of my purpose on Earth. An act that meant relinquishing control and abandoning perfectionism - two ideals woven as threads in my self-imposed protective cloak. Both were so ingrained that my mind could not fathom transformation.

Could I ever change? Was it too late?

Isaiah 43:14, 18-19 (NKJV) infused my brokenness and deafened my doubt:

> *Thus says the Lord, your Redeemer, ... "Do not remember the former things, Nor consider the things of old. Behold, I am doing a new thing! Now it shall spring forth; Shall you not know it? I will make a way in the wilderness And rivers in the desert."*

In that moment, I embraced hope. These sweet words refreshed my ears. I was washed in His grace. Though I could smell the soap's lavender scent, I breathed the sweet fragrance of heavenly peace as I sensed cool, comforting air blow across my bare body. The tension left me, and I raised my eyes to the heavens. Distinctly, God's words spoken centuries ago to a king and prophet penetrated my silence.

> *He says, "Be still and know that I am God; I will be exalted among the nations, I will be exalted in the earth." (Psalm 46:10 NIV)*

> *"For I know the plans I have for you," declares the Lord, "plans to prosper you and not harm you, plans to give you hope and a future." (Jeremiah 29:11 NIV)*

Naked and broken, yet covered and mended. There, on that cold porcelain floor, at my lowest point, I received His love. Tears streamed. I continued to pour out my heart and wash away insecurity, fear, immorality, and self-reliance. The need for human acceptance lost its grip as God immersed me fully in His never-ending and unchanging adoration.

Without warning, I was suddenly jolted back to those earlier hours in the darkness of the night when I once again failed to control my tongue, thoughts, and actions. Satan whispered ever so softly, "You are no better than you ever were. You will never be any better."

The battle for my mind was intense and relentless. However, instead of falling victim to shame, the Lord lifted me out of the miry pit. I stood with Him, renewed in strength, ready to face the enemy. His plan to kill, steal and destroy was disrupted by my Savior and Redeemer.

Let's go, God!!!!

Though I did not know the outcome, I trusted it would be good and right. Smiling, I looked forward to walking in the newness of a surrendered life despite the looming familiarity of fear and doubt. Slowly, I rose against the heaviness of my battered ego and lifted myself off the cold shower floor. I opened the glass door and faced the chill of reality waiting on the other side.

The next months were filled with ups and downs as I surrendered to God's will but still battled unforgiveness and codependency. My emotions concocted a blend of truths and lies that threatened my sanity. The only communication with my husband was business-related, pertaining to his permanent move or the division of our property, though I longed for so much more.

Without my husband to fill the God-sized void in me, I turned to my children. Diving deep into their lives, I attempted to meet all their needs and know all their business. I became involved in every sports booster club, fretted about the intimate details of their social life, and impulsively pulled the "parent card" to exercise control. Now teens, they further distanced themselves from mom's crazy-making cycle, and I reacted angrily to the rejection. I played tug of war with my old companions—jealousy, insecurity, and fear—while attempting to remain unreactive. Old battles perpetuated ongoing discontent and resentment. My soul fought for freedom while my body suffered more relapses with anger and codependency.

In time, it became painfully clear that my wounded children were not designed to fill that God-sized void in my soul. Only God could do that. Squeezing my sweaty palms, I stepped closer and fell into the open arms of Jesus Christ. The voice of truth whispered Proverbs 3:5: *Trust in the Lord with all your heart and lean not on your own understanding. In all your ways submit to Him, and He will make your paths straight.* (NIV)

February in North Florida can be fairly unpredictable. This year, however, was unusually pleasant with sunny warm days and cool nights. The view from my lanai boasted the promise of spring as buds began to pop up on the trees lining our yard's border. The grass, though void of green, was starting to show signs of awakening while the frost-bit broad leaf canna lilies swayed in the cool breeze. Cardinal families emerged with their young for breakfast while squirrels performed acrobatics in the tall pine trees. The days grew longer, and I frequently spent Saturdays sitting for hours on the screened-in lanai. My children were away at their dad's, so I was alone.

Alone. I can do this.

This covered porch became my sanctuary. Time did not exist. I learned to step away from the household work and sit at my heavenly Father's feet. I discovered promises provided in His love letters. His Words filled my broken places with healing salve and revival. I ceased filling my time with lunch dates so I could remain at the Father's table. Jesus Christ became my only life-giving source, and He blew new life into my suffocated soul. I was not alone, and I finally realized I had never been.

I am alone with Jesus. If only I could stay here forever.

Beyond the french doors into our home lay all the dirty piles of remorse and resentment. Codependency lurked, spilling disappointment. My motives to serve rose from selfish gain. My mind rationalized, *Christianity is about serving others.* Tired of the loneliness, I forced my care on others, but the help I intended ended up weighing others down. I craved a breakthrough to complete dependence on Christ alone and a release to joy-filled giving.

The war for my soul intensified as the enemy bombarded my waking and sleeping hours. My organic brain, spurred on by the enemy, fervently struggled to keep my old dysfunctional pathways alive. Battles raged in the caverns of my mind for ownership of my thoughts. Synapses fired back. New routes were etched. I audibly screamed 1 Corinthians 2:16 and 2 Corinthians 5:17 (paraphrased), "I have the mind of Christ! Therefore if anyone is in Christ, the new creation has come; the old has gone, the new is here!"

Thank you, Lord.

I grew closer to Christ and gained an understanding of my rooted conditions. The drive to bring health to myself and my children ignited my determination. As my days on the porch continued, angels fighting on my behalf brought gentle spring winds. The delicate pages of my grandmother's tattered black leather-bound King James Bible would blow intentionally to the words needed in my heart. Truths proven over the ages. My days and nights surrendered to the will of God. My heart declaring, *God loves ME!!!*

Finally, I received the courage to release control and allow myself to relax. The "Helicopter Parent" was grounded as my mindset began to change, and my children and I learned to enjoy each other's company. In the evenings, sounds of laughter replaced silence, and stories of the day's events replaced avoidance. Bible readings and discussions flourished as the Holy Spirit replaced our anxieties with promises. It seemed my world was turning on a new axis, and I was learning to enjoy the freedom to be the "me" who God created me to be. Unknowingly, my heart and soul were being strengthened for the coming days.

May on the beach boasts warm, comfortable temperatures and gentle breezes. The humidity had not arrived, and the porch was perfect for time with Jesus. I armored my heart and mind with God's love letters. In a few hours, I would officially be divorced. I woke with feelings of dread.

Divorce. Please, no, Lord. Isn't there any other way?

I prayed for a miracle, preferably before the judge's ruling, but there seemed to be angst in my spirit.

I know you got this. I mean, you don't like divorce anyway.

So, let's fix this.

My husband and I arrived at the county courthouse in separate vehicles. Quietly we ascended the stairs as our paths merged. Entering the judge's chambers reminded me of past meetings we each had with our ex-spouses.

We instinctively moved to opposite sides, already knowing the drill. The judge, seated at the head of the table, glanced up from her documents with a brief greeting. Surrendered to the Holy Spirit, I felt a nudge to be bold and request the seat next to my husband.

"May I sit next to my husband?"

The judge's eyes showed questioning concern for such an unusual request. Time seemed to stop for a moment, and I held my breath, wondering if I had heard the prompting wrong. Then, in an instant, she motioned to the chair next to my husband.

We sat quietly, and she guided us through the boilerplate procedures. The judge asked my husband to state his name, which he did automatically and void of emotion.

Then, she requested he state my name.

He attempted, yet the words would not, nor could not, leave his lips. I placed my hand over his, squeezed, and looked into his eyes as if to say, "It is okay."

Deep inside, I knew that God was in control. He whispered, "Remember the days I gave you free will? Trust me."

I discerned that, even if not today, He would restore us.

My husband cleared his throat, and just above a broken whisper, he slowly stated, "Stacy Thomas."

The words rang through my heart like a gong signaling the end. After today I would not have the right to carry that name ever again.

Though you take from me, I will trust you.

Startled, I heard the judge ask the bailiff to leave.

What was happening?

Gently, she redirected to my husband and asked, "Are you sure that this is what you want?"

He nodded. I breathed softly, murmuring pleads under my breath.

In my heart, I prayed that she would offer any answer besides dissolution. Instead, she gently shook her head as if she could not understand the events occurring in front of her and recalled the bailiff. We completed the documents, and within 30 minutes, we were divorced.

My emotions were a mixture of sadness and relief as I rose to leave. Sadness for our failure to love unconditionally and recognize each other's goodness. Relief that the cycles of insanity and pain would end.

I turned to leave, and my mind traveled back to a sunny day when I sat on my back porch. I remembered the gentle breeze intentionally turning the pages of my grandmother's tattered black leather-bound King James Bible. The next thing that happened is, by the world's standards, impossible and, to this day, never seen again in the same way. As Christians, we recognize that Malachi and Matthew are not even in the same part of the Bible. However, God wanted me to first see clearly on one page that God hates divorce (Malachi 2:16), while on the opposite page, I read, *With men this is impossible; but with God all things are possible.* (Matthew 19:26 KJV) In an instance, only by God's supernatural power, I rested on the promise that God would bring restoration in my now impossible circumstances.

Without my human prayers answered. I would return home divorced once again. Fortunately, I knew deep in my heart, with peace beyond all understanding, that there would come a day when we would be husband and wife once again. In the meantime, I vowed, *Lord, I live completely surrendered and purposefully yielded only to You.*

As the years progressed, the Lord removed my biggest fear; being alone. As a daughter of the Most High, I am never alone. My husband and I remarried after two years of divorce. The Lord continues to heal my pain and brokenness as I pursue Him as Lord of my everything. God is restoring me to my husband and our children while healing them in His time. I am learning to let go and trust that my heavenly Father is working all things together for our good.

The Lord used this storm in my life to teach me to trust Him and His plan even when I could not understand. Though there were many dark days, days that I begged and pleaded for a different way, I am thankful. The Lord walked with me and, at times, carried me through that difficult season. He never abandoned me. He transformed me. I will never know a greater love than the love of Christ, and I find great contentment in this truth. I continue to have my ideals of how I would like the marriage to be; however, God's ways are not my ways. Because His ways are perfect. For this, I am very thankful. Remembering His goodness helps me navigate our differences and disagreements in healthier ways. I know we are not perfect and won't be until we are through the gates of heaven. In the meantime, I can trust God, His will, and live surrendered.

Therefore I urge you brothers and sisters, in view of God's mercy, to offer your bodies as a living sacrifice, holy and pleasing to God - this is your true and proper worship. Do not conform to the pattern of this world, but be transformed by the renewing of your mind. Then you will be able to test and approve what God's will is - his good, pleasing and perfect will. (Romans 12:1-2 NIV)

Surrender Your Control

By Julie T. Jenkins

Control is something we crave. We want to effect outcomes and make sure things go our way.

I admit I don't do well handing over control, so it follows that I really dislike surprises. But twice in my life, my husband has thrown me a surprise party. The first one was for my 30th birthday, and the second was a shower for our third child. Before these events, if you would have asked me about surprise parties, I would have said they were my nightmare. But, despite being far out of my comfort zone, I loved both parties—because my husband knows me well and took everything that could have disrupted my joy into consideration.

First, he prepared me for what was to come. He lovingly made sure I left the house well-rested and feeling like I looked my best.

Second, he surrounded me with love. He invited those who meant the most to me. I will never forget walking into the restaurant on my 30th birthday and seeing everyone I loved. At first, I didn't even recognize that it was a surprise party for me—I was just overjoyed that we "happened" to run into our best friends! And at the shower, when I walked into my neighbor's house and saw my mom, who lived a distance away, I'm sure my smile lit up the room.

Third, he gave me what I needed even though I didn't know I needed it. I've never enjoyed my birthday because it means getting older. And thirty was a milestone (eye roll from the now much older me!). But my husband recognized that having my friends celebrate me would give me confidence as I entered my next decade. And a shower for a third pregnancy?! Each child is a gift from God, no doubt about it. But let's face it. Not many people celebrate the impending birth of a *third* child—but I can almost guarantee

Surrendered: Yielded With Purpose

that any pregnant mom of two needs more celebration than she receives!

As I reflect on these two surprises given to me by my imperfect yet loving husband, I begin to recognize how we can fully trust our *perfect* and *perfectly loving* God to control everything in our lives.

- *When we surrender our control to God, we can trust He will always prepare us for what is to come.*

The world is a tricky place. But in surrendering control to our God, who knows everything, we can trust He will prepare us for every circumstance.

God gave us the Bible, full of scriptures we can hold onto in times of uncertainty *(When I am afraid, I put my trust in you.* - Psalm 56:3 NIV, *Set your minds on things above* - Colossians 3:2 NIV) and stories from which we can gain truth (Job teaches us of God's unfailing love and presence). One of the best ways to allow God to prepare us for what is coming each day is to surrender our quiet time and allow Him to lead us to the Scripture and study of His choosing.

And when we give our lives to Christ, we gain the Holy Spirit, who prepares us with wisdom beyond our wildest imaginations. *The Holy Spirit, whom the Father will send in my name, will teach you all things and will remind you of everything I have said to you.* (John 14:26 NIV)

- *When we surrender our control to God, we can trust He will surround us with love.*

We can relinquish control to God because not only is His love for us unfathomable, but He also surrounds us with the love of a Christian family and community. *Therefore, since we are surrounded by such a great cloud of witnesses, let us throw off everything that hinders and the sin that so easily entangles. And let us run with perseverance the race marked out for us, fixing our eyes on Jesus, the pioneer and perfecter of faith.* (Hebrews 12:1-2 NIV)

As a Christian, you are never alone. Not only is God with you, but so are the saints and angels. Nothing can come against you—you can trust God's control of every situation when you remember you have an army on your side.

- *When we surrender our control to God, we can trust He knows just what we need.*

Sometimes keeping things on an even keel requires letting someone who has a better view of the situation take over. Who better to give control to than our God, who sees everything, knows everything, and governs everything? *I, the Lord, define the ocean's sandy shoreline as an everlasting boundary that the waters cannot cross. The waves may toss and roar, but they can never pass the boundaries I set.* (Jeremiah 5:22 NLT)

Surrendering our control can be scary. But God doesn't ask us to surrender to just anyone. He asks only that we give Him control. Our God—who always prepares us for what is to come, who loves us unconditionally and surrounds us with those who love us, and who knows exactly what we need even when we don't—wants to take the reins from us. He wants to guide us and lead us through every step of our lives. That sounds like the best surprise party of all to me!

. . . .

Sara Sahm

 From a very young age, Sara Sahm dreamed of sharing God's Word through music and word. As a child, her favorite quote was, "I love Jesus, and the devil is an idiotic brat." Through many ups and downs, her dream has become a reality. "To write for WWL and have an online ministry is a dream come true," she says. Sara enjoys writing not for the million readers, but for the one in a million who needs to hear what she wrote. Sara's favorite part of Women World Leaders ministry is coordinating worship nights and making space for women to come lay their burdens at Jesus' feet.

Sara is a published author with WWL and sings with her church along with other women's ministry teams. She credits God's never-ending relentless love for all she has today. Sara resides in Jupiter, Florida, with her family. When she isn't busy practicing or writing, she can be found scrapbooking and paddle boarding. Sara's music can be found on her website: sarasahmmusic.com

In His Time

By Sara Sahm

1 Peter 3:1-2 (NIV)

Wives, in the same way submit yourselves to your own husbands so that, if any of them do not believe the word, they may be won over without words by the behavior of their wives, when they see the purity and reverence of your lives.

When my husband and I met, God was not high on my priority list. It wasn't until our first daughter was born that I began to wonder and miss the God I had known so closely as a child. As I rocked and held our week-old baby, the question pulled at my heart, "What will I tell her about God?" It tugged at my soul. I felt an ache and a yearning and sadness. How could I no longer believe if it hurt so badly to imagine my little girl growing up without Jesus in her life? I couldn't shake the question. Every time I looked at her sweet innocent face, I saw God and felt Him drawing me closer. Like a quiet whisper, He waited for me to respond.

So, I decided I needed to know why I believed and what I believed. My brother, who loved the Lord and was passionate about his faith, had given me a book. He also gave my husband Doug and me a Bible with our names inscribed on the outside. The Bible sat wrapped up in the plastic sheeting for some time, but I began reading the book. That book opened my mind and heart to the possibility that what I felt as a child was not just a result of my childish imagination.

Little by little, God worked on my heart. He was patient and gentle. God didn't mind my questions or my fears and doubt; He already knew them. He was just waiting until the day I'd ask Him to show me what I hadn't been ready to know. It took some time and tears, but God won my heart again. However, my newfound faith did not come without a struggle. I looked forward to the time I'd be able to talk to our little girl about Jesus, but I didn't know if my husband would tell her something different. I worried that our conflicting ideas about God would confuse her. That fear cut deep and filled me with feelings of shame and regret. I felt scared our daughter would be confused and discouraged if we didn't agree on the Bible or who Jesus is.

Beyond the worry about my daughter's faith, I feared the loss of my marriage. My husband is and always has been my best friend, but I still was anxious that if I chose God, I would lose my husband. There were days I considered sacrificing my relationship with God for my relationship with my husband. But thankfully, God is good! A wise and trusted friend instilled in me that the Lord cherishes and values marriage. God didn't want to see my faith break our friendship or marriage. I held onto that belief with all my might for the next few years.

As I walked day by day, God steadily proved His faithfulness. We had another daughter and began to go to church sporadically. My husband never shamed me or degraded me for my faith as I feared he would. He would, however, sometimes laugh and be a little sarcastic when he referenced some of the stories he knew from the Bible as a child. That made me angry and irritated inside, but I tried to let it roll off my back. I knew he did not have the best experience with what he called religion. Deep down, I think he knew the Bible was true and Jesus was real. And just like I had been not so long before, he was comfortable and had become content with his own beliefs.

It had been a year or so since I had embarked on my renewed faith. I was hungry for God and to spend time in the Word. Since our newest addition was an early bird, I found this time at 5 am. One of the first ways my husband saw how important God was to me was when he began to notice I wasn't waking up so early to work out but instead to read my Bible. Usually, he would sleep through it. But sometimes, I would hear him stumbling down the hall to the kitchen where I sat. At first, when I heard him, I would run to put my Bible away and act like I was making coffee.

Every time I hid my Bible, however, I felt my heart ache inside my chest. I felt convicted and sad. I knew I couldn't grow in the Lord if I was hiding what I had found. I longed for my husband to know the Lord—to pray with me and to pray with our children. It was around that time I found Proverbs 31:10-31, sometimes known as *The Wife of Noble Character*. One verse stuck out to me, *Her husband is respected at the city gate, where he takes his seat among the elders of the land.* (Proverbs 31:23 NIV) I began to see my husband as this man. I always knew he was a leader and knew that, with the Lord, he would be unstoppable! I began to pray this truth over him. And from that day forward, I sat with my Bible opened when he woke up early. Sometimes he would ask questions; other times, it was just silent and weird. But it was the first step. And with God's help, I took it.

We were going to church more as a family. I still felt like it was just because of me. I had to do all the getting ready, and he would grumble about a football game here and there, but he was willing. It was exhausting, and sometimes I just wanted to quit going altogether. But I knew I couldn't. I knew our kids were counting on me, and so was he, even if none of them knew it. Through prayers, tears, and frustration, God showed me that my husband's faith was not up to me. My only job was to follow the Lord and let the seeds that fell as we walked take root. Doug and I had always been reading the same book; we were just on different chapters. And I had to be patient while God caught him up.

By the time the girls were 3 and 5, I had begun writing worship music again and felt like I was growing spiritually. Sometimes it hurt because I felt I was growing alone. I wanted my husband to be walking beside me in the Lord. I didn't want to feel like I was dragging him behind me. During those days, I held on to what my friend told me, "God cherishes marriage, and God loves your husband." I knew that God had been patient and gracious with me, and I could trust He would be the same loving father for Doug, too. I could trust that God saw my heart and heard my prayers. I could trust that while He was working on me, He was also working on Doug. And I clung to the hope that one day I would see the fruits of God's spirit well up in my husband.

Together, we decided to make a move to Florida. I gave my husband a couple of conditions: we would look at churches when we looked at houses, and when we found a church, he would support me in getting involved. He willingly complied, and we flew to find our new home. When we got to Florida, I was more excited to try the church I'd found than look at houses. Sunday came, and only the kids and I attended service. I felt that ache inside again. Being at church that day was bittersweet, but I felt I had found my congregation and pressed forward. We put in an offer on a house, flew home, and then COVID hit!

COVID made me question the move. I was scared, and things were uncertain. I worried I'd heard God wrong when it came to moving. But God has His ways of letting us know we are on the right path. When I opened my Bible that March morning, my eyes landed on Isaiah 7:4: *Be careful, keep calm and don't be afraid.* (NIV) Immediately I felt a wave of peace rush over me, and I knew God was in our plans to move.

In June of 2020, we drove our family to Florida. It was quite the road trip amid COVID closures and protests plaguing the country at the time. On our way, we decided to make an unplanned stop for the night—right before a massive protest that had overtaken a bridge in Tallahassee. Unbeknownst to us, we had been headed right for it. It was all over the televisions in the hotel lobby when we walked in. I remember telling Doug, "That's not a coincidence. That was God." I saw his eyes and knew he knew it too.

Since, due to the pandemic, most churches were closed when we got to our new home, I was back to only my morning studies and prayer. Desperate to find a church, I tried one that a new friend attended, which she told me had opened. Doug wasn't in a hurry to get into a church, so I went with just my girls. Finally, a couple of months later, he agreed to go. Once again, I was so excited, only to be let down when he didn't like the church. I enjoyed the community, but Doug felt it was boring. The kids and I had made friends, so when he suggested we look at other churches, I felt angry, and everything in me wanted to scream "NO!" Selfishly I wanted my way and, at first, didn't see the beauty in the fact that Doug wanted to look for churches with me. Thankfully the Holy Spirit opened my eyes and heart.

I felt the Lord telling me to let Doug lead us. My verse became, *Wives, in the same way submit yourselves to your own husbands so that, if any of them do not believe the word, they may be won over without words by the behavior of their wives, when they see the purity and reverence of your lives.* (1 Peter 3:1-2 NIV) I allowed the meaning of this scripture to flood my mind, and I realized if I wanted Doug to "sit among the elders," I needed to treat him like he already was. I walked by faith, without words, and without trying to control the situation. I gave up my way and what I thought was best for Doug and allowed God to do the work. My hesitance to let go shined a light on my lack of faith. But I chose to trust God and let Doug take the lead. I'll never regret that decision to let go, to surrender.

I was only able to let go because I realized it wasn't my job to make Doug believe, and I recognized that I couldn't change him. *My job is to trust in the Lord with all [my] heart and lean not on [my] own understanding.* (Proverbs 3:5 NIV) Although I had an idea of where I thought Doug was spiritually and where he should be, God knew where he was and what he needed more than I could ever comprehend.

Letting go of the burden of controlling a loved one's walk with the Lord is one of life's biggest challenges. God has given us this incredible gift of salvation and His daily presence, and we want to share that gift with those we love. And though we are to model and verbally share our faith, we must let God do the inner work on others. The biggest challenge I faced wasn't changing Doug but changing myself. Through this time, God showed me that as we love the Lord and keep our eyes on Him, others will follow our example. And when we walk with the Lord, His joy will emanate from us. *The joy of the Lord is...strength.* (Nehemiah 8:10 NIV) People are drawn to strength and crave joy. So I knew I had to love first and let God lead.

In the waiting, the in-between, my faith grew. I got to see God move in Doug's life. I saw changes that wouldn't have been possible beginning to show up all around me. One of my favorite memories is walking into the garage to find my husband working on a project with worship music playing in the background, loudly playing for our whole neighborhood to hear! This was the same man who had balked and complained if I ever put on Christian music. And watching the way he encourages our girls to love the Lord is the best part of all. Now they get to see their daddy loving Jesus. I prayed for that so many times with tears in my eyes and doubt in my heart. Still, God, in all his glory, answered! He gave me the desires of my heart, and He gave Doug a new life.

We each walk at a different pace at different times. Sometimes the pace is slow, sometimes fast; we may skip or run, or maybe even go backward or sideways. But we can't control the steps of another; that choice belongs to the individual and is directed by God alone. We are simply to *love because he first loved us*—with the perfect, grace-filled, and unselfish love that flows through us from God. (1 John 4:19 NIV) Our job is not to change our husbands. Our job is to love them as they are with all their brokenness—trusting God to take those broken pieces and use them for His glory.

When we married, neither of us knew how much we needed Jesus in our lives. But my brother saw the need and, through his obedience to the Holy Spirit, helped create the legacy for a family committed to God. It took me years and my husband even longer to open the Bible he gave us, but today my husband is a believer! Step by step, as I kept my eyes on the Lord, I began to see the seeds I left behind sprout. Ephesians 1:4 (NIV) says, *For he chose us in him before the creation of the world to be holy and blameless in his sight.* Doug was already chosen; he just had to surrender and choose God back.

Surrender Your Self-Image

By Julie T. Jenkins

As Christians, we are in a unique position to be able to surrender our self-image. Why? Because, as Christians, we are a reflection of God Himself. In God, we are perfect.

Society teaches us to put a good face out to the world. Beauty creams, make-up, and hair products flood the marketplace attempting to acquire our time and money. We are encouraged to make ourselves in the image of celebrities, who are often airbrushed and pictured in perfect lighting. And we model our lives after the perfection many portray on social media.

It is not wrong to want to put our best foot (or face!) forward, but when our obsession becomes how our lives look from the outside, it's easy to deceive ourselves and others about the state of our lives on the inside.

Gazing through the window of the gospels, we see a time when following the religious law meant everything. Time and again, the Jewish people were held to impossible standards. They lived in fear of being stoned or otherwise prosecuted should they appear to step outside the boundaries of the law and the ancillary rules put in place over the years. Jesus' own life was threatened for "working" on the Sabbath when he healed a man and permitted his hungry disciples to pick grain to eat. Jesus responded by going his own way. (Matthew 12)

I say that the Jewish people were threatened when they "appeared" to step outside the boundaries of the law because it was impossible for any human, other than Jesus, to keep the law in its entirety. The game of the day was to hide any imperfections—which they all had.

Does this sound familiar?

Jesus came to set us free from the need to stay within those boundaries and the need to uphold that impossible religious or society-driven image.

> *Therefore do not let anyone judge you by what you eat or drink, or with regard to a religious festival, a New Moon celebration or a Sabbath day. These are a shadow of the things that were to come; the reality, however, is found in Christ.* (Colossians 2:16-17 NIV)

As Christians, we are free to surrender the image of perfection that society tells us we must live up to.

The ironic part is that as Christians, our image becomes increasingly more perfect every day as we grow to reflect God's image more clearly. And we can surrender the worry and angst we may have over being perfect in the eyes of society, knowing all that matters is how we look in God's eyes.

And let me tell you, Christian, how you look in God's eyes. Better yet, let me tell you how GOD says you look to Him!

- You are chosen, holy, God's special possession. *You are a chosen people, a royal priesthood, a holy nation, God's special possession, that you may declare the praises of him who called you out of darkness into his wonderful light.* (1 Peter 2:9 NIV)

- You are forgiven. When you give your life to Christ, God blots out your past, and when He looks at you, He sees Jesus' perfection. *I am writing to you, dear children, because your sins have been forgiven on account of his name.* (1 John 2:12 NIV)

- You are light. The light of Christ shines through you to all the world. (Wouldn't Instagram love THAT filter?) *You are the light of the world. A town built on a hill cannot be hidden.* (Matthew 5:14 NIV)

- You are called. God has a plan for you! *But as God has distributed to each one, as the Lord has called each one, so let him walk.* (1 Corinthians 7:17 NKJV)

- You are victorious. *But thanks be to God, who gives us the victory through our Lord Jesus Christ.* (1 Corinthians 15:57 NKJV)

As we walk through this world, our days can be challenging. As we compare ourselves to others and even work to recognize and rid ourselves of sin, our self-image can become tattered. But Christian, I encourage you to surrender your self-image! God created YOU in His perfect image. You have been redeemed and chosen by our Lord and Savior, Jesus Christ. You are God's treasured possession. So lift that chin up, even when your mascara may be running down your face, and walk as the reflection of the Almighty you were created to be!

. . . .

Stephanie Winslow

Stephanie Winslow is the proud wife of Marshall and mother of two girls, Cora & Lydia. Stephanie helps business and ministry professionals develop leadership and communication skills to help them grow into a life of significance, impact, and abundance. She founded her company, Blind Spot Consultants, in 2016. Recently, she became a John Maxwell team certified coach, trainer, and speaker.

Stephanie's first book, *Ascent to Hope,* was published in 2018. She uses her gifts of writing, coaching, and speaking to inspire transformational change in the lives of those who need hope, healing, and restoration.

In her free time, Stephanie enjoys long walks on the beach, playing any sport or board game with her family, coffee dates with girlfriends, the comfort of a soft hoodie, and the pampering of pedicures.

Overcoming Shame

How Satan Uses Internal and External Shame to Keep You From Surrendering to God.

By Stephanie Winslow

"God, you are near to all who call upon you, and right now, I need you. I need you to fill me with your strength. Your Word says, *The Lord is near to all who call on him, to all who call on him in truth.* (Psalm 145:18 NIV) I can't have this conversation without you. God, I want to believe your Word that tells me *You hem me in behind and before, and you lay your hand upon me.* (Psalm 139:5 NIV) Help me to communicate your heart for this book. Prepare Zach's heart for what I am about to say to Him."

I prayed this prayer as I drove to meet with my brother to tell him that I had made a decision to say yes to God. It was not a decision I came to without a fight. I had battled with God in prayer for months. But I felt Him nudge my heart to "tell my story." This nudging was like a snapping turtle that wouldn't let go.

Once I felt the prod from God's heart to mine, I couldn't shake His message for me to "write and speak" and "tell your story." Everywhere I went, every song I heard, every commercial on TV and highway billboard were somehow related to writing or speaking. It was as though I was being chased down by God's call on my life for this season.

The truth is, I didn't want to write or speak. When God began speaking this message to my heart, I was running a company. Business and manufacturing held a higher position than writing and speaking. I was more comfortable with my "President" title than with the title "Author."

I knew I was good at business. I was confident in my own ability to solve problems and present solutions to customers. I learned to never say no to what the customer wanted; just make it happen.

But there I was at a different point in my life. God was calling me to trust Him and His ability to train, equip and lead me instead of placing my trust in my own talent and track record. And the fact is, at first, ignoring God's promptings was easier than telling a customer no.

I gave God every excuse why I was the wrong girl for the job. And I even explained to Him the shame my family would face. "Don't you understand, God? Too many people look up to my family. Too many people look to us as an example. What will this do to our reputation?"

That was a false selfless plight with God. Of course, I could justify that it was noble to say no to God for the family's sake. And, as I weighed the shame, embarrassment, discomfort, and exposure that would result if I followed God's voice with the seemingly more manageable consequences of disobeying Him, saying no seemed like my only option. In those initial months, I was unwilling to surrender my shame in exchange for obedience to God and blessing from Him.

It took months of contemplation and God's gentle nudges before I finally chose to be obedient. I still often wonder why He didn't give up on me. That's when God reminds me of His patience with the children of Israel who constantly disobeyed Him, yet He faithfully waited on them to return to Him.

Lamentations 3:22-23 says, *Because of the Lord's great love we are not consumed, for his compassions never fail. They are new every morning; great is your faithfulness.* (NIV)

I experienced the newness of His mercy every day that I chose to waiver in my decision. Every day I chose doubt and shame over following God's plan He was still patient with me. Finally, after months of experiencing God's faithfulness to me and His persistent call to write and speak, I surrendered my heart, mind, and soul to His will.

Even in surrender, though, I was not sure what to do with my feelings of shame. I didn't know how to move past them. How could I get beyond the monstrous mistakes I had made? Still unsure and with loads of questions, I timidly chose to take the new path with Him to write and speak. One day, one moment, one step at a time.

And so, there I was in my car, driving to meet my brother and following God's lead to tell my story. I knew I had to tell my brother what God was calling me to do, as my yes would impact him, opening the door for shame and stigma to pour into our family. To this point, our family was unscathed by tragedy, seen as a pinnacle of perfection to those looking from the outside. Now, all that was about to change.

But I knew it had to be done. I knew I needed to obey.

I pulled into the parking lot of the coffee shop where I was to meet Zach. I shut off the car. I pulled the visor down and looked in the mirror.

"Okay, it's you and me, God. Give me your words. Help me to let go and trust you," I prayed.

I closed the mirror and headed into the coffee shop.

"Hey, Buddy! Aren't you a sight for sore eyes!" I said to Zach with a giggle, trying to hide my anxiousness.

My hands trembled. My voice fought to form the right words. *Jesus, please help me,* I prayed to myself. Then I reached my arms out to hug my brother.

"Hey Steph, you're looking good yourself. Gosh, it's good to see you. It's been a while. Sorry about that," he said to me.

"It's okay. No apologies necessary. Life's been busy for us all," I said.

We made our way through the line at the coffee shop, making small talk. Then we found a booth in the back corner, which seemed appropriate for what I needed to unveil.

We sat down, and I took a few sips of my coffee. Then I took a deep, cleansing breath, and, with courage from God, I looked into his eyes.

I began, "I don't mean to be abrupt, but I do need to tell you something."

"Okay, shoot, what's on your mind?" He paused. "Wait. Are you and Marshall okay? The girls?" he replied with concern in his voice.

"Oh, me and Marshall. Yes, we are fine. The girls, too. They are a handful, but good," I said, slightly caught off guard by his question.

Okay, here goes, I thought to myself.

"Zach, I believe God is asking me to share my story. I know this may be hard to hear, but He's asking me to tell how I've walked through alcoholism with you. He's asking me to share the mistakes I made. He's asking me to help others not make the same mistakes. They need to know they are not alone. I believe God wants to use my story, well actually, our story, to help bring comfort and courage to others."

His face was blank. His eyes shifted from me to the coffee he held between his hands.

"I know this is a lot to take in. And I know sharing my story means also sharing your story. But I have to trust that God will use the isolation, shame, struggle, and hopelessness we've felt because of alcoholism and the hope we've found." I continued. "You must have a million questions."

Zach sat in silence for a minute with his head down. That moment seemed to last hours. My heart raced as I longed to know his response. Then he looked up at me - tears in his eyes - and spoke.

"If our story can help people, then you should tell it," he said.

Tears welled up in my eyes. It was as if a pressure gasket ruptured, and all the fear, worry, and concern about this very moment I had bottled up for months began to flood out of my eyes. I reached across the table and grabbed his hands. We sat and cried together.

He had no questions. No yelling at me. No running out. It was just a real, intimate, raw, and heartfelt moment between a brother and a sister. God allowed us to see the hurt was not in vain. He would use it - if we let Him.

"This is not at all how I had pictured this would go!" I said to him. "I was so afraid you would storm out and hate me forever."

I found out as we sat together, talked, and cried that day over coffee that Zach was sober. I had not seen him sober in so long. I think part of me doubted I would ever see that day.

When I walked out of the coffee shop and got in my car, I was in shock. I was in disbelief. I was overwhelmed by what God had done. God orchestrated the perfect timing for Zach and me to meet together. My brother was sober and clear-minded. And I was open to whatever God wanted from me.

I was in awe, humbled and grateful to God that He chose me. All the pain could now help others find hope.

Can you believe it? This story is just one example of how God walks with us every step of the way when we say yes to Him. He doesn't promise it will be easy. But He will be with us. God's Word confirms for our hearts that He is with us.

> Isaiah 41:10 says, *Do not fear, for I am with you; do not be dismayed, for I am your God. I will strengthen you and help you; I will uphold you with my righteous right hand.* (NIV)

I said yes to God. That was the first step. What followed was a montage of daily choices - a million little steps. A million decisions to continue to say yes to him, even when the voices of fear, shame, and doubt plagued my mind. This surrender - this obedience – was like standing on stage naked, ready to bear ridicule, shame, and judgment with no defense.

God asked me to confront not only the reality of addiction within the family, but also outside of the family. Sharing our story meant stepping headlong into an open forum in a society that says, "once you are an addict, you are always an addict." It's a stigma that can paralyze.

I was well aware of the external shame or stigma we would face. I was no stranger to the false assumptions, conclusions, and judgments that would occur. The shame and the stigma the world placed on us were hard to shake and out of our control.

From the time of the Garden of Eden, Satan has used shame to draw hearts away from God.

In Genesis 3:10, God talks with Adam after they had eaten the forbidden apple. *He answered, "I heard the sound of you in the garden, and I was afraid because I was naked; so I hid."* (NIV)

For the first time in humanity, Adam and Eve felt shame - because they chose to disobey God. Shame is fear of exposure, fear of being found out, fear of the truth being made known, and the humiliation that accompanies that.

As I look back over the months it took me to surrender to God's prompting on my heart to write, it's become clear that Satan was at work. He wanted to keep me from saying yes, from obeying God. Shame was his weapon of choice.

But besides the external shame, what surprised me as I began to write was the internal shame I also faced. Shame's presence reared up within me like an irritated stallion showing itself big to get control and get its way. I was not aware of how much internal shame I carried. I was not cognizant of how much I had beat myself up for "failing" Zach and my family.

Writing about and rehashing my own mistakes was a process that only God could see me through. Reliving the anger, worry, sleepless nights, fear of whether my brother was alive and the panic of not being able to get in touch with him unearthed all I had not previously processed through. But bringing these experiences to the light gave God the opportunity to heal me from the inside out.

Facing both the external shame from the world and the internal shame I hid from myself was a major part of my healing. Of course, Satan didn't want me to be healed. Because when I am healed, I am no longer held back by shame, embarrassment, or any discouragement he tries to throw at me.

Shame is based on lies that Satan whispers - seeds he plants that grow into weeds of accusation. He whispered to me that I didn't pray enough, that I wasn't involved enough or was too involved. He told me I was too bossy and pushy, that I had made too many mistakes and was a failure for my family. Satan told me that I couldn't solve any problem anyway, and he attacked my submission to God – even telling me that I shared the wrong Bible verses with people I loved. He was brutal.

I felt blown and tossed by the wind, like a boat in a storm, as I wrestled with the shame and doubt of all I had done or hadn't done.

Through this wrestling, God was maturing my faith. Like Ephesians 4:14 says, *Then we will no longer be infants, tossed back and forth by the waves, and blown here and there by every wind of teaching and by the cunning and craftiness of people in their deceitful scheming.* (NIV)

God didn't ask me to write about my wins. He didn't ask me to write about the solutions I had found or the business goals I accomplished. He did not focus on my strengths. In fact, this story was not about me at all. It was about Him. It was about His strength that was made perfect in me when I admitted alcoholism was not a problem I could solve.

It was my time to boast in the Lord that, though alcoholism was an issue I could not resolve, it was one God could. And no matter what happened, I chose to trust in Him. And that is what I wrote about, God's power at work in my weakness.

In 2 Corinthians 12:9, the Apostle Paul proclaimed, *But he (the Lord) said to me, "My grace is sufficient for you, for my power is made perfect in weakness." Therefore I will boast all the more gladly about my weaknesses, so that Christ's power may rest on me.* (NIV)

Through writing, God unraveled the shame that had built up within my heart, mind, and spirit. He exposed the internal shame - the weakness that Satan tried to use to keep me from maturing in faith. As I confessed my weaknesses to God, however, His power rested on me to tell the story.

By surrendering to God's call to write and speak, I was able to tell the story of God's power at work in my life. He took my shame, the very thing that made me feel most exposed, weak, and like an imposter. And He gave me in its place faith in HIS strength to move and work on my behalf.

His grace was sufficient for me in the moments of writing and facing the internal and external shame head-on. His power shone brightly through the weakness of my inability to solve addiction. Surrendering and saying yes to God allowed me to boast in all God was able to do in our family.

My conversation with Zach, telling him God asked me to write, was just one example of God's power and grace through this process. Surrender is our opportunity to allow God's power and grace to shine. And surrender to God puts Satan in his place, powerless to win.

We all face shame at some level, both internally and externally. What we do with it, or what it does with us, matters. We can let shame win, withholding our yes from God, or acknowledge its existence, not allow it to stay hidden, and become conquerors by stepping out in faith.

Shame is not of God. It is a tactic the enemy uses to keep us bound to the past instead of living fully in the light of God's promises. It's a tactic Satan has used since the beginning, since Adam and Eve. God taught me that Satan uses shame in my life the same way he used it in the garden, to keep me from living fully for God, to keep me from standing firm, to keep me from proclaiming my faith and trusting in God's power to work in my weaknesses.

Satan doesn't want us to be healed. He wants us to stay shame-sick. He doesn't want us to utilize the power of God at work through us and for us. But where does that leave us? Where does that leave you? I don't know what shame you may be facing, but I can bet shame has held you back in some area of your life.

I want to leave you with a final thought, a verse to remind you what the Bible says. I pray that you will pour over this verse, absorb it, and allow God to renew your mind until you believe it. Own this verse as God's personal promise to you so you will no longer be held hostage by shame but emboldened in faith that you are free.

John 8:36 says, *So if the Son sets you free, you will be free indeed.* (NIV)

Christ has set you free from the stigmas of this world, and you are free indeed to overcome shame! It's time to say yes to God and give Him a chance to heal you from the inside out.

Surrender Your Anxiety

By Kimberly Ann Hobbs

Have you ever been called a worry-wart? Do you know anybody you would label as a worry-wart? In writing these teachable moments, I often speak to myself and use my real-life situations as examples. And there are times I certainly worry or get anxious, only to realize things typically work themselves out for the good.

For instance, I tend to worry when I get ready for events. Whether they are in my home, in an event center, or at a church, any event I am a part of tends to make me anxious. I breathe a sigh of relief when it's over and everything has ended up working out. But the anxiety I experience while planning is not a good thing. So, I want you to know I am speaking to myself here, but hopefully for your benefit as well.

None of us can add a single moment to our lives by worrying. In fact, the opposite is true. We lose life when we worry. I know this, and I believe and understand this, but sometimes I still do not remedy it. Instead, I often spend time worrying, causing health issues that could eventually shorten my life.

God tells us not to worry. We can find freedom from our anxieties just by spending time with God. I know it often calms my soul when I take a quiet moment to sit and reflect with God, basking in His presence.

When anxiety was great within me, your consolation brought me joy. (Psalm 94:19 NIV)

I admonish myself, acknowledging that if I am anxious, I am not trusting God. And indeed, I AM NOT. So I intentionally turn it around and remember how God proves His faithfulness to me. He will never leave me alone, He is always with me, and He always guides me when I ask Him to, but I must ask Him and relinquish my control. Thankfully, this is pure truth. Surrendering your anxieties to our Lord may help you, as it did me. Jesus said,

> "And do not set your heart on what you will eat or drink; do not worry about it. For the pagan world runs after all such things, and your Father knows that you need them. But seek his kingdom and these things will be given to you as well." (Luke 12:29-31 NIV)

God tells us that we do not need to be anxious about anything; instead, we should just pray about EVERYTHING. (Philippians 4:6)

There is something beautiful to learn here. Do not allow your brain to tell you something is too small for God. Surrender the control of trying to accomplish whatever you are worried about to God. Prayer is that powerful connection with the One who is the source of our comfort, strength, provision, and hope. God can take care of all such worries and more if you surrender them to Him. Giving your worries to God means that you fully trust in the promises nestled in His Word and that He will make good on them.

When you learn more about the God of creation to whom you can give your ALL, surrendering the worry that you carry becomes easier and easier. The worry-wart syndrome disappears because God is ever-present and always will take control. So create the daily practice of surrendering to God without worry.

Not one of us can do things better than God. You may know the saying, "Let go and let God." Embracing this comment can become a source of comfort to us. Why? Because we take our worries about the future to the One who holds the future in His hands.

God has the whole world in His hands. That most definitely means you're included.

. . . .

Rusanne Carole

Rusanne Carole is a published author, speaker, and advocate for young people. She has served as a school chaplain for eight years and now teaches young people and supports parents and carers.

Born in Baton Rouge, Louisiana, Rusanne represented her state in the 1984 Miss USA pageant. She owned and operated children's clothing, women's shoes, and cosmetics businesses. After receiving a political science degree from LSU in 1989, she moved to The Gold Coast, Australia, her home for the last twenty-two years.

Rusty, as the Aussies call her, loves to study, write, walk on the beach, go to the movies, hang out with friends and family, and experience cuisine from around the globe.

She has studied and received recognition in Pastoral Care, Christian Counselling, and Bible School.

As a mom of four boys, Rusty's life is never boring. She is a full-time carer for her youngest son and is currently writing her memoir and mentoring carers around the globe who are preparing an upcoming book. Rusanne contributes to the Women World Leaders *Voice of Truth* magazine and is a co-leader for Women World Leaders Australia.

Footprints Toward Eternity

By Rusanne Carole

A Mother on Her Knees

It was a warm summer day in Australia.

We had been at the beach soaking up the sun and breathing in the salt air. This was our happy place, a place of freedom. Away from the busyness, away from our day-to-day responsibilities, routines, and endless therapy and doctor appointments. A place you could be you, the real you. We were free to walk barefoot in the sand, you following my footprints, placing your little feet in the imprints of mine.

We watched and listened to the birds, one of your favourite pastimes. I've never quite heard someone imitate their sounds so precisely as you do! I wondered what you and those birds spoke about to each other.

After our walk, we played in the park. The sun had set and said goodbye to the present day, and the darkness was approaching. You were suddenly on the other side of the road. A large patch of green grass stood in front of me.

It was as if the blades of grass were tall soldiers creating a barricade preventing me from reaching you. You looked so little, my son, so far away from me.

"Come, Christian, come on! We need to go home now!" I yelled out to my boy.

He began to run towards me, crossing the street. From the left side of my vision, something was coming. My eyes darted to the biggest 18-wheeler truck I had ever seen in my life. It came out of nowhere. It was coming down the street at a speed that would surely plough right into my son! I was frozen in the spot my feet stood. My body could not move, yet my insides were screaming, "STOP, STOP, STOP!!" I could do nothing. It all happened so fast!

Christian ran. Christian ran right THROUGH that massive truck! He made his way right into my open and waiting arms. I fell to my knees in relief and gratitude to have him safely with me. The driver of the truck, a man in his mid-30s with long dark brown, slightly curled hair, turned his head to look and wink at me with his piercing and captivating eyes as if to say, "I was never going to hit him. I was never going to hurt him." He quickly tapped his horn twice before moving on out of my sight.

I also felt the presence of someone next to me. I could not see him, but the word 'BIG' came to my mind. His presence was a comfort as I could feel he was there slightly to my left and behind me.

As Christian ran forward and through the massive truck, the man to my left said, "Wow! What a miracle!" He began saying the Lord's prayer, giving thanks to God, and praising His goodness and mercy. I joined him, reciting the prayer as I held Christian in my arms and fell back to my knees again in worship to the King.

Christian had run right into my arms.

"Thank You, God! Thank You for saving him. My son. My son. Thank You, Jesus!"

I had never held my son so tightly before. I did not want to let him go!

My phone, vibrating on the nightstand next to me, woke me from my deep sleep.

The dream was disrupted.

I wanted the dream to continue. Do you know the feeling? When you want to go back to sleep and hit play after pausing a movie that you are totally engrossed in? I wanted to see more. I wanted to see how it all ended.

I wanted to see that scene again. It would be etched in my mind forever. Christian, running with a supernatural superpower right through that truck to complete victory! I wanted to see that truck driver's glance, his sweet smirk, his whimsical wink letting me know my son was okay, even when it didn't seem like it. But most of all, I desired to see and feel the man's presence next to me and hear His voice again, His heavenly voice praying for my son. It brought such comfort and peace. I knew it was God.

But then the moment came that I breathed in a big, deep breath and released an exhaling sigh, thanking God it was only a dream. I had learned by now that sometimes God gives me dreams to teach me something, to cause me to reflect on the next lesson He has for me. And in my prayer time earlier in the week, I had asked God to come into my dreams.

God hears. God listens. And at times, He gives us what we ask for - but occasionally not exactly as we may suspect or even desire. His ways are so much greater, and He is so much wiser than we are.

What are You trying to say to me, God?
Was my son, Christian, going to be healed on this side of heaven?
Am I holding on too tightly to my boy?
What have I not surrendered to You?
Show me, Lord. Whatever You have for me, I am here to receive.

I knew God's answer would be made clear as I continued to seek and spend time with Him. There is an ongoing reception of revelation and knowledge of Him when we seek Him with all our heart. This had been shown to me over and over again in the years since meeting my Saviour.

Rising From The Ashes

We had taken many walks on the beach, but you often didn't seem to notice things other kids noticed. You had few words; most had been stolen from you when you were a toddler. It seemed like you looked right through me. You didn't even notice the footprints on the sand as you walked behind me. But ONE day, you noticed them! It was as clear as the perfect blue sky above. It was June 2016, a month before your eleventh birthday. I raced home and wrote about it in my journal. After that, you began stepping in my footprints, following me with a big smile on that beautiful, angelic face.

You SAW my footprints! Oh, my gosh, you really saw them!
You stepped inside each one, Christian, showing me with
your smile you SAW them!
And I know you see me too and how much I love you!

There are little things parents can take for granted. A child's first smile. Holding your hand. Looking in your eyes and saying, "I love you, Mama."

But I didn't know if my child would ever do these things, which brought me to my knees in despair and heavy-heartedness. All I had dreamed of for my son was taken away that December 13, 2007.

"Go home and enjoy him. It is most likely he will never speak and will need to be institutionalised. And I hope you'll be okay. I gave similar news to another mother last week, and she went home and attempted suicide".

That was the way the specialist delivered the devastating news. Fifteen years ago, my fourth son was diagnosed with autism spectrum disorder, and the future seemed dark and bleak. Little or no hope. Devastation rocked my world like a daily earthquake from which I could not escape. I had a choice; run away or run to Jesus. Bail or run through the 18-wheeler - pressing on, persevering, and trusting God to get my son and me to the other side.

I decided to surrender to God, but surrendering once was not the problem. Living each day in surrender is the challenge. I embarked on the ultimate test of trusting my Creator with my son's life and mine.

As parents, we are blessed to give life and love to another human being, to protect them with all our hearts. Except it is a different road for "forever mothers."

The mother who becomes not just a mother but a full-time 'carer' for her child has many unique challenges.

Her child may not move out.
Her child may not date or have a family.
Her child may not live independently, drive a car, or have a career.
Her child may not, without a miracle on this side of heaven, accomplish things we typically "expect" from our children.

So how do we surrender our lives and plans? How do we surrender the dreams we have for our child? And how do we surrender control, knowing it is likely that one day, we will join the heavenly realm before our child and we will no longer be on this earth to give them the care they need?

There is just one answer.

TRUST JESUS. When we surrender to Jesus, we can trust He will take control and provide all we need. He will care for our children and us. And He will provide through His people! This we must believe!

My real shift began when I started applying Scripture and God's promises not only to myself but also directly and personally to my son. Recognizing that God created my boy and has a good plan for his life allowed me to see more clearly that, just like God will never leave me, He will never leave my son.

Letting go of control can leave us feeling vulnerable. God's Word tells us not to worry about tomorrow, for tomorrow will worry about itself. (Matthew 6:34) And life tells us that when we focus too much on the future, we lose the joy of today. Still, that's difficult for us mamas who put our whole lives into caring for our children who depend on us for even their basic needs.

That's why I say that surrendering is not a one-off occurrence. It is a continual, day-to-day, moment-to-moment choice. But Jesus is always there - giving us the opportunity to renew our minds in Him each waking day. He is waiting to take over all that hinders us so we can run the race marked for us.

When we trust Jesus, we begin to trust those He sends to help care for our special needs children. I clearly remember one day when a carer was looking after my son. She did something for him in a different way than I would have. I was about to say something, and the Holy Spirit undeniably spoke to me! "There will be many people caring for your son, and not everyone will do things just like you. Your way isn't the only way."

That stopped me in my tracks. In His goodness, God corrects and teaches us constantly when we open our hearts to hear Him.

Who am I to say I'm the ONLY person who can look after my son? We are only given the role of stewarding these little souls, but God is their true Caregiver.

Fighting The Battle And Holding Close

Surrendering every day has not been easy, but God is always there.

He is there with Bible stories that give me freedom from guilt, blame, and deep heaviness in my soul. For instance, in John 9, the disciples asked Jesus whose sin had caused the man's blindness, and Jesus replied, *It was not because of his sins or his parent's sins...This happened so the power of God could be seen in him. We must quickly carry out the tasks assigned us by the one who sent us.* (John 9:3-4 NLT) This scripture released me from the guilt of feeling responsible for what happened to my son. As I got to know God more, I realised the truth. God did not cause my son's condition. It was not anyone's punishment. He is a good Father. Yes, I had anger and cried out to Him. I even spoke very unkindly toward Him (to put it mildly!). But in His grace, God patiently held me in His arms through it all. He still does when I struggle.

Our Father is there with comfort, even when we are at our lowest. Recently, when things had gotten really exhausting, and I felt that I could not take one more step, I caught myself saying under my breath, "Lord, just take me home. This is too hard! I don't know if I can do this anymore!" Anyone in a full-time caring role can feel overwhelmed and as if they are completely losing themselves. But God is always there, ready to hold us.

When we submit to His care, God will speak! One of the loudest ways He talks to me is through books. And in His goodness, when I was at my lowest, He spoke to me through an author's words, saying that when we ask the Lord prematurely to take us home, what we are really saying is life with the Lord is miserable. Ouch!! Sometimes God's comfort is a shove back in the right direction.

So, I regrouped and repented. I didn't condemn myself. This job is draining. It is the most sacrificial love I have known. I think of Mary, Jesus' mother, quite a bit and all she went through. She was the only person with her son at both His birth and His earthly death. She watched Him be mocked, misunderstood, and rejected.

Mothers of special needs children can feel the same.

But when I set my mind that ALL I do for my son is FOR the Lord, life changes for the better.

Are there still tough days I want to run for the hills? Heck yea! But I breathe, reset, and find my rest in Him. I just get the privilege of living this out and trusting God with the moulding process He has for me through it all. He is the Potter, and I am the clay. He is strongest when I am weak.

Maybe the greatest story I'll tell will be how I ENDURED rather than my son's miraculous healing I desire to see on earth. I will trust Him and His will.

Sharing The Blessings of Jesus

Christian cannot read the Scriptures, but I speak God's Word over him. And although he cannot study the Bible, he sings to Jesus beautifully, with a perfect tone. I know that the Comforter and Teacher, the Holy Spirit, does things for Christian I could never do.

Some of us who met Jesus later in life may regret not teaching our children in the ways of the Lord. Yet it is never too late, and the Lord redeems lost time.

There were many times when I could not go to church because it was too difficult. Christian would not sit still, and there were no "children's rooms" or ministries to support us. There were times when I left the service in tears because of the looks I received or the stinging words spoken directly to me or loud enough for me to hear that cut to the core. "You know, the devil uses those children to distract us at church!" "Why in the world would you bring a child who can't sit still to church?"

Forgive them, Father, for they do not know. They have no idea how much my heart aches right now because my son and I can't be here in YOUR house!

Then there was the time the worship leader said, "Hop up and dance and praise our God!" My little guy took that message literally and began hopping up and down the aisle and being very vocal, loving every minute of the song – to the horror of many people in the congregation. But I thought, *I bet that's how we're gonna sing and worship You in heaven, Lord! No inhibitions.*

As my guy got older, it became a little easier. I often play worship music at home, and Christian praises and sings to God. At church, He runs to the worship team as if running to the angels. One Sunday, He even grabbed the microphone off the pastor and shouted, "Take the Jesus!" Some people cringed, but most of the congregation smiled, including the pastor, who didn't quite know how to ask for the microphone back.

I've noticed Christian looking around as if he sees things. And I know he sees the supernatural. For example, the other day, he kept looking at the bookshelves in our home.

"Christian, what do you see? What do you keep looking at?"

He answered, "Jesus."

We should never doubt that those with "additional needs" don't have a Spirit that is whole, complete, and alive! Their body and soul may not operate at "full capacity," but the Holy Spirit lives inside them and is at work healing, teaching, and loving them.

Beauty From The Ashes

Not only does God have a plan for caring for our children, but He also has a plan for our children to make a difference in this world. EVERY life has value and is here for a time such as this. God doesn't make mistakes!

And I have seen firsthand how my son touches the lives of so many other people: his carers, teachers, family, and even strangers in the community. He is the angel through whom others see the glory of God abundantly shine. And Christian is the angel who led me to chase after God, to know and serve Him with all I have!

We continue to enjoy our walks on the beautiful beaches on the Gold Coast, Australia, where we are blessed to live. Christian (given his name before I became a Christian) walks by my side, holding my hand or swooping his arm inside mine as if he is escorting me to a ball. He may look at me and say, "I love you" or "We're a good team." My heart melts. My eyes meet his crystal blue eyes, more beautiful than the ocean water, and well up. I am reminded that God tells us in Revelation 21 that He will wipe every tear, and there will be no more death, mourning, crying, or pain. Our God has caught every tear that has run down our cheeks for our little ones!

Christian's footprints in the sand are now bigger than mine.

My 17-year-old is taller than me, and I must tilt my head to look up to him. But I do look up to him in many ways.

He has taught me so much more than I'll ever teach him.
He has taught me about the love of Christ.
He has taught me about having joy in the midst of suffering.

He has taught me about endurance, perseverance, and never giving up!
He has taught me that living with a diagnosis is difficult, but with or without a diagnosis, living without Jesus is impossible!

He has taught me about the importance of the simple things
in life and that everything is temporary.
He has taught me to appreciate stopping and the importance
of rest and self-care.
He has taught me about the beauty of the sunrise, the clouds, the moon,
and the stars as he gazes at them constantly and calls out to them.

He has taught me about LOVE, sacrificial LOVE,
and the daily surrender to God.
He is the angel sent to me by GOD to show me the way home,
my eternal home where this good team will be together for eternity!

I pray for all those whose lives have been interrupted to CARE for a loved one. Know that God is with you every step of the way!

> *"And the King will answer them, 'Don't you know? When you cared for one of the least of these, my little ones, my true brothers and sisters, you demonstrated love for me."* (Matthew 25:40 TPT)

> *Those who plant in tears will harvest with shouts of joy.* (Psalm 126:5 NLT)

A Forever Mom

I'm a forever mom
I didn't pick it or choose it. It chose me

I fought it at first, so angry with God
To be honest, there are still days I want to bail
But I have begun to see the blessings in the sufferings that sail

Sail through my days
Sail through my heart & soul, Lord

I'm still caring for a child, although he is bigger, stronger,
and taller than me
It's not an easy job, but God's strength is the key

Daily surrender to thee
Daily surrender to thee

Plans rearranged
Dreams disengaged

Buckle up for a new ride where exhaustion and tears come with a mighty stride
Constant advocating
Very few understand or can relate

A constant battle, often weary
Knocking down doors, every direction I take
Passing out each night only to live the next that seems a lot of the same

Daily surrender to thee
Daily surrender to thee

Oh, yet through the isolation, the deep lessons and revelations come
When face to face with Jesus – no desire to run

For I have fallen for the One
The One who restores hope deep within the mother's heart

A servant who no longer lives for herself but for Him and His divine plan

Opportunities to sit at His feet
To feel His breath upon your face
And to hear His heartbeat resounding in thy ears
To look in the eyes that see you and all you go through

Lay upon His chest
Rest
Wait
On His next 'love lesson' He has designed just for you!

Eyes on eternity
Eyes fixed on Him

God cares for the Caregiver, this I know
I pray you will know too

Daily surrender to thee
His will, not mine
Daily surrender to thee
To the only One who truly knows and cares about it all!

Surrender Your Children

By Julie T. Jenkins

Being a mother is a dream that many women hold in their hearts. And birthing and raising children is one of God's greatest gifts.

> *Children are a gift from the Lord; they are a reward from him.* (Psalm 127:3 NLT)

But any parent will tell you that raising kids can be difficult. And one of the most challenging things about raising our children is surrendering them to God.

In the Bible, there are many instances of God calling His followers to surrender their children to Him. In 1 Samuel, we learn of Hannah crying out to the Lord as she asked Him to grant her a child, *"Lord Almighty, if you will only look on your servant's misery and remember me, and not forget your servant but give her a son, then I will give him to the Lord for all the days of his life."* (1 Samuel 1:11 NIV) After her son, Samuel, was born, Hannah kept her word and surrendered him to God. She resolutely delivered him to the temple to be raised in service to God at the tender age of three.

This is an extreme example of surrendering our children. And yet we also read of Abraham, who surrendered his son as a sacrifice (which God pulled him back from at the last moment). And Mary surrendered her son Jesus to death—the ultimate sacrifice for the world.

In most cases, the surrender God asks of us regarding our children is not as extreme as these situations. But that doesn't mean what He calls us to is easy or simple. One example of surrendering our children is allowing them to be who God has called them to be.

It can be impossible to understand, when we are yet pregnant with our children, that each child is a complete person unto themselves with a lifetime of God's plans and promises ahead of them. *"Before I formed you in the womb I knew you, before you were born I set you apart."* (Jeremiah 1:5 NIV) While that is exciting to envision, as our children grow, it can be difficult to "let go" and allow them to become who God created them to be.

We have two daughters and one son. I imagined my daughters would be involved in musical theater, something I had always loved. And my husband dreamed our son would play football, something he had always longed to do himself. But, although my daughters sang in the school choir and one dabbled in theater, their interests led them elsewhere. And before my son was even the age to sign up for football, his apathy toward sports led us to realize that football wasn't in his future.

On the surface, surrendering to a child's likes and dislikes seems inconsequential. But the fact that parents often try to live vicariously through their children rather than supporting them as they grow into all God has called them to be can cause severe emotional and mental trauma. When a child isn't accepted for who they are and what they enjoy, they can feel unloved, unworthy, unimportant, and unwanted. And if they are forced to do activities that are not their passion or desire, they might miss out on developing the gifts God has uniquely instilled in them.

Unfortunately, in this sin-infested world, surrendering our children's desires and hobbies isn't the only thing we have to trust God with. As we've noted, each person is individually created by God; as such, they not only have God-given gifts and desires but also have unique issues, temptations, and obstacles. The job of parenting is one of ongoing guidance, love, and discipline. This three-fold cocktail is to be administered in different ratios throughout our children's lives. And the recipe—which must be reconfigured every season or even every hour—can only be known through Holy Spirit-infused wisdom.

As parents, we must surrender our children and their needs, wants, desires, and sins daily. We, like Hannah and Abraham and Mary, must give our children to God, trusting His care and protection. When we do, God will provide exactly what they need. Some days, that provision will come through us as we hold tight to God, seeking His wisdom. On other days, God's provision and care for our children will come through others. That can be a hard pill to swallow. But we must trust God's leading.

One day I was crying out to God on behalf of one of my children when He graciously reminded me, "Julie, I love your children more than you do. You can trust me."

When we surrender our children to God, we can trust Him. Because, as difficult as it is to comprehend, He loves our children even more than we do!

· ·

Arlene Salas

Arlene Salas is a Christ follower who loves Him with her whole heart. She is a devoted wife to Angel, whom she has known for over 38 years. They were high school sweethearts and now have two amazing children, Valerie and Fabian, and two precious granddaughters. Arlene has been in the medical field for over 27 years and currently works in account receivables for a hospital. She is also a district leader for her own financial services business. She loves helping people and is a greeter at her church.

Arlene was born and raised in New Jersey and is Puerto Rican by blood. She later moved to South Florida and still resides there. She loves spending time with her family and beautiful granddaughters and reading the Bible and other books that inspire her to improve herself.

Arlene is a leader with Women World Leaders ministry, using her gift of service to support others and help the ministry run efficiently, reaching many for Christ. She credits WWL as the catalyst for opening her heart to step into her God-given purpose.

God Is Always There

By Arlene Salas

Have you ever seen one of those television shows where the characters seem to go through trial upon trial? So much that you think about how unreal the scenario seems – no one would continually be hit again and again with such various issues. Not in real life, anyway. Looking back at the last several years of my life, however, I see a path full of ups and downs. And yet, through the highs and lows, the struggles and pain, I recognize that I was never once alone. My God was there – sustaining me, providing for my family, and growing me into the woman He has called me to be. My job was to surrender to Him through it all.

In August of 2012, my husband lost his job due to a back injury. As you can imagine, this led to various trials and financial hardships. Our home life struggled, and I panicked, unsure of how we would pay the mortgage, car loans, and all the other monthly bills. God was there. With His help, we received assistance from family members and made it through an impossible-looking situation. Following this, God helped me understand we needed a plan B to supplement my husband's income.

God provided by leading me to get my license in financial services. Obtaining the license was initially a challenge, but I remained persistent. In all of this, God continued to guide us. Still, I had so many questions for the Lord.

Why was it that we were enduring these struggles and pain? Why did you allow my husband to go through all the health challenges and not heal him? Why did you allow everything to fall apart? Why are you not making things better for us? Despite not having the answers, I pursued my faith and listened intently for God's voice.

> And my God will meet all your needs according to the riches of his glory in Christ Jesus. (Philippians 4:19 NIV)

The following year, we, as a family, experienced God's comfort. Though our hearts broke with the loss of our first family dog, Ginger, God was there.

Then, from 2015 to 2018, our family had to overcome numerous health challenges that impacted our livelihoods. And God guided us through the turmoil. The first situation involved my husband, who almost lost his life due to bilateral pulmonary embolism. Though he could barely breathe, our son wisely and immediately rushed him to the hospital, which saved his life. That same year, challenges with my 17-year-old son began to arise. Although he had struggled with depression from an early age, I was unaware of the severity of his illness and how deeply it affected him. Thankfully in retrospect, God gave him the courage to open up a small amount about some of his feelings. Never in a million years would I have thought to hear such hurt and misery from my son - I was so heartbroken. And I cried to God and asked again, *Why more pain on top of pain?*

Non-medical issues were happening with our family, too. For example, that same year, my daughter's fiancé broke off their engagement after she had already paid for her venue and dress - perhaps that was God's protection.

As if that wasn't enough, other health challenges hit my husband. The doctors discovered and removed a tumor from his kidney. I was utterly grateful the tumor was not malignant. But after surgery, he developed a left flank bulge hernia, a known complication of various retroperitoneal surgical procedures that involve flank incisions. As a result, to this day, my husband has not been able to recuperate to full capacity and now deals with chronic back and hernia pain in his kidney area. Then, within another year, he was again hospitalized, this time for pneumonia. But once again, our mighty God pulled him through the turmoil. As you can understand, I became angry, sad, and confused at this point in my life. I couldn't understand why we were going through all this and why challenges and hardships kept coming our way. At one point, I felt I no longer wanted to live. Thankfully I never tried to hurt myself, but I felt I could not bare the pain and suffering. Why was God allowing all of this to happen?

> *Be merciful to me, Lord, for I am in distress; my eyes grow weak with sorrow, my soul and body with grief.* (Psalm 31:9 NIV)

The truth is, I became enraged. The more I thought about everything negative that happened in our lives, the further I fed that internal fire. *Why, Lord? Why have you allowed us to go through all these challenges involving my husband's health, financial hardships, challenges with our son, and so much more?* At times I felt so alone, abandoned, and scared. No one other than my close friends and close family really knew how I was feeling, as I tried to hide it most of the time. Seeing people on social media who looked like they were living their best lives made me question further why God allowed so much hurt in *our* lives. And all this when I sought Him wholeheartedly, went to church, and served where He called. I asked, *Why Lord? Why is it that the people who don't seek you the way I do aren't going through all the hard times like we are? And why isn't my family seeking and worshipping you the way I do after praying fervently? Isn't that what you want all your children to do, Lord? So why aren't you answering MY prayers? This just isn't fair, God.* I just could not understand why He didn't do what I knew He could do.

Although I didn't always see it then, God never stopped blessing us.

Later, in 2017, our first precious granddaughter was born. After so much pain and sadness, our family finally had a joyous moment.

> *As for me, I call to God, and the Lord saves me. Evening, morning and noon I cry out in distress, and he hears my voice. He rescues me unharmed from the battle waged against me, even though many oppose me. God, who is enthroned from of old, who does not change - he will hear them and humble them, because they have no fear of God.* (Psalm 55:16-19 NIV)

Then, yet again, in 2019, God blessed us tremendously. At first, I was unsure how to feel after we sold our first home that I loved and was so emotionally attached to, but selling it enabled us to purchase our current home - closer to our daughter and her family. I was concerned about my long drive to work - 45 minutes on a good day. But, yet again, God showed up as He always does and blessed me with a new job with a great company – much closer to our new home. So again, I worried and stressed for nothing. Because God already had it all figured out.

Along with our ups, the trials of life continued. In April of 2020, my husband was hospitalized for chest pain. Thankfully his heart turned out to be fine, but in early 2021, they discovered he had three blood clots in his leg. He is now on blood thinners to treat the clots even as he battles with four herniated discs and arthritis in his back. Like, can the poor man get a break here? *God how much more pain does my husband have to endure?*

In July of 2021, my son admitted himself to a mental health facility for depression. After a month of inpatient treatment, he continued with intensive outpatient therapy. Although we were hurting so much for him, I was thankful to God for this answered prayer. For many years, I pled and cried that my son would seek help. We had unsuccessfully attempted throughout his youth to get him treatment. All the while, I continued to pray on my bended knee for him. When I let God do His work on my son, he finally decided to seek help on his own. Through treatment, he was diagnosed with Bipolar II and was put on the proper medications.

That same year I also grieved the loss of a long-time friendship that had lasted 15 years. Even now, I still don't understand why God also allowed that friendship to end. But I know He knows best, so I have learned to accept it.

Our second precious granddaughter was born in September of 2021. We could not have been more elated as we never thought our daughter would have a second child after experiencing Hyperemesis gravidarum with her firstborn. This condition consists of extreme, persistent nausea and vomiting during pregnancy. We prayed so hard that God would heal her and her husband's minds about not having another child due to her difficult first pregnancy. We also prayed for a better and healthier pregnancy, but unfortunately, it was not so perfect. My daughter experienced Hyperemesis gravidarum for the second time. It was so heartbreaking for us all to see her happiness affected by becoming so ill. As a mom, I felt helpless. My only hope was to continue to pray as our newborn granddaughter experienced acid reflux and failure to thrive. Soon the baby will be going for an endoscopy - a nonsurgical procedure used to examine the digestive tract using an endoscope, a flexible tube with a light and camera attached. Doctors are thinking of possibly inserting a G-tube or a feeding tube. The purpose of this small tube is to provide another way to offer food to the baby. At this point, we must continue to trust with our entire beings that God has our backs and will take care of our family. He knows what is best, and we trust His will - as painful as it may be to my family and me. This, too, I must surrender. I must trust God that everything will be fine and my precious granddaughter will grow up to be happy and healthy.

> *"Go back and tell Hezekiah, the ruler of my people, 'This is what the Lord, the God of your father David, says: I have heard your prayer and seen your tears; I will heal you. On the third day from now you will go up to the temple of the Lord.'"* (2 Kings 20:5 NIV)

Due to the loss of my husband's income and using credit cards to help pay the bills to keep us afloat, we incurred much credit card debt, which resulted in us filing for Chapter 13 bankruptcy. I struggled with that so much due to shame and because I felt I had let God down after He had entrusted us with all His money. Unfortunately, we could not afford to pay the mortgage, monthly expenses, and credit cards, so we had no choice but to file for bankruptcy.

Throughout the years, I have lived in fear of the unknown. As time passed, my depression, anxiety, and fear grew. Finally, I had to learn the skill of letting go of the things I could not control. I did not know how to surrender, but I realized that I could not change or help my loved ones. Only God can do such things. When I finally surrendered it all to Jesus, I began to feel at peace and see some of the things I had been praying for come to fruition.

> *Peace, I leave with you; my peace I give you. I do not give to you as the world gives. Do not let your hearts be troubled and do not be afraid.* (John 14:27 NIV)

As believers, we do not associate God with pain. We pray and expect Him to answer our prayers right away. But He wants us to continue to trust in Him no matter how difficult the journey is. I've learned there's a reason for all the good and not-so-good He has allowed me and my family to experience. He wants us to depend more on Him and to fully trust Him. I must surrender it all to Him, so He can take me where He has called me to be. I have prayed and asked God to forgive me, admitting I am sorry, and I surrender.

Come, let us sing for joy to the LORD; let us shout aloud to the Rock of our salvation. Let us come before him with thanksgiving and extol him with music and song. (Psalm 95: 1-2 NIV)

As tough as it has been, I am beyond grateful for all the challenges and lessons I have learned throughout this journey. Without this path, I would not be the woman I am today. I have experienced many disappointments from as far back as I can remember. But if God did not allow me to go through the challenges, I would not have recognized my need for Him. And we must always stay close to Jesus, not because of what He can do for us, but because of who He is. He is love, sovereign, and compassionate.

In this life, we will always go through trials and tribulations, but if we steadfastly stay close to God, we can know that the weapons formed against us shall not prosper, and what the enemy has meant for evil, God will use for good. Feeding ourselves constantly with His Word and promises gives Him a pathway to our minds that He can use to sustain and guide us and reminds us of His glory. *I will extol the LORD at all times; his praise will always be on my lips. I will glory in the Lord; let the afflicted hear and rejoice. Glorify the Lord with me; let us exalt his name together.* (Psalm 34:1-3 NIV)

I will always choose God - in good and bad times. He is the only one who will always be there, even when no one else is. He does not judge us because He is a loving and merciful God who always hears our cries.

"For I know the plans I have for you," declares the Lord, "plans to prosper you and not to harm you, plans to give you hope and a future." (Jeremiah 29:11 NIV)

As you read my story, you may or may not relate to how I have felt at times - angry, sad, confused, lonely, and depressed. If you can relate, I encourage you to always remember that you are not alone - God is always with you. He knows you, all about you, and exactly what you are going through. You can always go to Him; He is always there to listen. The Lord will renew and restore your strength. He loves and cares for you like no other and longs for you to come to Him and depend on him for everything. My prayer today is that you learn to fully surrender your fears, hurts, worries, family, and all your concerns to God. It can be difficult to release control, but once we do, we allow God to do what only He can do while we will experience His true peace and joy. God has gone before you, and His treasurers are bountiful and plentiful.

Surrender Your Doubts

By Kimberly Ann Hobbs

Whenever we venture out to conquer new ground or fulfill something God has called us to do, opposition seems to follow. One reason is the enemy can stir up doubts and past failures that haunt our mind. God may be bringing us through situations, but more times than we care to mention, we have these doubts in the darkness that do not go away. Why do we do this? It is because the enemy wants us to take our eyes off Christ, so he stirs in our mind.

Do you ever feel the enemy attacks just before God does something great in your life? That is me regarding my writing. I started writing years and years ago, but until five years ago, I did nothing with it. Why? Partially because I was dealing with some of the worst pain I have ever experienced in my life—the pain of heartache. I was carrying guilt on my shoulders. Unfortunately, during those times of hurt, I doubted what my purpose was, and then the doubting spilled over to my writing. I felt like a failure in my life as a mom. As thoughts arose, the enemy attacked. He knew the impact my writing would have, so he interfered with it. Finally, I had to begin fighting those doubts! But I could not do it alone, though I tried.

How do we combat doubts with truth? There is a voice of truth that tells us a story better than the lies we believe. When we hear this special voice, we can hit the pause button, regroup ourselves, and press on. We need to familiarize ourselves with this voice—God's voice. If we surrender our doubts to God whenever the enemy throws a lie our way, He will hear our surrendered heart, and the lies will be short-lived. We will recognize that the opposite of the lies we have been hearing is waiting for us on the other side. We need to silence the insecurities and past mistakes the enemy uses to taunt us, putting them to rest by fully surrendering our doubts to God. God's voice will become louder and louder the more acutely you listen for Him.

If I can be vulnerable for a moment, I would like to share how the voice of truth told me a story much different than the enemy wanted me to believe. For years I heard this doubting voice in my head from the liar, the accuser—the one who confused—saying, "You will never amount to anything in your writing," and asking, "Who will ever want to read what you write?" That is what the enemy told me for years and years. It stifled me and kept me from publishing many stories I wanted to share for God's glory. I allowed it. I hid behind every doubt the devil imprinted in my mind. Because I believed the lie, many more negative thoughts popped up over and over. I developed a pattern of doubting and stopping, doubting and stopping, all inside that cycle of darkness as I listened to the wrong voice. Doubts arose in my mind continuously because they were attacks from the enemy that I did nothing about, but I did believe them.

Understand that God has called us to newness in Christ. When we surrender our doubts to God, there is no condemnation for us who are in Christ Jesus. Pray that you will be healed, restored, strengthened, and mobilized. That gets me through my doubts when they occur. I pray for my walk of faith. I pray for it every day, every hour, every minute—because I need it. If you commit to doing this and praying through the "doubts in the darkness," surrendering them to God, He will show you the truth in His light. He is your forever source of truth. You have life in the Spirit. And you have the opportunity to walk in the Spirit continuously.

My prayer over you is that Jesus will make a public spectacle of the powers that oppose you, causing you to doubt. Jesus went to the place of utter public humiliation for you and me, and He won the victory over your doubts. Be encouraged by the apostle Paul when he puts emphasis on forgetting the past, that which is behind us, and straining forward to what lies ahead.

> *Brothers and sisters, I do not consider myself yet to have taken hold of it. But one thing I do: Forgetting what is behind and straining toward what is ahead, I press on toward the goal to win the prize for which God has called me heavenward in Christ Jesus.* (Philippians 3:13-14 NIV)

Do not let yesterday's failures derail you, in the form of doubts, from reaching the goal of your upward call of God in Christ. Press on for the gold medal that awaits you when you surrender all your doubts to Christ.

God told me to author this book with Julie Jenkins. Any doubts that arose in preparation—and trust me, they did—I stamped out with trust in God and by fully surrendering. I no longer allow the enemy to throw dirt at me when God clearly gives me a vision. Instead, I stop right away, acknowledging where the doubt comes from. I make a conscious effort to seek God the moment the doubt hits. I do not view myself as covered with smudges of past sins and failures any longer—they are gone, wiped clean. I encourage you today to lay hold of your life, forever free of condemnation. When we release the guilt about past failures and obediently do what God calls us to, our doubts in the darkness will cease. And instead, we can accept in full surrender the newness God is showing us in the light.

. . . .

Christina Hjort

Christina Hjort, originally from San Diego, California, has made central Florida her home for almost four decades.

She and her husband, Matthew, married in 2015 and, in 2021, accepted a call to marriage ministry. Together, they cofounded Narrow Path Marriage Ministries, aiming to restore and strengthen marriages through biblical truth and godly direction. Their hope is to positively impact marriages by encouraging couples to live a life of abundance, as versed in John 10:10. Christina and Matthew also serve on the Welcome Team at their church, HighPoint, in Lake Wales, Florida. They have a blended family with four children and three grandchildren.

Christina is an AACC Certified Professional Life Coach, has a bachelor's degree in Business Administration from Warner University, Lake Wales, Florida, and is co-owner of Narrow Path Lawn Control, LLC. Additionally, she served honorably in the United States Marine Corps for five years during Operation Desert Storm.

In her downtime, Christina enjoys spending time with family, attending church, helping marriages, and relaxing by the pool.

The Road to Brokenness

By Christina Hjort

You saw me before I was born. Every day of my life was recorded in your book. Every moment was laid out before a single day had passed. (Psalm 139:16 NLT)

My father, Gerald, was a handsome man. He was a brilliant computer programmer, a semi-pro tennis player, a wine connoisseur - and an atheist. The only memory I have of him and my mother Peggy together was of them arguing in the kitchen and him throwing my mother against a refrigerator out of anger. My father had been severely abused as a child, and now he had become the abuser. When I was five years old, my mother and father divorced. I went to live with my mother and my brother Jeremy went to live with my father. I don't remember much from those days. I remember good times with my mom and some weekends with my father. When I was at his house, he would take me for donuts and ice cream to enjoy all the wonderful things in life. I was his princess. But my brother's life was hell on earth, filled with abuse and pain. He was physically abused by our father.

When I was eight years old, my mother met Ronnie Ashley, Master Sergeant of the United States Marine Corps. He was being reassigned to a military base in Virginia Beach, Virginia – a long way from San Diego, California.

My Mom and Ron had a whirlwind romance. They got married in January of 1980 and relocated to Virginia. Ron was a good man, willing to take responsibility for a single mom with two children. He had a wonderful sense of humor and a strong, protective way about him. Over the years, I found out that he suffered from post-traumatic stress disorder (PTSD) from being a Vietnam Veteran, and he struggled with alcoholism. He could be a hard man to please.

That summer in 1980, my brother was flown out to visit us. One evening, shortly after he arrived, we were sitting at the dinner table. My mother handed my brother a plate of food which he commenced shoveling down as fast as he could. My mom said to Jeremy, "You don't have to eat so fast! No one is going to take your plate from you." I pulled my mom aside and politely advised her that Jeremy regularly had his food taken from him as a form of punishment at our father's house. My mother was shocked and heartbroken. She contacted our father and informed him that their son was not leaving Virginia and that she would be assuming full parental custody. After that day, I did not hear from my father for another 21 years.

Unfortunately, even at that early age of 10 years old, it was too late for my brother. He was broken from the abuse of our father. As the years passed, he was in and out of counseling. He struggled in school. He used marijuana to ease the pain from the past. He was manic-depressive. I was not aware of any of this at the time. To me, my brother was the most amazing person I knew. He was funny, popular, athletic, and an artist. He did everything right in my eyes! He used to wake me up in the mornings, tickling me until I could not breathe. He was the first person to tell me about Jesus.

After high school, Jeremy went into the Army, and then, shortly after, when I graduated, I went into the Marines. I will never forget getting a phone call from Jeremy for Thanksgiving in 1990 while I was on duty. Jeremy told me to resolve any disputes with our mom and step-dad and to take care of them, and he told me that he loved me – something he rarely said. Then, on December 6th, I got the news that would change my life forever. My beautiful brother was dead from suicide. My world came crashing down in an instant.

Brokenness to Surrender

The abandonment of my father, the inadequacy I felt from my step-dad, then the loss of my brother broke me. Was all of this my fault? Was I to blame? What could I do differently to be worthy of love? So many questions and no answers! I spent the next 20 years going from relationship to relationship and religion to religion, trying to fill the hole in my heart. I was in a relationship with the alcoholic, the addict, the abuser, and the adulterer – trying to fill the emptiness that only God could fill, each ending in disaster. I was baptized three times in different denominations trying to wash off the shame and guilt of my life, only to come up out of the water each time feeling even dirtier than before. I went to counseling for five years, trying to put the puzzle pieces of a shattered heart back together but somehow still felt broken. I was living a life of self-destruction because I did not believe I deserved goodness and peace.

Even through all this, deep down in my spirit, I knew God was always there. He was watching over me, walking before me, and would make a way. Through my brokenness, now God could meticulously chip away at each area of my life, leading me and calling me to surrender each area a little bit at a time. In Lamentations, Jeremiah called God's people to repentance after years of disobedience. We see God's compassion and comfort in sparing His people. No matter how devastating our sin is, our Father invites us to repent and be healed by the blood of Jesus. *"For I know the plans I have for you," declares the Lord, "plans to prosper you and not to harm you, plans to give you hope and a future."* (Jeremiah 29:11 NLT)

Change of Mind

In 2012, I had just bought a house in Winter Haven, Florida. I was divorced (again), and I had three children – Austin - 13, Ryan - 10, and Maggie - 9. I was trying a "fresh start" even though I was still stuck in my ways and blind to God's will for my life. One day while driving my daughter to school, she said, "Mom, why don't you stop listening to this kind of music on the radio and turn on Joy FM?" (our local Christian station.) Jesus tells us in Matthew that *out of the mouth of babes...You have perfected praise.* (21:16 NKJV) Oh, how true that is!

My daughter reached over, changed the station, and started singing along with the next Christian song. I remember that morning being so amazing - filled with words of hope and joy and love! Music to my ears! I vowed to leave that radio station on in my car from that day forward. That day something changed in my mind.

> *The Lord is my strength and my song; he has given me victory.*
> (Psalm 118:14 NLT)

Listening to Christian music, a daily renewing through song, began to change my way of thinking. Leading me to how the Lord would have me think.

> *We take captive every thought to make it obedient to Christ.*
> (2 Corinthians 10:5 NIV)

> *Do not conform to the pattern of this world, but be transformed by the renewing of your mind. Then you will be able to test and approve what God's will is – his good, pleasing and perfect will.*
> (Romans 12:2 NIV)

Change of Heart

I always struggled with right versus wrong, good versus evil. *For I do not do the good I want to do, but the evil I do not want to do – this I keep on doing.* (Romans 7:19 NIV)

I wanted to be "holy," but I didn't understand how to get there. I imagined the God of the universe in heaven ready and waiting for me to screw up again so He could rain down His wrath, something which I believed I deserved for my wretched life. Oh, I loved Jesus! But did I believe that I deserved the gift of His death, burial, and resurrection? Certainly not! How could a good God love a person like me? It was a struggle until 2013, when my dear friend, Lisa, pulled me aside and told me something I needed to hear.

She told me that God is not like my earthly father, who fell short and abandoned me. Rather, God is the best Father a girl could ask for - a Daddy who loves His daughter more than words can say. He is a Pappa who will never leave me, who will never abandon me, and who will always take care of me. He is a Father I can trust! I can have a personal and intimate relationship with Him! The light bulb came on that day! My Father God was not condemning me. *I* was condemning me! I had a change of *heart* and knew I was safe with the Father. *Trust in the Lord with all your heart, and lean not on your own understanding; in all your ways submit to him, and he will make your paths straight.* (Proverbs 3:5-6 NIV)

Surrender of My Will

With the change of mind and heart, little by little, my life started to look different. Until one day in 2014, I found myself face down, weeping on my bedroom floor. Alone and worn out from years of self-abandonment and sin, I cried out to God and told Him that I surrendered my will to Him. I had been a "religious" Christian for many years, but now I wanted a *relationship with Him* - and I knew He wanted one with me! I made a commitment to get to know Him better, wait on Him, and obey Him. Less of me, more of You, God. *He must increase, but I must decrease.* (John 3:30 NKJV)

In that moment, I felt His warm, loving arms wrap around me while I was lying there completely broken. Somehow I knew that things were going to be different. God was calling me to surrender my will – not my will Lord but yours, just as Jesus said. He wanted me to call out to Him when I was scared, lonely, or confused. But He also wanted me to talk to Him about the daily things. Nothing is too big or too small for Him. He would guide me with His provision and protect me if I would trust His will for my life. And He wanted me to rejoice and celebrate with Him when the victories came. *So do not fear, for I am with you; do not be dismayed, for I am your God. I will strengthen you and help you; I will uphold you with my righteous right hand.* (Isaiah 41:10 NIV)

Surrender of My Relationships

One of the first areas of my life God called me to surrender after my will was my relationships. God wanted me to surrender my relationships to Him and stop listening to the voices in my head left by words from friends and family. He wanted me to get alone with Him so that I could hear His voice. I was no longer trying to please people in relationships while neglecting to please my Father.

I stopped trying to live up to others' expectations and paid attention to what God expected from me and our relationship. Once my relationship with God was aligned, my feelings about myself started making sense. I no longer did things to impress others or to be noticed. Oh, there were times of loneliness, but in those times, I turned to God, talked to Him, and drew closer to Him.

When God takes something out of our life, and we are obedient to Him, He gives us back something greater - with a multiplier! I may have moved away from old relationships, but now I've been given many more relationships with faith-filled men and women who build me up, encourage me, and reinforce what I know to be true about my relationship with God. My relationships take on a new meaning now. They are not about what I get from others or how they make me feel. I now have people in my life who point me to the Father, I can serve with, and encourage me to practice my role as a Good Samaritan – helping others in need. *Am I now trying to win the approval of human beings, or of God? Or am I trying to please people? If I were still trying to please people, I would not be a servant of Christ.* (Galatians 1:10 NIV)

Surrender of My Selfishness

Once I surrendered my relationships, God called me to surrender my self-serving and instead serve others. He called me away from my own self-pleasing and desires and pointed me to other people. Going to church was no longer about listening for what I could get out of a message. Rather, it was a calling to step out, serve others, and be a light to other believers and people who are still searching for the answers to life. God prompted me to start loving people right where they are and minister to *their* needs – not my own. When we surrender our selfishness and serve mankind, God invites us to share in His happiness!

"His master replied, 'Well done, good and faithful servant! You have been faithful with a few things; I will put you in charge of many things. Come and share your master's happiness!'" (Matthew 25:21 NIV)

When we serve others, we are invited to share in the delight of our Lord! Then, the Lord grants authority to us for a broader scope of responsibility with endless opportunity.

Surrender of My Finances

Another area God called me to surrender was my finances. I always found ways to juggle and stretch my money through worldly ways - like credit cards and loans - but I always struggled. As a single mother of three children, it was difficult to figure out how to pay the mortgage, feed the family, buy school clothes, and still tithe. I had no one to count on but myself, so I did whatever I had to do to make it work. I certainly did not count on God to help me financially.

I knew my way was not profitable, so I tried Dave Ramsey's *Financial Peace University* but never fully implemented it. Then one day, God said enough is enough. The Lord prompted me to cut up all my credit cards, tithe, and trust Him. He called me to surrender my finances to Him. Matthew 6:26 tells us to *Look at the birds, they do not sow or reap or store away in barns, and yet your heavenly Father feeds them. Are you not much more valuable than they?* (NIV)

Now, I realize I can do more living off of 90% and giving 10% to God than I can by hoarding the 100% for myself. I have seen a dramatic change in my finances. God has blessed me more than I could have ever imagined. Now I tithe my 10% and give additionally out of abundance. God has called me to be a good steward of the things He has blessed me with so that I can bless others. When I surrender my finances to Him, He blesses me, not to line my pockets or to buy more things, but to pour into others and to use my resources for the Kingdom.

Surrender of My Life

In 2018 I was diagnosed with Melanoma which had metastasized into my lymph nodes. It was a trying time. I remember laying on the cold bed about to get a body scan, receiving a painful injection in my arm, and looking over and seeing a picture of Jesus on a corkboard. It was as if He was looking at me. I felt His eyes meet mine, and, in my spirit, I heard Him asking me if I was willing to surrender my life – even unto death! Without hesitation, I told the Lord that whether I lived or died, it was well with my soul. I trusted God no matter what the outcome was. If I were healed and lived another day, I would be here to do His will. And if I died, then I would be at home with Him.

It seems that we walk through our Christian lives dealing with day-to-day circumstances and are okay turning it over to the Lord, but when it comes to our *LIFE,* that is a completely different story. We want God to spare us or take that cup from us. But we all will encounter the time when our life here will be over. The end of this life is only the beginning! Do we believe what Jesus said when He promised us eternal life? *"Very truly I tell you, whoever hears my word and believes him who sent me has eternal life and will not be judged but has crossed over from death to life. Very truly I tell you, a time is coming and has now come when the dead will hear the voice of the Son of God and those who hear will live."* (John 5:24-25 NIV)

From Broken to Healed – Fully Surrendered

Brokenness is a path we don't have to walk. In my life, God used people like my daughter Maggie, my friend Lisa, and others to change my mind and open my heart to Him. I started to trust that God cared about me and had my best interest in His mind. Once I began to trust Him, I surrendered my will and declared my obedience. I continued to surrender daily to each thing God called me to lay down – my relationships, my selfishness, my finances, and my life. In the process, He has given me back fellowship, unity, security, and hope. These things have brought me so much joy and peace and love. This is the best part of having a relationship with my Father God. Once broken, I now live my life fully surrendered and healed. You can, too. God is waiting to walk with you.

Surrender Your Desires

By Julie T. Jenkins

> *The world and its desires pass away, but whoever does the will of God lives forever.* (1 John 2:17 NIV)

There is much to desire in this world. After all, God is perfect, and He created the world and recognized that it was good. So in and of itself, the feeling of desire is not bad. But succumbing to the desire for something not meant for us can get us in trouble.

After God created all that was good, He added His crowning glory—man and woman. And they lived in paradise. In the middle of the garden where they spent their days were two trees, the tree of life and the tree of the knowledge of good and evil.

> *And the Lord God commanded the man, "You are free to eat from any tree in the garden; but you must not eat from the tree of the knowledge of good and evil, for when you eat from it you will certainly die."* (Genesis 2:16-17 NIV)

God gave Adam and Eve everything they needed to thrive and lead happy and fulfilled lives. And then He gave them wise counsel and instruction: they were not to eat from the tree of the knowledge of good and evil—because it wasn't meant for them. But Eve, with a little help from the serpent, looked past the glorious creation God had made specifically *for her* and set her sights on something that would only bring her pain.

When the woman saw that the fruit of the tree was good for food and pleasing to the eye, and also desirable for gaining wisdom, she took some and ate it. (Genesis 3:6 NIV)

We often "credit" sin to Eve as she was the first to reach out for the forbidden fruit, to hold it in her hand, examine it with her eyes, contemplate its luscious scent, and, with her mouth watering, take a bite.

But we, too, have difficulty walking away from some things that were never meant for us. Resisting our desires can be even more difficult when we, like Eve, take time to gaze on them, contemplate our longings, and allow our cravings to wash over us. The more we focus on what we do not hold, the blinder we become to the glorious gifts and pleasures God has created specifically for us.

We must face the reality that everything in this world is not for us.

But perhaps it can help if we remember that those things that are not for us are dangerous or, at the very least, detrimental to us.

So how do we know which of our desires to surrender and which we should hold on to?

Sometimes the answer is clear. For example, if the object of our desire is another woman's husband or takes us out of our own marriage, that is a longing we must certainly surrender. If our desire leads us into substance abuse or a harmful addiction, we must lean on God to take the pining away. When we recognize that the object of our yearning is not intended for us, we must intentionally surrender it to God, asking Him to hold us close in protection. We must petition Him to focus our eyes on the good things He has provided specifically for us and cloud our vision and senses to those fascinations not designed for us.

But often, the answer to which desires we should surrender is challenging to discern because the devil specializes in making things murky. So what do we do then? The key is to know that any good desire will come directly from God, so when we are unsure, we can ask Him! "God, is this desire from you?" And petition Him, "Please make me desire only what *your* heart desires! Give me the wisdom to strive toward what you have prepared for me and remove any yearning that is not from you."

God is most eager for us to be with Him, so being with Him should be our greatest desire. God knew that if Eve ate from the tree of the knowledge of good and evil, she would be separated from Him. And she was. But Jesus came to earth and, by His crucifixion, enabled the chasm between God and man to be eliminated. So all we need to do now in order to spend eternity with God is to come before Jesus and surrender our lives to Him.

God places good desires in our hearts that are intended to bring us closer to Him. But the devil tempts us with longings meant to pull us away from God. So examine your desires objectively – will obtaining what you long for bring you to a closer relationship with God or pull you away from Him? And then surrender those desires that do not come from God as He guides you toward the desires of *His* heart.

. . . .

Elizabeth Anne Bridges

Elizabeth Anne Bridges is one of seven children from an Air Force Family and has traveled the world, even living in England briefly during the Vietnam War with her British-born mother and grandparents. Her two adult children and two stepchildren are her joy.

A graduate of Pembroke Christian Academy in Pembroke Pines, Florida, Elizabeth received a Business Administration degree from Cumberland University in Lebanon, Tennessee. She has worked extensively with human resources, payroll, and time and attendance software implementation for over 20 years. She is a consultant specializing in organization, efficiency, and client relationship management.

Elizabeth enjoys giving books and resources to charitable organizations focusing on young women and children. She posts scriptures and devotions, called Warrior Strong, on social media, encouraging others to know Jesus Christ. She serves in Women World Leaders and United Men of Honor and sends old-fashioned cards to encourage and inspire others to stay strong in Jesus Christ.

Elizabeth loves animals, the symphony, theater, and spending time in museums. She can be contacted at Elizabethwarriorstrong@yahoo.com.

Surrendered to Joy During Health Trials

By Elizabeth Anne Bridges

I was diagnosed with multiple sclerosis (MS) and fibromyalgia in 2003. And then stage 1 breast cancer in 2017. And then I had a horrific car wreck in 2019.

That is a lot of mess and a lot of stress.

When we go through trials, it is easy to question God, "Why me?" It is understandable to do this when we suffer. But we must trust God with our lives, trials, and suffering, just as Jesus did in the Garden of Gethsemane before His crucifixion.

> *I have refined you, but not as silver is refined. Rather, I have refined you in the furnace of suffering.* (Isaiah 48:10 NLT)

> *The Lord is my strength and shield. I trust him with all my heart. He helps me, and my heart is filled with joy. I burst out in songs.* (Psalm 28:7 NLT)

As I reflect on the last three years, I recognize they have been full of trials and refinement by God with twists and turns I did not expect. Some were the direct result of my own mistakes and immaturity. I was living alone, enduring emotional and physical pain, and questioning God. Worries about the future were ever present in my heart. Let me go back to the year 2017 as I shine a light on God's glory.

I had been dealing with my diagnosis of multiple sclerosis and fibromyalgia for numerous years. Then, in November 2017, I was diagnosed with stage 1 breast cancer after a biopsy confirmed a cancerous lump. A lumpectomy was scheduled for December. The pain in my upper right breast near my armpit had become a constant companion, and mammograms, diagnostic mammograms, an ultrasound, and a biopsy confirmed the breaking truth. I had cancer. It was a moment in time that you wish would go away. My mom died of leukemia when I was five. I was only beginning to understand her pain and suffering.

Getting rid of the "C" involved not one but two surgeries and thirty radiation treatments. The first tissue pathology from surgery revealed that I needed an additional upper right quadrant mastectomy. I chose to forgo traditional chemo after surgery due to my family's history of heart problems and strokes. After radiation, I took tamoxifen, a chemotherapy pill, at night. Fortunately, after the second surgery, the pathology showed that the cancer had not spread further into my breast tissue or lymph nodes.

You never imagine walking alone through a journey like this, but that is exactly what I had to do. I had just left my husband of 33 years, who had been living a single social life while being a married man. His relationships and social activities told me I was no longer important to him. I left him after my diagnosis with breast cancer. Sadly, he told me I had gotten cancer to receive alimony from him. I never asked for or wanted his alimony despite being on disability for multiple sclerosis. Having 33 years of marriage dissolve into nothing but money obligations is heartbreaking.

As I faced the surgeries and radiation alone without my husband, the grace of God showed up, and He provided for my needs. My older sister, who is a nurse, flew in for the two surgeries. My older brother's wife (my sister-in-law) helped pay my rent, which was difficult for me to manage alone due to the added bills of moving and leaving my husband. My brother bought me some household items necessary to set up my new residence. Another church member who "happened" to be selling an Airbnb gave me furniture. And a good friend brought food. Even though I was alone for the bulk of the time after surgery, these acts from God's faithful servants helped me so much. Although I was numb due to the trauma and pain of the situation, including my changing figure, I was so appreciative of the added support.

Except for one session, I drove myself to my first fifteen radiation visits. My skin began to burn and peel. It was terribly painful; it just began to hurt so much. I told my 81-year-old neighbor I was not going anymore. I just could not. I sobbed and held my head in my hands. She said, "You are going, and I am going to ride with you for the rest of your sessions." She had breast cancer years before. So, each day for the remaining fifteen visits, I picked her up. She would sit faithfully in the waiting room, watching the three shows they kept on constantly—*Andy Griffith, Bonanza,* and another western that I do not remember. The knowledge that she was in the waiting room enabled me to lay on that table as technicians adjusted and taped my breast up and down or moved me to get the exact spot of radiation done. Again, the grace of God had shown up. I completed my treatment. And I began taking a chemo pill at night. To date, I am cancer free. As I completed that trial, this scripture kept coming to mind. *Each time he said, "My grace is all you need. My power works best in weakness." So now I am glad to boast about my weaknesses, so that the power of Christ can work through me.* (2 Corinthians 12:9 NLT)

I have always had a husband and children, but in this season, I was single and alone. My children were adults—both working full time. One was in another state with my grandchildren. Both were young with new careers that would not provide much time off. But what I thought was an impossible journey alone became doable as God provided the right people and support.

I was feeling so much better and enjoying life when the unthinkable happened. I was driving home from a friend's house, about to head to church, when a person ahead of me on the highway lost control of their car and hit another car at a high rate of speed. It caused a chain reaction pile-up of three vehicles, and I hit the back of a vehicle going sixty miles an hour. It broke my sternum (breastbone), right ribs, gave me whiplash to my neck, and injured my left shoulder, abdomen, and bladder. It also killed my dog Ezekiel (Zeke) in the wreck. He was a Yorkie and my medical support pet. I had gotten him after breast cancer, still dealing with the MS I had had since 2003.

Once again, I was alone on this impossible journey. I was transported to a hospital via ambulance and was told that I only had broken ribs. Sadly, it was not a level one trauma hospital. A friend drove me home from the emergency room, and I found a note the police left in my purse about my dog. I called the animal control near my home, who told me the news that my dog had died of his injuries. Heartbroken, I called the friend who had brought me home and went to her house for the night. The next day, after she went to work, I was sitting in a recliner and tried to stand up. The pain in my chest and ribs shot through to my back. I could not push myself up to stand. I thought that if I could slide down onto my knees, I could use my legs to stand up. But that did not work. I ended up lying on the floor and was able to call my friend. Her boyfriend came, and by the grace of God, my daughter called and was able to arrive quickly. I was transported via ambulance to a different hospital—this one was a level 1 trauma hospital. I was in the trauma unit alone for several days as my adult children were working and my grandchildren were in school. My daughter was able to visit just once at night due to her hectic schedule. I never felt alone, though. God provided kind doctors and nurses, and I was eventually released after four or five days.

Still, my pain level was unreal—off the charts. I ended up taking two more trips to the emergency room due to the side effects of the wreck. My church family bought a box spring and frame to lift my mattress, allowing me to get in and out of bed more easily. Before the accident, I had the mattress directly on the floor so my Yorkie could get on it. Again, God's grace brought me the kindest people for over a year as I healed from the wreck.

The occupational therapists and physical therapists who came to my home were impressive. Later, I attended a physical therapy center that employed the most cheerful and positive people. They were kind but made me work hard so I would heal correctly.

My biggest challenge by far has been my bladder. Due to multiple sclerosis, I have had urgency and hesitancy. After the wreck, I had to start bending over to empty my bladder and cathing once at night as needed. It has been a blow emotionally to have this added to my existing challenges. I began taking bladder spasm medication again to help, which added some leakage. And at times, it caused infections. I also took antibiotics off and on, which caused yeast infections. My bladder was spasming, and my vagina spasmed as well from MS. They prescribed Valium or opium suppositories to help with that. I even ended up at the emergency room with such terrific pain from it. I was reduced to tears. But that day, a miracle happened. My OB/GYN was on call in the hospital and was able to prescribe what I needed. Again, another miracle from God.

While I was healing from the car wreck, I was also trying to help an immediate family member. She is so talented in computers and customer service and was just a few credits from earning a human resources degree. But things went downhill for her after a devastating divorce. Right after the divorce, she was coping well. I had moved into a bigger apartment so she could live with me, but she finally got her own apartment.

Then I received a very disturbing call, alerting me to her struggles. My relative had someone who influenced her to take ecstasy. She would do great at times but then would abandon everything she owned and come stay with me. That happened five times. I have managed this mostly by myself, except for some help from my son, her ex-husband, and a great former boss of hers. Most of the family on both sides backed away from her due to her drug-induced thoughts and conversations, which I totally understand. Her conversations were not rational. She made scary comments and later angry, aggressive comments towards others. She did things that did not seem to make sense. But that left me fielding those scary calls alone.

Concerned that she might have multiple sclerosis or lupus, which both run in our family, I kept trying to help her. She did scary things while in my home, such as putting water in my needed medicines, stealing medicine to sell, urinating in my mouthwash, or putting cleaner in my face lotion. The list went on. I eventually, for my own safety, had to ask her to leave. It broke my heart. I am not sure why I hung on so long when it was so dangerous for me to have her there, except I had that unconditional love for her. My family told me over and over to let her fall so that she would get help. They were right to help me realize this. But it was a hard tightrope to walk—helping too much versus letting her fall. The results of which can be success or death.

I made numerous calls to prayer lines daily—reaching out for others to cry out to the Lord with me. I prayed myself, asked for prayer from prayer partners, and posted my requests on prayer walls. Today, I still constantly reach out to others to pray with me daily. I have also been on the phone with mobile crisis centers, state troopers, police stations, and local law enforcement navigating two frightening situations with her.

Back to my physical situation, I was still working to heal. I began to feel beaten down and hopeless from everything. But with God's grace, so many people prayed and rallied around me, providing me the encouragement to keep going. Fellow church members supported me. People sent cards. A few friends brought food. My church Sunday school teacher brought flowers and candy. Just when you are ready to give up, God steps in and gives you the strength to go on. *That is why I take pleasure in my weaknesses, and in the insults, hardships, persecutions, and troubles that I suffer for Christ. For when I am weak, then I am strong.* (2 Corinthians 12:10 NLT)

I was still losing hope, though, due to the physical pressures. Listening to God's voice, I looked for ways to begin serving others again. Through my church, I helped get food and baby supplies for a single parent living in a hotel. I began sending cards to cheer people who were sick or had lost loved ones. I helped provide Christian adult devotionals, children's books, clothing, and toiletries to a domestic violence center. I also set it up for that center to receive multiple copies of *Voice of Truth* magazine from Women World Leaders to encourage each woman who was escaping domestic violence. (Women World Leaders is a ministry whose purpose is to grow and encourage women to serve Christ and can be reached at womenworldleaders. com.) I helped hand out supplies after a tornado ravaged our community and destroyed lives, homes, and a school.

Even as I served and relied on God, trusting in the knowledge He gave me of His grace and love, I began to lose my hope and joy. The physical and emotional challenges began to drain me. I visited a church and heard a sermon from an Assemblies of God minister about walking without joy. He said, "Joy withers due to ignorance of our freedom in Christ in trial and trouble." I used to try and have the visual picture of Jesus with me wherever I went. Now I realize the Holy Spirit lives in me, and Jesus is walking by my side. I am never alone. A prayer partner said she felt like if she laid her hand on her chest, she remembered Jesus was with her. But the Assemblies of God minister gave a better visual that restored my joy.

He took two people, one short and one tall. He put the short person first and the second tall person behind him like they were standing in line. He put his hand on the short person's chest and said these are my trials and troubles right in front of me as I focus on them. Then he moved the tall person in front of the short person and said this is what it looks like when you know God is in front of your trials and tribulations. My joy was immediately restored during the prayer that followed.

God's power is ever-present. He is always in control.

> *I have told you all this so that you may have peace in me. Here on earth, you may have many trials and troubles. But take heart because I have overcome the world.* (John 16:33 NIV)

Ladies of God, do not let Satan steal your happiness or joy during physical and mental hardships or trials. Ask God for the strength you need in all areas of your life. *But even now I know that God will give you whatever you ask.* (John 11:22 NLT) We need to walk in the freedom that God is in control, no matter what. I love this scripture; I breathe it in daily. As we walk with joy through the troubles and trials, we become more like Christ and are given the opportunity to give others hope. I do not know what my future holds. But I choose to surrender this and walk in the joy God meant for me, knowing He is holding me in His hands. I know the promises in His Word, the Bible, are true. And I claim those for myself and my family. As time goes on, my relative has shown some small signs of recovery. I keep holding on to faith in God. And stand in the gap for her in prayer as so many have done for me.

> *Lord - who is the Spirit - makes us more and more like him as we are changed into his glorious image.* (2 Corinthians 3:17-18 NLT)

Surrender Your Health

By Kimberly Ann Hobbs

We all have friends and family hurting due to their health; they surround us. And we may even be one of those people. Usually, we can name an unhealthy, hurting person quite quickly. But some unhealthy people may be very silent about their needs, while others are loud, crying out for help.

How can we be a positive influence for ourselves and others when it comes to achieving healthy living? The first step is to surrender your health and how you care for yourself to God. Allow Him full control when making decisions about your health. And ask Him for His wisdom as you process the best ways to care for your body.

Sometimes seeking an accountability partner to help you pray over your own health, whether staying healthy or getting back to health, is a promising idea.

> *Therefore encourage one another and build each other up, just as in fact you are doing.* (1 Thessalonians 5:11 NIV)

God is our way, truth, and life. (John 14:6) As such, He is the ultimate truth and means for healthy living, and we are to exude His truth to the world. We can be a joyful and positive influence on others and maintain healthy living by doing five simple things:

1. *Lead by example.* There is no better way to lead others than to be the first to do something significant for your own health. Ask God to help you make a healthy change in your lifestyle. Whether dealing with physical, spiritual, or emotional health, we all should desire to be healthy. If we want to help others in our families who are suffering and need to make

changes, we should set an example by changing first. We will capture their attention with our actions, not just with our words. God will help us do this with our full surrender to Him. Step out in faith and do it!

2. *Make new friends.* Surround yourself with others who wish to support and affirm your healthy path of living. God will guide you to the right person who will encourage you, and then you can also be an encouragement to them. Together you could influence each other into healthier living.

3. *Share your joy.* Share the Lord; share the desire to be healthy along with new products, stores, books, and other helpful information that God shares with you. God will lead you to ways that will help you get healthy if you ask Him to.

4. *Be bold.* People may fight against you as you make a heart surrender to God to change your health for the better. Others may be afraid of change or seeing you change your old ways and habits, but understand that God will lead you to healthy change; you must trust Him and not what others say. Love on those around you with your new healthy lifestyle; do not preach, but encourage them. Do not be shy. Continue to pass encouraging words and helpful information as God gives it to you through the wisdom you have asked for. That is what kindness is about, and kindness helps promote change!

5. *Pray for others.* Those actively trying to better themselves health-wise and those who wish to help a loved one may need you. You might be the one placed in their life to assist them. So many goals are accomplished through the power of prayer. When we surrender our health and the health of others we love to God, we don't stop praying until we see God move through our continuous prayer. Miraculous changes occur when we seek God. *I urge you, first of all, to pray for all people. Ask God to help them: intercede on their behalf, and give thanks for them.* (1 Timothy 2:1 NLT)

I believe we all want to make healthy changes in our bodies. We can help influence each other. We can surrender our health, not for just our own benefit, but for the purpose of helping others. We can make a significant impact if we allow God to use us. He cannot use us if we are constantly in the way.

Believe it.

If you lack wisdom regarding your health, ask God for it. He will not withhold it from anyone who asks. Then, make healthy choices in how you live from the moment you open your eyes to the time you close them at night. Be the example first by surrendering your health to God.

> *If any of you lacks wisdom, you should ask God, who gives generously to all without finding fault, and it will be given to you. (James 1:5 NIV)*

. . . .

Carolyn Joy

Carolyn Joy is a Southwest Florida Real Estate Agent, mother of three married children, and Nonna to eleven grandchildren. She serves in her church and helps lead a women's Bible study in her community. Additionally, she loves vacationing with her family, playing pickleball, hiking, writing, the beach, and watching sunsets.

Carolyn is also a previously published author. Her two devotional journals, *The Overflow of the Heart* and *Let Your Heart Overflow with Joy,* encourage scripture memorization and writing prayers. Her fiction novel, *Out of the Grey Zone,* demonstrates God's grace, mercy, forgiveness, and unconditional love. Carolyn also writes "Nonna's kNOWledge," a column published in *Voice of Truth* magazine.

Her favorite scripture verse is Proverbs 4:23, *Above all else, guard your heart, for everything you do flows from it.* (NIV)

Never Say Never

By Carolyn Joy

I was born into a Christian home where we went to church every Sunday morning, Sunday evening, and even mid-week for Wednesday evening service. I was involved with my Sunday school classes, a girls' group called Missionettes, and eventually, youth group. Many would think it is a blessing to be raised with strict Christian principles; however, even families with strong faith can have sin issues in their homes. My early Sunday School teachings revealed that even the mighty biblical leaders such as Abraham, Sarah, Moses, David, Solomon, Jonah, Peter, Paul, and John (to name a few) all had struggles in their life. My journey has been no different.

My rigid Christian upbringing made me rebellious toward my parents at a young age. To try to fit in at school and make friends, I compromised my faith and did things I knew to be wrong. However, by seventeen, I dedicated my heart back to the Lord, realizing God's ways are always better than the world's ways.

I met a man at church whom I married when I was nineteen and had three precious children by the time I was twenty-five. My children went to a private Christian school, and we were very involved in our church. We looked like the perfect family, but the walls told a different story. The marriage lasted twenty years.

After we divorced, I did not date for the next seven years, while my children were still living with me. I believed that if the Lord wanted me to meet someone, He would put that special man in my life. It was important to me to be available in my children's lives and be a good example to my ever-present, impressive, almost adult children. When I was in my late forties, however, my last child went off to college, and I recognized my heart was yearning for a relationship.

I have learned not to judge anyone's journey and never to say "never" because when Satan twists your heart, you don't really know what you will do.

For the first time in many years, I desired a relationship; my calculated, protective, hard-shelled exterior had an internal heart beating for love. The Bible says, *Above all else, guard your heart, for everything you do flows from it.* (Proverbs 4:23 NIV). That is so true! The heart's only purpose is not just to pump blood! A heart is the central location in our body where we experience all our emotions. When we love with our heart, we might say, "I love you with all my heart." When we feel joy with our heart, we might exclaim, "I can just jump with joy." When we experience excitement, we can say, "I am going to explode with excitement." On the contrary, when hurt, pain and sorrow creep into our heart we say, "I have a broken heart."

All these extraordinary emotions with which God created us come from deep within. The Bible says in Psalm 139:14 (NIV), *I praise you because I am fearfully and wonderfully made; your works are wonderful, I know that full well. We have feelings that well up in our hearts as God has designed us intricately from birth. For you created my inmost being; you knit me together in my mother's womb."* (Psalm 139:13 NIV)

Although I always had a strong faith, when the devil crawled his way into my heart, he knew how to throw me off course into the deep, dark pit of sin and despair. Suddenly, the familiar adage "blinded by sin" took on new meaning. When we are blinded by sin, we cannot glimpse Christ's best for us because our hardened hearts cannot see the knowledge of the truth. Sin blinds us from bad situations which are clearly visible to those without sin. That is why it is essential to surround yourself with Christian friends who can speak truth into your life when you get off course.

I was at the height of my walk with the Lord; however, I was lonely. Although I was serving through various ministry opportunities and working for a Christian organization, I felt alone. I was filled with joy as I worked for the Lord, loved helping both local and international ministries, and was surrounded by amazing Christian people and wonderful relationships. But I was empty. And no one in my busy world knew the emptiness of my heart. On the outside, I appeared content and happily immersed in my work, ministries, family, and friends. But Satan knew my one aching desire to love one special person and have that one special person love me.

With my heart intent on finding a relationship, I got involved with the wrong man. Although everyone thought he was a strong Christian (he was, in fact, a leader in our church), he had a secret life that would be uncovered over the next four years. This man had perfected the art of grooming his next desire while brainwashing her to keep his behavior confidential. Unbeknown to me, I was his next object of affection. He used his cunning words, demonstrative demeanor, and extreme kindness to pull me into his world of secrets and lies. My heart and mind conceded. When you enter the grey zone, a slow, steady spiritual blinding beyond normal comprehension comes upon you. Knowing this relationship was not God's will, I told no one.

After being swept into the relationship, the ups and downs, secrets and lies engulfed me for the next two years. Then, without warning or caution, the Lord blew off my blindfolds; I was left broken, ashamed, hurt, guilt-ridden, and suicidal. You can choose your sin, but you cannot choose your consequences. The reality and vastness of my sin were beyond what I could physically bear. The loss of the love I had felt in my life was heart-wrenching. The unveiling of the man I had fallen in love with was despairing, and his swift disappearance was catastrophic. The thought that his words and actions were all lies was intolerable.

His secret life was mind-boggling, beyond words, and devastated all that knew Him, especially me.

I was caught in a web of despair with no do-over. There were times I did not get out of bed for days. For months I thought dying would be the easy way out of the pain and sorrow. I was a Christian mom who had raised my children in fear of the Lord and taught them right from wrong. Now, I was the sinner that needed God's redemptive power and forgiveness.

When the devil gets a hold of your heart and mind, he can turn the most intelligent person into a pile of mush. I was that pile of mush, not knowing how to receive the grace, mercy, and forgiveness the Lord so freely gives. I thought I knew how to pray for forgiveness, but how does a Christian mom confess to her children and family or walk back inside her church when she has fallen so far? *If we confess our sins, he is faithful and just and will forgive us of our sins and purify us from all unrighteousness.* (1 John 1:9 NIV) The only way I could go on in life was to surrender everything to the Lord. I needed to surrender my heart, mind, and soul. I had to surrender my life. For me, it was not instant, and it didn't feel immediately healing. It took time.

My first step of surrender was to offer forgiveness. Unforgiveness in your heart is like drinking poison and hoping the other person will die. Life moved on for the man I once loved who had devastated me, and I had to learn to forgive and pray for him. Understanding and realizing he needed Jesus helped me take this step.

Then, I had to offer my apologies. I went to the people I knew had prayed for me throughout this time, those I lied to, and those I offended. It took time and prayer to arrange all those confessions. Included in my list were church leaders, friends, and my three children and their spouses. To my surprise, everyone was supportive and forgiving. It was a noose around my neck breaking free.

Next, I sought a Christian counselor so I could talk through my trauma. I began writing and journaling my thoughts, hurt, pain and sorrow. For me, surrendering meant writing it all down. I wrote scriptures over and over until I memorized them. *For the word of the God is alive and active. Sharper than any double-edge sword, it penetrates even to dividing soul and spirit, joints and marrow; it judges the thoughts and the attitudes of the heart.* (Hebrews 4:12 NIV) Reading, writing, and memorizing scripture is life-changing. The Word of God goes deep down into the soul, changing our heart, mind, and life from the inside out! God's Word will never return void! It is alive and life-changing!

I wrote my prayers so I would not forget them. I constantly re-read my prayers so I could visually see how my God was answering them. That was the beginning of my love for writing. I found a new path to release my hurt, sorrow, and pain. Once I surrendered to God, He did not leave my pain unnoticed. God will always turn our sin, pain, and suffering into something that will bring Him glory.

I returned to church and joined a women's small group Bible study. Having women in my life to talk to and having a weekly Bible study plan to keep me on track helped heal my mind.

Healing from trauma in life is not an easy process. Just like a physical injury may leave a scar, emotional injury can also leave a scar. But what we do with our hurt and pain will direct the path of our life. *Your word is a lamp for my feet, and a light on my path.* (Psalm 119:105 NIV) We can choose to stuff the pain inside and pretend we are not hurt, but that can lead to us becoming like a volcano, just waiting for the right trigger to make us explode.

Although I felt I was healed, I still hid the pain in my heart for years, unable and unwilling to move forward in another relationship. I was mad at God for my "life story." I wanted a different and better life story. I was filled with all kinds of questions. *Why did God let this happen? Why did God give me that path? Why didn't God make me and the others around me aware of what was going on? Why? Why? Why?*

Unable to bring my own pain into the light, I hid in shame and went through the healing process alone. That shame had me weighed down in despair. The devil whispered lies that no one would forgive me. No one would want to be my friend. No one would understand. As long as I believed those lies, I couldn't break free. I lived in that cycle for years, unable to move forward. As a Christian, I had all the head knowledge but could not move it to my heart. I knew Jesus died for all my sins, and through His grace and mercy, I was forgiven. However, I did not realize I was not moving that knowledge into my heart.

My secrets had a hold on me. The devil wants us to keep our secrets locked up because hidden sin can wreak havoc in our lives and hearts. However, when we release our secrets and realize that our sin is covered in the blood of Jesus, that is when we can surrender all that we are to Him.

I have since learned that we cannot change the past, but we can change the future. I did not want my past hurt, sin, and pain to hold me in bondage any longer. Although I had been through the healing process and taken all the right steps towards healing, I was still living in a cloud of shame, at times lying about my life story instead of using it to bring God glory through His redeeming love.

Satan is the keeper of secrets. He uses those secrets to torment our minds and our hearts and our souls. *What will people think? What if they do not like me? What if I lose friends?*

I used to avoid that part of my life story. When questioned about my past, I skipped over those eight years of my journey, feeling like a liar. Although I was careful not to change the truth, I would omit significant parts of my experiences. Eventually, I was able to talk about my past as part of my life story. I learned to surrender! Recognizing my story is God's story to tell. Exodus 14:14 says, *The Lord will fight for you; you need only to be still.* (NIV)

As I embraced my life story as a tribute to God's grace, mercy, and forgiveness instead of one of shame, guilt, and despair, I was able to admit a very dark period of my life. When I began sharing my story, other people came forward and shared their buried secrets and hidden life stories. Encouraged by my testimony of redemption, others admitted their own hidden pain. There is freedom in being able to confess and talk about your own life.

Life will always have its ups and downs. Satan knows how to attack and throw our life off course. Living under an umbrella of shame and regret only eats away at our innermost being, causing everything from health problems to relational and mental issues. Christ came to set the captive free. He loves us, no matter what we have done, and wants nothing less than to bless us with abundant life.

When buried pain begins to surface in a healthy way, it is like peeling back an onion. The painful layers of smelly shame will probably burn and bring tears. But those tears are usually accompanied by a sense of freedom, which enables a person to finally surrender their life of carefully hidden shame to a life of freedom. Surrendering your life story to the Lord means no more fear of questions or avoidance of social events and meeting people, and no more shame of someone "finding out." Philippians 1:6 says, *being confident of this, that he who began a good work in you will carry it on to completion until the day of Christ Jesus.* (NIV)

A surrendered heart is a heart rooted in peace and joy. Joy is deep down confidence that God is in control. Once you live in the certainty that God is in control, you can let go of all the fears that prevent a heart from surrendering to God's will. You will also have a keen awareness and knowledge of the control of sin and a remarkable understanding of the power of the cross. You will think before you pass judgment on anyone again, and scripture will have new meaning and come alive with truth as you learn that your relationship with God is not inconsequential and will be forever cherished.

God has a plan for each one of us.

> *"For I know the plans I have for you," declares the Lord, "plans to prosper you and not to harm you, plans to give you hope and a future."* (Jeremiah 29:11 NIV)

Sometimes, our foolish choices make us wish there was a different plan. However, God is sovereign, and when we confess our sin and believe in the Lord, He will always use our life to bring Him glory. Our honesty helps others to know we are real people with real lives. Our life story is unique to each of us. God will never leave us, even when we stray off the path. He is faithful to extend grace, mercy, and forgiveness and fill us with abundant life. There is nothing better than a surrendered soul walking and talking with Jesus! *She is clothed with strength and dignity; she can laugh at the days to come.* (Proverbs 31:25 NIV)

Surrender Your Temptations

By Kimberly Ann Hobbs

Even though we go to church, sing hymns, and set our minds on things in heaven, like a Christian is taught, temptations are all around us.

Jesus was tempted in the middle of the desert, even with nothing visible to come against Him. Likewise, we may never see where temptations are lurking until they hit us smack in the face. We can innocently turn on the television or check social media, exposing ourselves to posts, ads, and movies full of sex, violence, and devastation. Although we think we are strong enough to handle anything that could steer us from obedience to God, there is no telling what could easily drag us down at any given moment, tempting us to be filled with ungodly things. Even going about our daily business by taking a walk in the park or circling together with friends can put us face to face with temptation that arises out of nowhere.

How do we overcome temptations?

No temptation has overtaken you except what is common to mankind. God is faithful; he will not let you be tempted beyond what you can bear. But when you are tempted, he will also provide a way out so that you can endure it. (1 Corinthians 10:13 NIV)

Too many people struggle against and fail to successfully turn away from temptations presented through contemporary living, including lust, perversions of truth, and more. They fight, harnessing their own willpower and offering tearful prayers, but still cannot genuinely change how they handle what they have succumbed to. We cannot cleanse our hearts by merely modifying our outer behavior alone. Does "just saying no" work?

Surrendered: Yielded With Purpose

Jesus says that if our eye offends us, we should pluck it out. But He didn't mean that literally—praise God because we would not have any body parts left if everything that offended us had to be cut off. Walking with God, we know who we are and whose we are. And we can be free from what has its hooks in us by yielding to something we want more—a stronger relationship with our God who loves us unconditionally. By surrendering all our temptations fully to Him, we can have victory because God is bigger, better, and more powerful than all our desires. Our victory comes when we release our temptations to God and allow Him to stake a claim on our life.

> *Now to him who is able to do exceedingly, abundantly above all we ask or think, according to the power that works in us.* (Ephesians 3:20 NIV)

May we come to understand that our abundant life is not about quieting down or repressing our God-given life force. It is about surrendering things we think we can handle to the One who CAN handle them. God can filter, focus, and turn on something beautiful in your life through His power and word of truth. Just saying no to the sins that so easily trip us up is a start, but when we resolve to surrender as an apprentice of Jesus, we begin to change our behavior authentically.

Countless people have overcome struggles, but when you have a desire to change, a desire to emulate Jesus, and He becomes your source of satisfaction through prayer and reading the Word, you are on the first steps of real and lasting heart change. You can combat temptation as you surrender to the Holy Spirit at work within you. It is His working inside you which allows victory in any spiritual battle of the flesh.

Today, remember to say no to the lures that will set you up for failure. However, also say yes to surrendered intimacy, love, and POWER of what Jesus can do through you.

Kimberly Ewell

Kimberly Ewell has been walking with the Lord for 11 years. During that time, she learned to walk in faith and obedience, which brought her to where she is today. After years of healing and training, Kimberly founded WildFire International Ministries in 2021.

Because of Kimberly's personal experiences of childhood trauma, abuse, pain, grief, and loss, Kimberly has been given a powerful testimony of God's love and healing power.

As part of Kimberly's journey, the Lord called her to Colorado Springs, Colorado, to learn ministry work at Focus on the Family. There she gained experience of what it's like to be on the battlefield's front lines. The Lord opened Kimberly's eyes to the depths of the brokenness that runs rampant across the world. During her time at Focus on the Family, she ministered, counseled, and poured out the love of Jesus to many people across the nation.

Kimberly firmly believes that every person should be empowered to fulfill their God-given calling and destiny. She desires to see God's people healed, equipped, and live in freedom.

Kimberly can be reached at wildfireintl.us@gmail.com

Tell Him You Love Him!

By Kimberly Ewell

> *And Jesus said to them, "I am the bread of life. He who comes to Me shall never hunger, and he who believes in Me shall never thirst." (John 6:35 NKJV)*

Every day coming home from work, I would turn off the 101 freeway onto the Victoria Avenue exit. There, standing at the end of the off-ramp, was a homeless man holding a sign which read, "Hungry, please help."

He was an older man who, day after day, wore the same worn-out blue jeans, long-sleeved grey shirt, and shoes that were falling apart. I noticed he may not have had a shower for some time as his hair looked unclean and his beard was scruffy.

I don't believe it was a coincidence that the traffic light would turn red, causing me to stop where he stood every time I approached it.

As I waited for the light to turn green, he would stare at me but not ask for any money. I wondered why he would only stare. Was he an angel sent from heaven, being used by the Lord to test me to see if I would help a man in need?

As I sat there each day, I thought about the fact that this man was once a child. I wondered if he had ever dreamed he would find himself homeless and holding a sign at the end of an off-ramp asking for help. And then, I wondered what I would do if my son, who was 20 years old at the time, ever became homeless.

Seeing this poor man broke my heart; to this day, I can still see his face as he held that sign.

"Hungry, please help."

I am a mom of five. But it was my oldest son whom I thought about every time I saw the man at the end of that off-ramp.

Let me share with you a bit about my son, Christopher. I always knew there was something special about him. A mother sees what is unique about each child, and Christopher had something special. We had a connection I can't quite explain, but I'll try.

I wasn't allowed to call him "Chris" like everyone else. Instead, I called him Christopher. A sign of the special bond we shared.

Christopher was a protector. He would never leave his little brother alone. One day, when he was around three years old, he crawled into his younger brother's crib while he was supposed to be napping.

Christopher was a mischief-maker. Once, I found him sitting on the bathroom floor, covered in his father's shaving cream. He was so proud because he was trying to be like his daddy.

Christopher was always entertaining others. He told some funny jokes that would make you laugh until your belly hurt, and some you'd scratch your head while trying to figure out the punchline.

But above all, Christopher had a big heart for his family and others. That was what I loved most about him. He would give his last dime or the shirt off his back for another human being.

These are some of the traits that made my Christopher so special.

In the late spring of 2010, when I was working for a plumbing company in Ventura, California, I received a phone call from Christopher, then 22 years old. I answered the phone and heard him say, "Mom, please come pick me up; I'm ready to get help."

He was at the Volkswagen dealership about 10 miles from me. My heart began to race. My stomach was nauseous, and anxiety and fear started to overwhelm me. I didn't know what to expect or do other than to pick him up. I thought to myself, *It's happening. Today's the day I've been waiting to hear those words.*

"Mom, I'm ready to get help."

I didn't know what to say to him other than, "I love you, son; I'm on my way."

I hadn't seen my son in a few months, and I didn't know what to expect when I saw him. Was he going to be healthy? How was he going to act?

Christopher had been homeless, living on the streets and under bridges near the beach. Law enforcement friends told me they saw him begging for money at gas stations. They offered to help him and encouraged him to go home; however, he chose not to. Christopher had an addiction to drugs and decided to live a reckless lifestyle.

My worst nightmare had come to pass. Christopher became the homeless man at the end of the off-ramp I repeatedly saw two years earlier.

Christopher had been sixteen years old when he started to get into trouble. First, he was arrested for stealing from a Walmart shopping center. As a result, he went to juvenile hall, and I let him stay there overnight to learn a lesson. I was sure this would open his eyes to see what direction he would go if he didn't make some changes in his life.

I disciplined him, went to counseling with him, and sought help anywhere I could find it, but nothing seemed to work. I tried everything I could to help my son, to the point where I started to enable him—bailing him out of trouble and making excuses for his behaviors - trying to keep the peace in the house.

Over the years, his behavior got progressively worse. I finally got to the point of giving up. I learned to wear a mask and act strong as if I had it all together; however, on the inside, I was falling apart. Guilt and shame tormented me. I felt I had failed him as a mother.

Six years later, after he had had several outbursts of anger, we got into a heated argument, and he pulled back his fist as if he was going to strike me. And this wasn't the first time. So, I had to make the most challenging decision I had ever made. I told him to leave; he could no longer live in my household because I was afraid of him.

Shaking my head, I was brought back to reality, remembering I needed to pick up my son. I pulled myself together and asked to leave work for the rest of the day. I calmly started the car and raced off to the car dealership.

As I drove, my mind flooded with memories of when Christopher was little. We had a very close relationship back then. We talked about how we were so much alike; he liked being like his mama.

So, WHERE did I go wrong?

How did he get to where he was that day?

As parents, we want our children to grow up to be the best they can be. We want to love, guide, encourage, and provide the best life possible for them. I never thought my son would be an addict and live under bridges. My heart had broken, not knowing how to handle his angry outbursts, addictions, or emotional roller coasters. I felt lost and helpless, wondering if I had let him down as a mother. I felt like I had messed up my own life and his.

But I hadn't given up. Even before Christopher made that life-saving call, his aunt and I had been looking for a Christian rehabilitation home for young men with addictions. We researched many rehabilitation centers on the internet and located a place in Oxnard, California, called Victory Outreach. This faith-based program relies on biblical guidance, prayer, and Bible studies. They require young men to stay in the rehabilitation program for one year, providing an atmosphere of God's love as they heal. I was prepared to offer Christopher this life-changing opportunity.

As I approached the turn to the car dealership, I took a deep breath and turned the corner to find my 6' 3" boy standing on the curb, weighing about 120 pounds. He was skin and bones. All he had were the clothes on his back. I gasped for air because it took everything I had not to fall apart.

"Keep it together, Kimberly. He can't see you fall apart," is what I told myself.

Christopher checked into Victory Outreach. He couldn't have visitors for three months. After his probation period ended, I was able to visit weekly. With each visit, I saw improvement; he was in the Word of God every day, growing in the Lord and healthier week after week.

I had my son back!

Then Philip said, "If you believe with all your heart, you may." And he answered and said, "I believe that Jesus Christ is the Son of God." (Acts 8:37 NKJV)

When I visited, Christopher asked if I would attend church with him. My response was always, "Next time, Son."

I didn't feel I needed church, and the church wasn't for me. The fact is that I wanted nothing to do with God because I thought He had let me down. Why? When I was five years old, God allowed me to be molested by a neighbor. Then, He allowed my parents to divorce when I was seven years old and He allowed me to be sexually abused at nine years old by my brother's friend. When I was 12 years old, I was attacked by a soldier in the middle east where we lived, but I was able to get away before he could sexually assault me and maybe even kill me. By my teen years, I had been sexually abused so many times I had given up; it was normal. I was broken, beyond broken; I couldn't be destroyed any further; I went numb and felt nothing. I wanted nothing to do with a God who would allow this to happen to an innocent little girl.

But Christopher never gave up asking me to go to church with him. Finally, on Christmas Eve, he asked me to go to a Christmas service, and I reluctantly agreed. I met him at the church a few hours later. He introduced me to his roommates from the rehab center. Service began, and Christopher and his friend sat in the front as we all found seats. The praise and worship started, and all the men ran up to the front praising the Lord and singing,

"I am free!"

I will never forget that day, I knew my son had found the Lord, and he had been set free.

Christopher only stayed at Victory Outreach for nine months of the twelve-month program. I begged him to stay, but he felt he was ready to go to another men's home, where there was more freedom. The new program would allow him to work and start a new life, so the staff at Victory Outreach allowed him to leave against their recommendations.

Christopher continued to improve in his new home. He became the person all the other young men looked to as a leader. I was so very proud of my son. We talked daily, and he would share his accomplishments with me.

Several months later, Christopher called asking me to pick him up; he was asked to leave the men's home. He told me he didn't know why they had kicked him out, only that he wasn't allowed to return. I tried to get the truth from him, but he became angry and started to yell. I explained that I could not pick him up because I had the flu. I instructed him to return to the home and see if they would allow him to stay a few days so I could get well and figure out what we had to do to rectify the situation. But he became hostile toward me on the phone and hung up. That was the last time we spoke.

After he hung on me, I attempted to call and text him, but he never answered. Later I learned he went to live with his father in San Clemente, California. I called and texted Christopher for two months, but he never responded. I was lost and couldn't understand what to do.

It was October 24, 2011. I woke up and started my daily routine before going to work.

And this is where my journey began on the road to Damascus.

I heard a voice say, "Tell him you love him."

When I heard this, I stopped what I was doing and then listened to the Lord say, "Tell him you love him."

These words penetrated my heart. I had a sense of knowing. I knew who was speaking to me and who He was speaking of - Christopher. There was a sense of urgency I felt in my soul. I was immediately obedient to text Christopher, saying, "I love you, son."

> *As he journeyed, he came near Damascus, and suddenly a light shone around him from heaven. Then he fell to the ground, and heard a voice saying to him, "Saul, Saul, why are you persecuting Me?"* (Acts 9:3-4 NKJV)

Saul, a man who had turned his back on Jesus and even persecuted Christians, heard the Lord's voice when he was on the road to Damascus. And it penetrated his heart. Likewise, the Lord spoke to me; I recognized His voice immediately and, believing, surrendered to Him in obedience. This was my first surrender to the Lord.

I hated God. And although I may not have persecuted Christians as Saul did, I had rejected Him.

But for five days, I heard the Lord tell me, "Tell him you love him." And I surrendered to His instructions, remained obedient, and texted Christopher for four days,

"I love you, son."

He wouldn't respond to my texts, however. Then, on the fifth day, I heard the Lord say three times to tell Christopher I loved him. I was disobedient and went to bed.

The following day at seven in the morning, I woke up to a voicemail from my sister-in-law. I returned her call, and she told me to call Christopher's dad. I knew something was wrong, but she kept repeating that I should call his dad.

"What's wrong! Why won't you tell me!" I said with a loud voice.

I begged her to tell me because I knew something was wrong.

"Please tell me!" I screamed.

"Christopher died in a motorcycle accident this morning around 5 am," she blurted out in tears.

I let out a blood-curdling scream from the depths within me and fell to the ground.

NO! NO! GOD, NO!

My world crumbled around me, my life stopped, and I could no longer breathe. All I could do was lay on the floor and cry. I was devastated! I didn't know where to go or what to do.

On October 29, 2011, Christopher passed away, and my life changed on the road to Damascus, where I met Jesus. Jesus had been preparing me for this day. When I heard His voice, I chose to surrender and be obedient, and because of my obedience, I was able to tell my son I loved him before he went home. I will treasure this precious gift that the Lord gave me in my heart forever.

Each person's surrendering to the Lord is different. It isn't a cookie-cutter experience or a script. We are all uniquely made. Our circumstances may differ, and our life experiences may not be the same; however, the destination remains the same: a closer relationship with Jesus.

When I surrendered to the voice of the Lord, He was changing my direction. My identity changed; I became a new creation in Christ. My community changed; brothers and sisters in Christ now surround me. My mission changed; I am currently on a mission to fulfill the calling God has given me, which has a purpose. I made a complete turn, allowing God to draw out the old me and put in place a new creation. In my surrender, I believe Jesus is the Son of God, and He is my Salvation.

Over the last ten years, I have realized why I couldn't get the image of the homeless man out of my mind. It wasn't about Christopher; it was about me. Like that man, I, too, was holding a sign, "Hungry, please help."

I was hungry for God and didn't know it. In my deepest pain, I cried out to God but couldn't speak the words until I heard Him that October day. Now I have a hunger for more of Jesus. To know His truth and grow to be more like Him.

> *Trust in the Lord with all your heart and lean not on your own understanding; In all your ways acknowledge Him, and He shall direct your paths.* (Proverbs 3:5-6 NKJV)

God has transformed my life. Every day I strive to surrender to His will and not mine. Proverbs 3:5-6 is my go-to verse when I try to lean on my understanding. I have learned that when I depend on my understanding, it creates obstacles. I become distracted from His path. I'm still not perfect, but I am learning.

> *That Christ may dwell in your hearts through faith; that you, being rooted and grounded in love, may be able to comprehend with all the saints what is the width and length and depth and height.* (Ephesians 3:17-18 NKJV)

The Lord has revealed His love for me. And He shared with me that when I was a little girl hiding under my parents' bed after a neighbor molested me, He was under the bed with me, crying too. I am His precious child. And so are you. I pray you will know the width and length and depth and height of His love for you, too, as you surrender to Him.

Surrender Your Fear

By Kimberly Ann Hobbs

Fear is a subtle attacker. It can burst out at any moment, causing us to idle where we are. And at other times, it can slowly gnaw away at us until we are consumed by it.

The Bible tells us that *Such love has no fear because perfect love expels all fear. If we are afraid, it is for fear of punishment, and this shows that we have not fully experienced his perfect love.* (1 John 4:18 NLT)

There is often a reason we fear. At times, it is because our trust has been violated in some way or another. Allowing the Spirit of God to take charge of your mind and sort out the tangles of deception that have been inflicted requires surrender to Him. When I find it difficult to trust in someone or something, I revert to the inner voice inside me—God's voice of truth. It almost always turns my bad story around to something positive. That voice of truth is where you receive trust.

When no one else seems to understand you, I suggest you draw closer to the One who understands you most, who loves you completely and perfectly— the One who created you. Confide in Him, releasing every situation of fear that creeps in to dwell in your place. Surrender any fear you hold onto and any fearful situation you may face with the ultimate trust that God will move and come to the rescue. God wants us to put all our trust in Him in all circumstances.

Begin with praying, surrendering all fear to Him through that communication. Be still in His presence and ask Him to show you how to get through your circumstance. Then go to His Word. He will equip you to get through your situation victoriously. I can combat my doubts and fears that rise out of nowhere because I have the voice of truth residing inside of me. God allows me to identify where those fears are coming from—the lies that try to encompass my thoughts are from the enemy of my soul. It is a daily battle to cast down fears and listen for the voice of truth.

Tomorrow is busy worrying about itself; do not get tangled up in that web of worry. Trust God one day at a time, one step at a time. Instead of trying to fight your fears, concentrate on completely surrendering your specific fear to God alone. When you relate to God in trust, there is no limit to how much He can strengthen you. By trusting God alone, you will find it will allow His channel of peace to flow through you. His greatest work happens when we can have a surrendered, trusting heart. This is not something that happens on its own; we must seek it with purpose. Believe in what you are doing by surrendering your fear to God, giving it 100% to the One who can conquer all fear. Believe with all your heart and mind and without doubts, and God will produce a paradigm shift that will completely alter your life.

• •

Wendy Arelis

Wendy Arelis lives in Kelowna, British Columbia, Canada. She worked as a registered nurse on the maternity ward and intensive care nursery for forty-two years. Her story about overcoming challenges like childhood abuse, cancer, and divorce is told in her book, *The Other Side Of Fear. My Journey Into Perfect Love* (pen name W. Veronica Lisare).

Wendy was one of the authors in the Women World Leaders book, *Embrace The Journey: Your Path To Spiritual Growth.* In her chapter, she describes her cancer experience and how God spared her life.

Wendy has traveled extensively on mission trips. She loves meeting new people. Attending the YWAM and Bethel schools were highlights in her life. She is passionate about leading believers into their freedom using the Sozo ministry tools. Wendy has also served as an elder, prayer team and home group leader in her church.

Wendy is blessed with two daughters, six grandkids, and three great-grandchildren. She was married for twenty-seven years. She loves sharing her personal testimonies of God's amazing goodness throughout her life.

Acceptance Granted

By Wendy Arelis

Desperately seeking acceptance and approval from others has been an unquenchable force throughout my life. Like dry, parched land, I longed to be watered by words of affirmation to quench my thirsty soul. And yet, never satisfied, this addiction always begged for more. Compliments lifted me only momentarily, sliding off me like melting butter on a hot skillet. I didn't believe them. My heart ached to hear that I was beautiful, intelligent, loved, and accepted, replacing the lies that I wasn't good enough. Little did I know that my true value and identity would be made known to me from an unexpected source.

Anger, criticisms, volatile arguments, and physical punishment flooded my childhood home. Although my parents argued with each other often, their hostility seemed to be directed at me most of the time. Doing my best in school subjects was never enough to reach their invisible standard. As a result, report card days were especially full of tension. The enemy of my soul whispered many lies to me, and my experiences told me they must be true. I often thought, "There is something wrong with me," and "I am stupid, fat, unwanted, and ugly," as feelings of loneliness, powerlessness, and despair silently crept into my heart. "I will just have to try to hide from my parents as much as possible," I reasoned, "then I can move away and live a peaceful life." My life goals were short-sighted.

I enrolled in nursing school because they offered free accommodation and training. But, a new kind of fear met me there with the challenges of caring for vulnerable adults. The lies I believed continued to haunt me. "You are not capable." Being very shy, I went through the motions and did what I was told, feeling much like a robot. Early into my second year, I was surprised to learn that the school was closing. Uncertain about pursuing this career, I decided that getting married would solve my problems. I just wanted someone to take care of me as I felt incapable on my own. It seemed I was hopping from one piece of ground to another, looking for a safe place to dwell. But it turns out that my "ground" was not solid nor safe. It was like pieces of ice melting beneath me. A very lonely life greeted me as I entered into marriage. Unlike my childhood home, the new atmosphere was very silent. My husband barely spoke to me. Rejection in a different form reared its ugly head again. This began a twenty-seven-year journey of searching for answers about how I could change into a loveable person.

My husband and I had a baby daughter, which added to my insecurities. The reality was that I felt unequipped to be a mother. And my daughter seemed to cry endlessly with her colic pain. "Failed again," I believed. Still striving and despite my fear of failing, I applied for a local nursing program two years later, reasoning, "My daughter will be much better off with good, kind women at her daycare."

After a year in my second round of nursing school, I was shocked to learn that I had earned the scholastic achievement award. Not for a moment did I accept the possibility that I might be capable of earning this prestigious recognition! Instead, I believed that it was just luck and that I was good at memorizing facts. Upon completing my second year, I was honoured again with two awards for highest marks and general proficiency. And still, I didn't believe that I was intelligent. Meanwhile, not a word of praise came from my husband's lips as I looked to him to tell me if I deserved to celebrate my accomplishments. And so, I continued to believe that I had fooled them all and would need to keep up the charade in my career.

For the next four decades, I worked in my nursing profession riddled with constant fear and feelings of inadequacy. Although the nursing school had blessed me with awards for book knowledge, the training and experience I received were sadly lacking. I was hired to work on the maternity ward, which seemed like a cruel joke as I believed I had seriously failed in the mother-baby department. Asking for help and explaining my lack of skills to other nurses was only met with remarks such as, "Oh, you just have the new grad jitters!" My anxiety went through the roof each time the elevator doors opened to bring a labouring woman into my care. Before this position, I had only watched one birth and had a baby myself. That was it! Suddenly, I had up to seven labouring women to manage.

After a year, I transferred to the newborn baby nursery. I assumed this department would be much easier, but it came with its own challenges. Years later, I learned that I hadn't valued my gift of compassion for people nor recognized that knowledge and skill grow with years of practice. Still, teaching new mothers what I hadn't known as a mother became my passion as my confidence grew with experience. Additionally, I found myself watching a couple of nurses who seemed so full of joy and peace, no matter what was happening. Oh, how I longed to find out their secret.

One day, after moving into a new neighbourhood, a lady from across the street invited me to a Bible study. I was intrigued and found the information fascinating. I had never learned about Jesus or thought about God, even though I cried out to Him when I was in trouble. Then one weekend, I gave my life to Jesus at a "Life in The Spirit Seminar," still not understanding what He paid for by dying on the cross for me. However, I did see those two nurses there, leading me to sign up for this group so I could receive that peace and joy. That was forty-seven years ago, and what a journey it has been!

One of the most important things I learned on my journey is that I am saved by God's grace alone.

Ephesians 2:8-9 (NIV) says, *For it is by grace you have been saved, through faith-and this is not from yourselves, it is the gift of God-not by works, so no one can boast.* I would have loved to have known and understood that verse right from the start. Instead, I spent many long years trying to be a good Christian in my own strength. I didn't understand the scripture, *My grace is all you need. My power works best in weakness.* (2 Corinthians 12:9a NLT) I believed that I could read the Word of God and fulfill my needs by doing what it said using just my willpower.

Failing to be obedient consistently led me to frustration and more condemnation. I eventually learned I needed the Holy Spirit to fill me. He would be my Guide and Helper. Surrendering to Him and welcoming Him to be in control would be the key to my obedience. As I grew to know my Heavenly Father and His unconditional love for me better, my trust in Him also grew.

Galatians 5:22-23 (NIV) says, *But the fruit of the Spirit is love, joy, peace, patience, kindness, goodness, faithfulness, gentleness and self-control. Against such things there is no law.* I began understanding the necessity of being filled with His presence and living a surrendered life. I longed for a relationship with God. Knowing relationships don't become intimate quickly, I spent much of my spare time reading, praying, worshipping, and listening to messages about God. I knew my mind and thinking needed to align with the Word of God.

Another important thing I learned is that our God is a loving Father, not a harsh taskmaster.

I finally renounced the lie set in my heart by my earthly dad's example of fatherhood. I began seeing myself not only as God's servant but as His beloved daughter. Inserting the word "daughters" where it says "sons" gave me a more personalized meaning to the scripture Galatians 3:26 (NKJV), which says, *For you are all sons [daughters] of God through faith in Christ Jesus,* and Galatians 4:7 (NKJV), *Therefore you are no longer a slave but a son [daughter], and if a son [daughter], then an heir of God through Christ.*

Out of that unconditional loving relationship, I now serve my Heavenly Father, knowing my true identity is not dependent on my performance. I never have to earn it. This revelation is almost too wonderful for words. Our culture teaches us that we are rewarded for doing well and drives us to perform and compete with others. But that isn't the Kingdom of God. Religious legalism tells us that we need to do well to succeed and avoid punishment. But, on the cross, Jesus took the punishment we deserve for our sins. This revelation of my redemption took me thirty-eight years to fully comprehend. Along the way, God gave me the perseverance to continue to seek Him and understand what He requires of me. I am so very grateful that He planted me in a wonderful church during those years. Speakers from places all over the world came to bring us anointed messages. Worship was glorious as we sang songs like "I Surrender All," even though I didn't realize the impact of the words. God doesn't want us to do it all and lose our peace. He is not like my earthly father in that way. God is loving and kind. I needed to release my control and allow God to take over, fully led and dependent on the Holy Spirit, the source of my strength.

As I served in many areas of my church, I was temporarily satisfied by my delight in being needed. But adding these duties to my already full life of working stressful twelve-hour shifts and being a wife and mother to two health-challenged daughters took a toll on me. Eventually, I burned out and got sick with cancer. I didn't know much about being led by Holy Spirit or depending on Him or that motives for service based on the desire to be accepted don't produce good lasting fruit. But one day, God would receive the glory as He changed my motives from wanting praise for myself to desiring to bless Him because I loved Him.

The third thing I learned is that, as a Christian, the most important words I can listen to come from God.

The harsh, critical words spoken angrily by my parents and the silence of my husband were unhealthy ways to define myself. Depending on others' feedback stole my power to be who God called me to be. People-pleasing led to an endless pit of disappointment and despair. Self-analyzing became a habitual form of self-judgment. And I found that even as I read the Word of God, I beat myself up for not reaching the standard of perfection I wrongly thought God required.

Although the enemy worked to deceive me, the Holy Spirit took over and taught me truth. Scriptures like Matthew 5:48 (NKJV), which says, *Therefore, you shall be perfect just as your Father in heaven is perfect,* once caused me to feel hopeless, believing that it was all up to me to earn God's love and favour. But the Holy Spirit led me to read and understand other translations. He taught me through study that the meaning of the English word "perfect" originally meant "mature, complete, and set apart," not "without sin." This makes sense because Jesus is the only one without sin, so He was the only one who could pay for our sins by dying on the cross.

God's Word taught me that I am set free from the penalty or punishment of my sins because Jesus paid for them all in full. 2 Corinthians 5:21 (NIV) says, *God made him who had no sin to be sin for us, so that in him we might become the righteousness of God.* What a Saviour and Redeemer! As we accept His sacrifice, He forgives us and sets us free from striving and performing for love and acceptance. Philippians 1:6 (NKJV) says, *being confident of this very thing, that He who has begun a good work in you will complete it until the day of Jesus Christ.*

Further, God is committed to using my life circumstances to mold me into His likeness and image. Isaiah 64:8 (NIV) says, Yet you, *Lord, are our Father. We are the clay, You are the potter; we are all the work of Your hand.* He uses the trials and challenges we face to develop the fruit of the Spirit in us.

And God's Word taught me to rejoice in Him, enabling me to stand against the enemy. *Do not sorrow, for the joy of the Lord is your strength.* (Nehemiah 8:10 NKJV) My joy now comes from knowing that I am God's unconditionally loved daughter. When He looks at me, He doesn't see my sin but Jesus' robe of righteousness. My sin, which once separated me from knowing the Lord as a Good Papa, is no more.

It has been a long road, but recognizing God's unconditional love and acceptance has allowed me to forgive my earthly dad and my husband for hurting me. Although my marriage ended, God had a new life of faith for me. And this ground was solid. My dependence on God grew as He healed my broken heart, provided all I needed, and continually coached me through my fears. Shortly after my divorce, I bought a new Bible and asked Holy Spirit to give me a new life verse. I opened to Jeremiah 29:11 (NKJV) *For I know the thoughts that I think toward you, says the Lord, thoughts of peace and not of evil, to give you a future and a hope.* He is SO good. Yielding to Him daily is a conscious choice I make as I welcome Jesus to take His place on the throne of my heart. Only God can meet my need for love.

My heavenly Father has set me free, and spiritual growth has become my passion, opening the door to His peace. Romans 8:1 (NKJV) says, *There is therefore now no condemnation to those who are in Christ Jesus, who do not walk according to the flesh, but according to the Spirit.* I don't stand before God alone, but I am in Christ Jesus, clothed with His righteousness without condemnation. What freedom!

Every day, I feed on the truths of God by reading, praying, and declaring His Word. This practice renews my mind and grows my faith in Him. Scriptures come tumbling from my lips as I pray for others. Having laid the foundation of God's promises, we then stand on them and call for them to be fulfilled in our lives. The Holy Spirit has opened many doors for me to be in leadership and teaching positions where I can share all He has shown me. Feeling like I have found a priceless gold mine, I can hardly wait to tell others. He has blessed me with an inner healing prayer ministry where I lead believers in forgiveness, renouncing lies, and declaring truths. It thrills me to give others the same keys to freedom I have received.

Having surrendered my need to gain affirmations from others, I know I have my Heavenly Father's approval as He fills me to overflowing with His love and purpose for my life. I no longer feel like I am hopping from one piece of ground to another because Christ is my solid rock. My true identity and value are clear to me.

God promises He will never leave us or forsake us, no matter what. We can be assured of His unconditional love and commitment to meet our every need as we fully surrender to Him. I often think of the iced tea commercial on TV that shows a person falling backward into a swimming pool. I imagine myself falling back into His loving arms. Trusting Him with full surrender takes faith as we learn that His ways are much better than our ways, even when it feels like we are walking through a dark passageway. Ask Holy Spirit what lies you are believing about Father God, renounce them, and ask to understand the truth. Declare the realities that He shows you, even if you haven't seen them yet. Forgiving others who have failed to meet your needs is key. Only Father God is perfect. And His perfect love is more than enough to give you all you need. He is waiting to grant you the acceptance and love you have longed for.

I leave you with a prayer captured in the verse Romans 15:13 (NKJV) *Now may the God of hope fill you with all joy and peace in believing, that you may abound in hope by the power of the Holy Spirit.*

Surrender Your Work

By Julie T. Jenkins

What is one of the first things you ask someone you've just met? I'm betting what they do for work ranks up near the top.

The question, "What do you do?" has long been an awkward one for me. Right out of college, I began climbing the ladder to an illustrious career in television production. But upon getting married and having our first child, my husband and I heard God's distinct call for me to quit my job and stay home with our children. At that point, my answer to that ever-present question changed from an animated conversation describing what it is like working with national sponsors and professional sports team franchises to a short sentence: "Nothing, I stay at home with our kids."

My husband was always quick to jump in and vindicate me, saying, "She works harder than anyone I know."

Over twenty years later, I can now look back and recognize that the day-to-day tasks I did in those "hidden" years of my life were some of the most essential responsibilities God has ever trusted me with. But wearing a spit-up-covered t-shirt and having remnants of finger paint and glitter under my nails never felt glamorous.

When we surrender our career to God and trust His wisdom and guidance, we can be assured that the work He puts in front of us will be Kingdom work. God has a perfect plan for each of us, with outcomes and rewards that are far beyond what we could ever imagine.

Esther was taken into the King's palace. She was groomed and adorned and became Queen. She had no choice but to surrender to her role, but in doing so, she discovered that God had a plan to use her in that position to save the

Surrendered: Yielded With Purpose

Jewish people. Her Uncle Mordecai spoke these wise words to her, *"And who knows but that you have come to your royal position for such a time as this?"* (Esther 4:14 NIV)

Following God's call for our lives positions us to accomplish great things. Though we may not be able to see what God is doing, when we obediently surrender to His plan, we can be assured that He will use each step along our path for His purposes. God cares so much for His children that He has opportunities all planned out for each of us to contribute to His ongoing work in this world.

> For we are God's handiwork, created in Christ Jesus to do good works, which God prepared in advance for us to do. (Ephesians 2:10 NIV)

Wherever God has led you, your job is to work with excellence and joy, trusting His provision and guidance, because we can know for certain God will always lead us into the holy and sacred.

> Whatever you do, work at it with all your heart, as working for the Lord, not for human masters. (Colossians 3:23 NIV)

> You should mind your own business and work with your hands, just as we told you, so that your daily life may win the respect of outsiders and so that you will not be dependent on anybody. (1 Thessalonians 4:11-12 NIV)

Though we are to surrender our careers to God's call and work in excellence and joy while trusting His meaningful outcome for our lives, we must remember that it is not our work that makes us worthy. You are worthy because God created you in His image and you are His child. God tells you that you are *precious and honored* in His sight (Isaiah 43:4 NIV), that *the very hairs of your head are all numbered* (Luke 12:7 NIV), and He takes *great delight in you.* (Zephaniah 3:17 NIV)

God loves you just the way you are! It is simply an added bonus that we get to work for Him and that He allows our accomplishments to have eternal significance.

God gives us the opportunity to surrender our work to Him, and He promises us that when we do, He will guide us to Kingdom productivity. *"Remain in me, as I also remain in you. No branch can bear fruit by itself; it must remain in the vine. Neither can you bear fruit unless you remain in me. I am the vine; you are the branches. If you remain in me and I in you, you will bear much fruit; apart from me you can do nothing."* (John 15:4-5 NIV)

I pray that you keep this teaching close to your heart as you rise to start a new day tomorrow. Work in excellence and joy as you surrender to God – that is one of His beautiful gifts to you.

. . . .

Mendez Vaughn

Mendez Vaughn loves the Lord and serving His people. She is energized by sharing His love and emotional healing with women and teenage girls.

Since becoming born again in 2003, Mendez has served the Lord in multiple ways, including participating in mission trips to Romania, Honduras, and Ecuador. She volunteers with and has held leadership positions with Kairos Inside Prison Ministries, Walk to Emmaus and Chrysalis Ministries, and SOULWELL ministries. Additionally, Mendez has served on the board of her local Crisis Pregnancy Center for the past 12 years.

Mendez has a Bachelor's in Occupational Therapy and has served special needs children in school systems for 25 years.

She enjoys spending time with friends, traveling, and spoiling her 4 dogs.

Mendez is a strong believer in prayer and in the power of God. She loves participating in Bible studies, especially one she has attended on Wednesdays since her new birth in 2003.

Mendez has always felt called to write, and this chapter is her first attempt!

Freedom From Emotional Prison

By Mendez Vaughn

Surrender, by definition, is giving up control to someone else. My problem with that is my flesh likes to be in charge. I am reluctant to let someone else decide what happens. So, for many years, I lived life my own way. I made decisions and acted based on what I thought was best. I was not willing to fully trust God. Could I truly release my grasp on my plans and believe that He had something better for me than I could give myself? I was unaware of the bondage this attitude caused; however, when I finally surrendered to God's purpose, He transformed me.

As Christians, we battle the daily choice of yielding to the flesh or the Spirit. God created us for a purpose and has special plans for our lives. He is good. God loves us. And He can be trusted. Are you finally ready to submit it all to Him so He can free you?

Have you ever felt trapped? Stuck? Discouraged? Disappointed? Heartbroken? Hurt? Ready to give up? We were not designed to live this way. God's original intention was for us to live free in perfect paradise in fellowship with Him. Sin changed all that, and our enemy has been trying to imprison us with his lies ever since. The good news is we can be set free!

The Bible tells us in Galatians 5:1, *It is for freedom that Christ has set us free. Stand firm, then, and do not let yourselves be burdened again by a yoke of slavery.* (NIV) And in John 8:36, we find that *if the Son sets you free, you will be free indeed.* (NIV) Then in Isaiah 61:1, we read that Jesus was sent *to proclaim freedom to the captives and release from darkness for the prisoners.* (NIV) So, if He came to set us free, why are we not living as if we are free?

My niece, an animal lover, found a wounded dove and wanted to help it. She put it in a cage to nurse it back to health. Her dove became very special to her. She wanted to keep it as a pet forever, but she knew the bird wasn't intended to stay in a cage. Since she loved her little dove, she knew she had to let it go when it got better. She tenderly nurtured it every day. Finally, the time came for the healed bird to be set free. As soon as she swung the cage door open, the dove hurriedly flew away. She was sad to see her beloved bird leave, but she was so happy it could fly. She thought she would never see her precious dove again, but surprisingly, it returned to the cage every single day!

We sometimes do exactly what that little dove did. Although God has sacrificed His only Son to provide freedom for us, we allow ourselves to be placed in bondage to darkness again. When we get wounded, we can grow accustomed to an environment we weren't designed to be in just because we have become so used to it. We can stop this cycle by surrendering to God and yielding to His purpose for our lives.

For years I lived in what I refer to as an "emotional prison." By that, I mean I had an inward feeling of being trapped inside a cold, dark, lonely cell, with broken emotions like isolation, fear, loneliness, sadness, and pain constantly looming in my thoughts and feelings. I told God if He would get me out of this imprisonment, He could use me to help rescue others from their emotional prisons. How did I get into this horrible place? My struggles first began in childhood.

My mother wrestled with depression and would stay in bed for long periods of time. My job was to keep other people from finding out about her struggles; therefore, when someone would call or stop by, I would tell them she was taking a nap or a bath. I was sad to see her staying in bed, but I could not show that sadness, so I learned to pretend everything was fine, which was extremely difficult. I put aside my own needs, and the people around me never saw my inner turmoil and pain. No one knew what I was going through; therefore, no one was able to help me. I longed for someone to read my mind so they could make it all better. I got so good at hiding how I felt that I eventually became numb to my true feelings. No one ever saw my sadness. I always pretended to be happy. Meanwhile, the enemy told me lies that I believed—the biggest ones were that no one liked me and I had no friends. These lies only added to my feelings of loneliness, sadness, and isolation.

I was not yet aware that I had a soul consisting of my mind, will, and emotions and that God's Word gives specific instructions for handling these parts of ourselves. *Give all your worries and cares to God, for He cares about you.* (1 Peter 5:7 NLT) I also had no idea how my coping mechanism affected my intimacy with God and other people. It was putting me in bondage to isolation. I felt alone all the time. I thought I had to take care of myself. My heart ached to be free from this horrible imprisonment. I just needed to disappear. I longed to be somewhere else. I wanted to be someone else— anyone but me. I did not like my reality and longed to escape it.

Even when my parents went through their divorce, I did not talk to anyone about it. I was not equipped to deal with it on my own, but I continued pretending everything was fine by stuffing my real feelings inside. Even though I struggled with so much pain and fear, I refused to show emotions in front of people. I desperately needed help but did not know how to get it. I needed comfort but didn't know where to find it. I eventually turned to food, becoming an emotional eater. Stuffing myself full of food seemed to cover up the hurt and emptiness. When I was eating with other people, I would hide extra food in my pockets and then disappear into another room to continue eating so they could not see what I was doing. This led to a sudden weight gain of thirty pounds in less than two months. I could not fit into any of my clothes. Still, the biggest issue was not the food I forced inside myself. My more significant problem was the anger, pain, bitterness, fear, shame, resentment, unforgiveness, loneliness, and other negative emotions that I also packed down deep inside. If I had somehow let my feelings out, I might not have needed all the food. And no amount of food would be enough to help me cope with what happened next.

I had one sibling, a brother named Keith. Since he was just two years and three days younger than me, we were close. We played together all the time. Our house was in the middle of a cattle field with a wooden fence around our yard. Keith and I always climbed the fence into the pasture. We never used the gate. The open field and nearby wooded areas afforded us opportunities for all kinds of adventures. We loved riding our bikes, swinging on the tire swing, climbing trees, and swimming in the pond. Keith and I loved being outside. Being inside was too hard. Mama was always inside, lying in bed. Mama and Daddy constantly fought, but we never talked about how that made us feel. Sometimes Keith and I would cry and hug when they were fighting at night. I think this was the beginning of my struggle with anxiety. Thankfully I had my brother, who loved me unconditionally. Everyone liked Keith, and he showed love to everybody. He was always smiling and happy. He did not stuff toxic emotions inside himself like I did. Or did he? I will never know the answer to that question because Keith took his own life.

I will never forget how I felt when I heard the news that he had committed suicide. I was completely devastated. Any joy I had was gone. Any feelings inside me that were not already numb were now completely dead. I wanted to die, too. I was angry. I couldn't eat or sleep, yet I was still unable to talk about how I felt inside. I needed something to turn to that would help ease the pain.

It was then that I discovered smoking cigarettes. I loved smoking—it worked for me. The deep breathing helped relax my mind, which was always racing in circles. Holding the cigarette somehow felt comforting to me. When no one else was there for me, I knew smoking was. I still could not see the walls I had built around myself that were keeping other people away. I believed lies from the enemy telling me my struggles were too hard for others to understand. I grew lonelier and more isolated. I was constantly battling feelings of anxiety and depression.

Four months after my brother's death, God sent an incredible Christian man into my life. His name was Chad. He had black hair and bluish-green eyes and would listen to me talk about missing my brother. Chad encouraged me to open up to him about how I was feeling. I had never done that before. It turns out he hadn't opened up to people about how he felt inside either, and he began to open up to me as I opened up to him. Our friendship and intimacy grew until we fell in love and got married. My relationship with Chad was very extraordinary because I knew I could talk to him about anything. Thankfully my walls were coming down. My husband had become a safe place for me to open up about past wounds that needed healing. However, I didn't realize that new ones were coming.

Marriage isn't easy, and couples don't always agree. On our second anniversary, an acquaintance of Chad's stopped by our house as we were leaving for dinner. My husband continued talking to him instead of taking me out to eat to celebrate. We never went to dinner, leaving me hurt and angry. I gave Chad the silent treatment. This event led me to return to stuffing my feelings inside again. The man I adored, idolized, and thought was perfect had let me down. I closed myself off to him emotionally so he couldn't hurt me anymore. He closed himself off to me, too. It seemed easier for us to deal with life on our own.

I began once again to handle my life situations in unhealthy and unholy ways. I felt trapped in an emotional prison again. How could this be happening to me? Where did my freedom go? Why didn't Chad care about what I needed? Feelings that are not dealt with steal our joy. They rob us of peace and eat away at our very souls. Holding on to past hurts can be deadly to our minds and relationships. I needed to learn a way to cope with pain that didn't involve stuffing it all inside, which only led to bigger problems.

Chad was no stranger to trauma and difficulty himself. He was only eleven years old when his dad was killed in a car accident. And then he became paralyzed from the waist down in a fall from a bridge the month before he turned seventeen. Even though he had encouraged me to open up about how I felt, Chad did not like talking about his own emotions regarding the pain he had endured. He thought it would not do any good because it would not change anything.

But despite going through so many hardships of his own, no matter what I did, Chad was always able to forgive me and show me unconditional love. I did not understand this at all. What I understood was blaming my problems on whoever I thought was responsible for how I felt. Love and forgiveness to me were conditional and needed to be earned.

Chad liked to work toward reconciliation which was foreign to me. But still, I knew he was right, and I wanted what he had. Chad had Jesus. The way he loved and forgave me led me to my salvation. Although I had grown up attending church and had even been baptized, I had not been truly born again. Finally, I accepted Jesus as my Lord and Savior, and my life was transformed. I was a new creature, and it felt good. I enjoyed my early days as a Christian, but I continued to struggle with completely opening up with others.

Seventeen years after our anniversary fiasco, Chad got sick with a horrible infection and was hospitalized for a long time—almost a full year. He required a hospital bed when he returned home. In total, his sickness lasted for four years. Although he was tough and fought hard, Chad continued to grow weaker. His illness was unbearable to watch, and I reverted to those same old coping skills I had turned to whenever something extremely challenging occurred in my life. Unfortunately, Chad reverted to his silence as well. We could not look at each other and discuss his life coming to an end and how we felt about it.

I was holding Chad's hand when he took his last breath.

I did not want him to leave me—we had been together for 24 years. What was I supposed to do now? I could not handle the devastatingly painful emotions on my own. Up to this point in my life, I had coped with my feelings by stuffing them inside. But this method would no longer be effective in dealing with how I felt about losing my husband.

Thankfully God is a good Father and always has a plan for us even when we cannot see it ourselves. He led me to the SOULWELL Ministries Journey in Texas, where I began the process of learning to live an emotionally healthy life. There I was taught how to give my emotional bondage and baggage to God. SOULWELL teaches emotional healing by inviting Jesus into our emotions and seeing His loving presence in our painful memories. Jesus had always been there with me and for me. God was waiting for me to surrender my feelings to Him. He did not want me to live isolated and imprisoned by negative emotions. At SOULWELL, I became aware that either I can own and control my emotions, or they will own and control me. Ephesians 4:26 in the New Living Translation states, *Don't sin by letting anger control you. Don't let the sun go down while you are still angry.* I was completely unaware that I had given the devil a huge foothold in my life. Instead, I thought someone else was responsible for how I felt. So caught up in blaming the people who had hurt me, I could not own my part in building and maintaining my emotional prison.

God used the SOULWELL Journey to equip me with tools to overcome my emotional immaturity. I first had to become aware of it, and then I had to give it to God. When we have become accustomed to responding a certain way our entire lives, we do not even notice our reactions that have become programmed within us. I became aware of being emotionally withdrawn and that God desired me to live differently. I began to long for freedom. God had unlocked the prison door I had been hiding behind, and it was time for me to walk out of it. I surrendered to His plan of living emotionally free and healthy. SOULWELL taught me to welcome the painful experiences from the past and hand them over to God. Now when adversity comes my way, I can deal with it in a manner that reflects my Christ-like character.

For the first time in my life, I am finally comfortable with being me! I have learned to like who God created me to be.

I am God's beloved child, and so are you. You can live in freedom, too! You can learn to like who you are and who He created you to be. God desires to teach you how to take the first step. He is longing for daily fellowship with you. It all begins with surrendering yourself to His will and His plan. God designed our lives to be lived one day at a time. Our responsibility is to learn to yield our souls to Him daily and trust His plan is for our ultimate good.

God is longing to heal your wounded heart. He is waiting to free you from your emotional prison. Freedom is possible. You no longer have to live in bondage to the enemy's lies.

Begin by spending time in God's Word. *Then you will know the truth, and the truth will set you free.* (John 8:32 NIV)

Never forget that God is listening to the cries of your heart. He is waiting to take you on the journey to living emotionally free. Right now is the time to take the first step. Enjoy your freedom!

Surrender Your Past

By Kimberly Ann Hobbs

> *"Forget the former things; do not dwell on the past. See, I am doing a new thing! Now it springs up; do you not perceive it? I am making a way in the wilderness and streams in the wasteland."* (Isaiah 43:18-19 NIV)

When you accept Christ as your Lord and Savior, you are a new creation. God's love for you never ends. Your past does not matter. Whether you were a liar, a prostitute, an addict, a thief, or filled with unforgiveness and disobedience to God and His Word, God says He will forgive you and remember your sins no more.

Letting go of the past can be difficult for many. Holding on to guilt and shame because of past mistakes made by you or someone close to you could rob you of your beautiful present life and the fantastic future God wants for you. The enemy comes to kill, steal, and destroy and wants nothing more than to throw all your past mistakes in your face. An unreleased painful past can put you into a vice that slowly squeezes the life out of you. God does not want that, but the enemy of your soul does. He wants every extremity and internal organ to die. That way, you will no longer be a threat to him. Surrendering your past to God serves a purpose—it allows Him to freely use you as the masterpiece He created you to be. God will use you to bring glory to Himself and bring others to His Kingdom.

Walk faithfully with the Lord and put the past behind you in full surrender to God. As you do, keep in mind that God is at work in your life even when you do not see it, feel it, or think it. With Christ's power, put on a new mindset, and don't look back. Allow the inner peace you desperately desire begin to flow. Trust in the Lord with all your heart. Understand that mistakes may still happen, but we can use them as an opportunity for growth. This idea may be difficult and challenging for some, but God will help you make stronger and wiser choices as you ask Him for help each day.

When you wake up each morning, look at that day as a new start. You are alive and a child of the King. Work heavily on putting your past behind you and look to God from the moment your eyes open, not allowing anything to hinder your relationship with the Lord as you enter the new day. Your attitude must be one of looking to God to guide you, strengthen you, and equip you as you walk in the newness of life He has for you. If you feel yourself slipping, remind yourself of your full surrender. You are NOT to look back; you've already given your past to God. Instead, look ahead and read scripture to strengthen you. Ask the Holy Spirit within you to refresh your thoughts.

Instead, let the Spirit renew your thoughts and attitudes. Put on your new nature, created to be like God—truly righteous and holy. (Ephesians 4:23-24 NLT)

You must understand that God can work even through the bad situations in your life, bringing good out of it all. It may seem unimaginable when you begin this process of release to God, but the good yet to come is a promise from His Word. God wants your thoughts, actions, and words from the past that still haunt you. He wants all of it surrendered to Him so that He can be God and work them out for His glory and your good.

And we know that God causes everything to work together for the good of those who love God and are called according to his purpose for them. (Romans 8:28 NLT)

Your past does not define you; God says who you are in Christ.

> This means that anyone who belongs to Christ has become a new person. The old life is gone; a new life has begun! (2 Corinthians 5:17 NLT)

Allow God to take away the heavy laboring you grapple with from your past as you surrender it to Him. He wants to give you rest by teaching and strengthening you to let go, forgive, and forget it all. Then move on, focusing on the present moment with Him. God has a plan for your life; trust Him with it.

. . . .

Michelle Hiatt

Michelle Hiatt is a wife of 18 years, a homeschooling mama of five, and an entrepreneur in Orlando, Florida. Through her conversations on The *Surrender Driven Success* podcast and in one-on-one coaching, she loves bringing a Biblical perspective to everyday life while helping other women find more purpose and peace as they balance business and nurture their families with God at the center.

She truly believes that 'THE most important work you will ever do is within the walls of your home.' Michelle helps other busy mamas expand their vision by connecting the work of their hands with their influence at home so they can leave a lasting legacy through the next generation.

Michelle is passionate about encouraging others to pursue their greatest potential as an excellent wife, an intentional mother, and in kingdom business by FIRST pursuing the presence of Jesus!

Sunsets are her favorite and date nights or walks with her husband are the highlight of the week. However, she finds no greater joy than soaking up time with her incredible family and watching her children grow.

Surrender Driven Success

By Michelle Hiatt

Do you have big dreams in your heart but are stuck living small? Perhaps you are working hard to do all the "right" things but struggling to find peace and purpose in the midst.

Do you feel called for MORE? Do you ask yourself, "HOW? Where do I start? How can I possibly honor the Lord and pursue my God-given potential while balancing ALL—The—Things?"

I know how overwhelming it can feel! As you read the next few pages, I want to encourage you to be aware of your dreams and open your heart to discover what GOD'S DREAMS ARE FOR YOU. There is a deep peace and a greater purpose to be found ON THE OTHER side of SURRENDER as you balance your family and work with Christ at the center.

I'll never forget the look on my male Bible teacher's face when I showed up for 8th grade career day with my best friend, both of us dressed up as pregnant ladies. We had balls under our bellies and Starbucks coffee cups in our hands as we proudly declared that our big dream was to be wives and moms when we grew up. Of course, in our minds, this looked like taking walks with our friends with a fancy coffee in hand.

Boy, did I have a lot of LIFE to learn?! Haha

Since I was a little girl, my deepest desire was always to be a wife and mom. It was the dream I held in my heart, and I knew the greatest gift. However, I was also full of ambition and goal-oriented by nature. I was the straight-A overachiever, captain of the team, president of the class, and winner of every trophy type of teenager. I felt called to DO big things, although I had no idea what that would look like once I graduated.

From when I was young, the message subtly implanting itself in my heart and mind was that my worth was found in my accomplishments. My childhood paved the way for my workaholic tendency to thrive as I proudly wore the word "busy" as a badge of honor. My heart and intentions were SO pure that I was blinded to the reality that self-sufficiency and striving were becoming a way of life.

My dreams came true at a young age when I married my incredible husband just after I turned 19 years old. Several years later, I had my first child and began experiencing all of the ups and downs that adult life and motherhood had to offer. I truly believe that "the most important work you will ever do is within the walls of your home," yet I also felt the tension of being labeled "just a mom." I found comfort in staying super productive at home. Being a wife and a mom was everything to me and has always been my priority, yet something in me yearned to do MORE. I knew deep down there was more potential to be found.

After nine years of marriage and three kids under my feet, the suppressed desire to do more "outside of motherhood" became a NEED to do more as our financial situation took a turn. Although finances were tight, our home life was settled, and I felt ready! I knew that I could bless my family and work from home to help bring in some income, but what would I do, and what would be the right fit?

Through much prayer, Holy Spirit inspiration, and the support of my husband, I began my entrepreneurship journey. I was determined to not only maintain health and wholeness in marriage and motherhood but also thrive in business.

As I pursued my goals in business, I dove into the inevitable self-development required for growth. I pushed out of my comfort zone to become a stronger and more resilient version of myself as I managed my home and worked with excellence. Although my heart was to partner with God in my endeavors, I began feeding the subtle lie that I must work for my worthiness and that my value increased the more I accomplished. My ambitious, goal-oriented nature rose, and a heart posture of "hustle" and control drove my efforts. I invited Jesus into the passenger seat of my business rather than trusting Him to take the wheel as Lord over all.

I was working and DOING "good" to honor God, bless my family, and serve others the best I knew how, but throughout 2020, the true motives of my heart were revealed and came crashing down.

We all know what happened this pivotal year when COVID hit, and everyone's world was rocked. When circumstances change, it challenges us to respond. For many, this was a time when life slowed down. However, in my world, life sped up faster than ever. I resolved to see the good in everything and chose to seize opportunities while I put my head down and got to work! I was going to make what many felt like was a setback into my BEST year as I showed up for high achievement. My goal was to create more income for our family while serving others well and shining God's light during a dark and challenging time. I would have to dig deeper into self-development and see what "I" was made of.

I flowed with grace during this intense season, and God truly held me through the fast-paced progress. My marriage was strong. In fact, we had never been on more dates or vacations than in the year 2020. My home was ·

in order. The kids were continuing with homeschooling, and their minds and hearts were healthy and nurtured. From that foundation, I gave myself permission to work every waking minute!

By the end of the year, I found myself managing my home, marriage, friendships, homeschool, motherhood, and activities while working THREE businesses from home!

Although on the outside, everything was thriving, "I" was suffering. One word sums up the path that I was on—burnout. But God, in His goodness, began preparing my heart to adjust my sails, find a better balance, and reorient with a sustainable pace. Clarity came as I took each new baby step toward God's slow-down strategy

I crossed the finish line of 2020 running on fumes, and after the first week of the new year, I was finally positioned to set all business aside, take a month off, and unplug! This was going to be a well-deserved allotment of "me time." I was desperate to rest and embrace self-care after the business beating I had taken the year before. Yes, this was MY time to get renewed!

As I lay in bed one Sunday morning, ready to begin my self-prescribed "staycation," exhausted beyond measure, I felt the Lord distinctly invite me to join my husband on a 21-day fast. He whispered in my ear, "This is MY time, and I love you more than you know. I want to consecrate you and do a NEW thing."

I gave God my yes of obedience, which became the first sacrificial act that would begin a journey of shifting me from self-absorbed to surrendered. My soul would find rest, and my life would find new purpose as I laid it down for His glory!

In January 2021, I was completely spent from the previous year of responsibilities, and on top of that, I wasn't eating because I was on a spiritual fast. I was literally on empty. As I lay in bed feeling weak, helpless, and desperate for a fresh touch from God, my only prayer was, "God, I have nothing to give, but I'm making room for you. So, come and do whatever you want to do. Do what only you CAN do in my heart. I invite you to change me...but it has to be YOU."

This heart posture of dependency was a sacred place because I was beginning to experience true surrender. Pages of journaling marked this time of stillness and wrestling as the Lord began speaking to me about learning to rest in Him for true restoration. He revealed that even with servant-hearted intentions, I had unknowingly become self-focused. He wanted me to learn to be strong in the Lord and in the strength of HIS might. He shifted my heart from striving and awakened a fresh SURRENDER. More than anything, God gave me a deep hunger to intimately know Him and hear His voice—not know about Him, not be satisfied with what I had already learned or what others had told me throughout my Christian life. I yearned to make Him my primary pursuit—my first love once again.

Coming off the fast, I sought to get my bearings and begin getting back to "normal," only to find that there was no more getting back to the way things were. I wasn't the same and wasn't supposed to fall back into my previous life rhythms. Instead, I needed to embrace the humbling process of learning to live from a heart posture of surrender, as foreign as it felt. So, I entered a place of unwavering obedience, deep trust, eternal perspective, and embracing the fullness of the gospel—a life laid down.

Through the refining, God reminded me of His desire for us to KNOW Him and pursue Him as the ultimate goal, the most important treasure to be found.

Seek the Kingdom of God above all else, and live righteously, and he will give you everything you need. (Matthew 6:33 NLT)

Seeking God first is the starting point of the abundant life of a believer. The message is not "set your goals and pursue your dreams and add Jesus to the process so you'll be happy and blessed." Rather, being a follower of Christ is about prioritizing His presence, and from THAT place, all blessings can flow and all dreams can follow. Seeking God first is a posture of the heart—and it looks like surrender.

Throughout 2021, the Lord redefined what success meant to me and stirred up a hunger for Him, rooted in humility, unlike I had ever known. Pursuing my greatest potential as an excellent wife, as an intentional mother, and as a kingdom entrepreneur meant pursuing the person of Jesus! My Martha-minded self was learning to become like Mary. To SLOW down, to sit at Jesus' feet, to look at Him and listen, and to be satisfied with only Him.

All the "worthy" and "necessary" things I was doing FOR God were simply distractions from His ultimate. God's perspective matters more than our good intentions, and not all good things are God's best for our lives. From His point of view, ONE THING is necessary and, like Mary in Luke 10:42, we are to choose the good portion by choosing Jesus above all.

Oh, if we can learn to continually posture our hearts on our knees at the feet of Jesus and truly lay down our dreams and desires in exchange for KNOWING Him. If we can grasp the love of God and find fulfillment in WHOSE we are, not in what we do. From that place of kingdom identity, every action we take will be bathed in peace and purpose because His presence will precede productivity.

Through the pressing and pressure in my heart over the past few years, God has taught me to choose the hard but holy work of surrender. It's not in our human nature to lay aside our plans, but He is worthy of our trust. Yielding to Christ transforms us to look more like Him, which is the goal! This life is not about getting what we want, but it's about giving God what He wants—a bride that looks like Him.

Surrendered: Yielded With Purpose

There is joy to be found on the other side of surrender because Intimately knowing Jesus is the greatest reward. There is purpose in every trial and tear—when you give it to God. You cannot rush the process or strive for His presence; you YIELD to Him. Fixing your attention on Jesus as the "One Thing" and submitting yourself to letting Him rule and reign in your life is where you must start with every desire and dream you ponder in your heart.

But that's only the beginning! Learning to abide and let God's love continually *nourish our hearts* (John 15:9 TPT) is where we want to remain. After understanding the importance of truly seeking God first and experiencing the sweetness of His presence, my next step of desire was wanting to stay, to abide—to DWELL.

> The one thing I ask of the LORD— the thing I seek most— is to live in the house of the LORD all the days of my life, delighting in the LORD's perfections and meditating in his Temple. (Psalm 27:4 NLT)

My prayer became, "Lord, I don't want to come and go from your presence. I want you to find a habitation where you can dwell in me...where there's continual peace because the Prince of Peace is ruling in my heart as I balance family and work." Everything I do and become must be fueled from a heart of surrender, or there's no purpose in it.

God desires us to bear much fruit from a place of abiding. *But if you remain in me and my words remain in you, you may ask for anything you want, and it will be granted! When you produce much fruit, you are my true disciples. This brings great glory to my Father.* (John 15:7-8 NLT)

This is the 'surrender strategy' that allows us to remain in His love while making progress toward our goals for His great glory. I am learning and growing in this every day. However, I am determined to surrender and

RE-surrender relentlessly, trusting that fruitfulness will flow out of my faithfulness. More than anything, I will transform to look more like Jesus in the process.

Additionally, my heart awakened to another beautiful truth in this uncomfortable "slow down" season! I wasn't on earth to write my own story, but rather I was here to fulfill my part in HIS STORY. I received a fresh revelation that God actually has dreams for me!

What is His ultimate dream for my life?
What are His goals for me?
What is His desire?

On my entrepreneurship journey, I had been so focused on MY 'good' goals that I failed to realize God Himself has dreams for my life! It's so easy to ask God to partner with our plans without ever realizing that everything we desire and do should first align with HIS dreams. As a follower of Christ, this life is not our own, and we must continually remember that what we do is not about us. It's all for His glory, and we must cling to this eternal perspective and conviction in our hearts!

In John 17, immediately before Jesus gives Himself over to be crucified as the greatest act of surrender of all time, He prays to God for His disciples. But do you know what He does next? He prays for YOU and ME! In His prayer, He reveals His dreams for us.

Jesus prays,

> *"I ask not only for these disciples, but also for all those who will one day believe in me through their message.*
>
> *I pray for them all to be joined together as one even as you and I, Father, are joined together as one. I pray for them to become one with us so that the world will recognize that you sent me.*

For the very glory you have given to me I have given them so that they will be joined together as one and experience the same unity that we enjoy. You live fully in me and now I live fully in them so that they will experience perfect unity, and the world will be convinced that you have sent me, for they will see that you love each one of them with the same passionate love that you have for me." (John 17:20-23 TPT)

At the brink of His death on the cross, in the most vulnerable moment, Jesus reveals through this passage that the greatest desire of His heart before leaving earth is that we will be ONE with the Father. His dream is that we can enjoy a deep relationship with God, just as He experienced. As believers, He wants us to embrace and enjoy His powerful love that it might flow through us and pierce the hearts of others because we walk in perfect unity with Him. This brings glory to God here on this earth!

Friend, I don't know what season you are in or all that you are carrying. Maybe you're juggling marriage, motherhood, managing a home, building a business, navigating challenging relationships, serving in ministry, or any combination of these and more! I know you deeply desire to leave a lasting legacy through the work of your hands. However, life feels overwhelming far too often, and it can be challenging to know where to start and how to honor God successfully in the midst of balancing so much.

I want to remind you that you are called and chosen, designed with purpose. Yet the call of the gospel is not about you accomplishing great things FOR God through your well-intended efforts. The invitation is to experience oneness WITH God as you follow Him, *"disown your life completely, embrace my 'cross' as your own, and surrender to my ways."* (Luke 9:23 TPT)

Your desires and dreams matter, but what matters most is that your heart prioritizes God's dreams because, as Jesus says, *"my glory is revealed through their surrendered lives."* (John 17:10 TPT)

The world is shaking, and there are more uncertainties about the future than ever. However, your soul can find peace in His presence regardless of the circumstances. Your heart posture of surrender will cultivate sweet unity with your heavenly Father while fueling a life of purpose and eternal impact in your work and in your family. Most importantly, you have the opportunity to reflect the image of Jesus on this earth and shine brightly for SUCH A TIME AS THIS.

As you set your goals, establish your intentions, and faithfully move forward, keep in mind that God's ultimate dream is that you would walk in oneness with Him. This is success! Seek God first, abide in His love, and choose to surrender daily, trusting that God's dreams for you are better than you could ever imagine!

May this be the prayer of your heart:

Thank you, Lord, that your glory is revealed through my surrendered life. In other words, you reveal your glory in and through my life as you and I are one. May perfect unity be the dream of my heart because it is your dream and design.

I've already received all of you but may my heart grasp the fullness of the gift I received in you through salvation. May I abide in your love and let your love nourish my heart as I seek you first in all I do. May I enjoy your presence and find rest for my soul in letting you rule and reign in my life.

Lord, give me the grace to get out of my own way and to surrender my goals, my dreams, my passions – all of me – in exchange for more of you. May I seek you as the 'one thing,' and may oneness with you be my primary pursuit as I work faithfully at home and in business.

Thank you for the simplicity of the gospel and the peace of your presence. Thank you for the joy of knowing you. Thank you for the purpose you have on my life and the fire that burns in my heart for more. May I impact the world and leave a lasting legacy from a heart and a home that's in order and a life surrendered to your ways, yielded with purpose.

Surrender Your Viewpoint

By Julie T. Jenkins

We all hold deep convictions that are often well-supported by sound reasoning. For example, many of us have strong feelings about politics, including gun rights or the treatment of immigrants. We may stand on a civil rights platform or have definitive opinions on how children should be raised or money spent. Personal experiences shape our beliefs. We learn from what we have seen, how we were raised, and even our faith community's interpretation of the Bible.

One thing is certain, although we all walk on this same planet, we each have a unique viewpoint on the world around us. Is it our responsibility, or even our place, to urge others to see everything as we do, or should we surrender our viewpoints to God?

The apostle Paul addressed this topic in his letter to the Romans, written to *all in Rome who are loved by God and called to be his holy people.* (Romans 1:7 NIV) Although all in the Roman church were undoubtedly loved and chosen by God, they did not necessarily love and choose each other. Many had different backgrounds and, as such, different viewpoints on how "religion" should work. Does this sound familiar?

Paul offers two points in chapter 14 that we would do well to take notice of today.

First, as Christians, our primary calling is to follow the Lord. Being a Christian is about relationships. And our number one relationship is to be a personal one between us and God.

> *One person considers one day more sacred than another; another considers every day alike. Each of them should be fully convinced in their own mind. Whoever regards one day as special does so to the Lord. Whoever eats meat does so to the Lord, for they give thanks to God; and whoever abstains does so to the Lord and gives thanks to God. For none of us lives for ourselves alone, and none of us dies for ourselves alone. If we live, we live for the Lord; and if we die, we die for the Lord. So, whether we live or die, we belong to the Lord. For this very reason, Christ died and returned to life so that he might be the Lord of both the dead and the living.* (Romans 14:5-9 NIV)

You, Christian, belong to the Lord. Your responsibility is to make sure that what you do is okay with the Lord. Pray to Him. Read the Bible for yourself. Ask God for His wisdom. And then act decisively and intently, giving the Lord alone all the thanks and praise.

Second, as Christians, we are called to be in relationships with each other. And to do that, we must recognize that we all have different viewpoints—we were created differently and have had unique experiences.

> *Accept the one whose faith is weak, without quarreling over disputable matters. One person's faith allows them to eat anything, but another, whose faith is weak, eats only vegetables. The one who eats everything must not treat with contempt the one who does not, and the one who does not eat everything must not judge the one who does, for God has accepted them. Who are you to judge someone else's servant? To their own master, servants stand or fall. And they will stand, for the Lord is able to make them stand.* (Romans 14:1-4 NIV)

Christians in the Roman church were experiencing conflict because they held different viewpoints on what kind of food was spiritually acceptable. Paul taught that the relationships Christians have with God and with each other are far more important than the policies followed.

> *Let us therefore make every effort to do what leads to peace and to mutual edification. Do not destroy the work of God for the sake of food.* (Romans 14:19-20 NIV)

> *So whatever you believe about these things keep between yourself and God. Blessed is the one who does not condemn himself by what he approves.* (Romans 14:22 NIV)

To follow Paul's teaching to the Romans, we must first focus on our relationship with the Lord and, second, nurture our relationships with others. By surrendering our viewpoints to God, we can trust that He will guide us when and if to have a conversation about our viewpoint—which can be powerful if done in God's time at His command. But following our own agenda and pushing our perspective on someone can harm the very relationships God has blessed us with.

St. Augustine said it well: "In essentials, unity; in nonessentials, liberty; in all things, charity."

And in the words of Elsa, "Let it go!"

Surrender your viewpoint. God is more than capable of leading and guiding those He has chosen.

> *How good and pleasant it is when God's people live together in unity!* (Psalm 133:1 NIV)

Donna Stinson

Donna Stinson is a born-again believer and follower of Jesus. She is a mother, grandmother of nine, and has been married to her better half, Ron, for nineteen years and counting. Donna works as an office manager for a gifted physical therapist and is an office assistant for a talented chiropractor in her small town of Sequim, Washington.

Donna has a huge heart to help anybody in need and has a strong gift of administration. She and her husband serve at their church as greeters and volunteer as co-leaders of their local Community Emergency Response Team. Additionally, she has volunteered with numerous other organizations, including Law Enforcement Chaplaincy of Sacramento, Big Brothers Big Sisters, two different pregnancy centers, a local community theatre, and many other places.

She loves coffee, singing, sushi, camping, gardening, playing games, and spending quality time with her husband, their fur babies—Wookie and Smokey—and her extended family.

Out of the Pit

By Donna Stinson

It took me 33 long, painful years to surrender a lifetime of fear and heartache and find deliverance through Jesus. I am forever grateful that He loves me and forgave me for my many sins. This Scripture defines me, and I proclaim it as my own: *He lifted me out of the slimy pit, out of the mud and mire; he set my feet on a rock and gave me a firm place to stand.* (Psalm 40:2 NIV) There is hope even when there seems to be none.

I was born in Florida in the 60s and, for the first years of my life, grew up with a mom, dad, younger sister, and brother. We attended church three times a week and prayed before every meal and at bedtime, but I didn't see Jesus lived out at home. As I grew older, there was a lot of tension in our house; I often felt like I was walking on eggshells. I wore my feelings on my sleeve and wanted people to love me, so I became a people pleaser.

My dad worked long hours as a lineman to support us. He smoked unfiltered Pall Mall cigarettes and, together with his brother, started a nursery and built a brick home for our family. He loved getting his back scratched by my sister and me, and we loved being on the receiving end of his back scratches. He was often serious, always busy, and usually just had to give that "look" to make me straighten up quickly to avoid getting yelled at or spanked. I never wanted to disappoint him and didn't like seeing him angry.

Mom stayed home with us the first few years as Dad didn't want her working an outside job. She later briefly worked as a waitress and then eventually sold Avon. She kept the house, sewed, made our meals, and was always busy. I remember wanting to be close to her yet feeling like I couldn't quite connect with her. She often seemed sad to me. I don't remember much laughter or fun times in our home. One Sunday, Mom didn't come to Sunday school with us, and my stomach was in knots the entire time. Afterward, I begged Dad to take us home early to check on her. He listened, and that decision probably saved her life as she had taken an overdose of pills and was passed out on the bed when we arrived.

One particular summer, my mom got into the habit of dropping us off at a park or the movies, leaving me in charge of my siblings. While many children might enjoy such freedom, this always frightened me. My school had shown films about kidnappings and how to react to "stranger danger." At the park, I remember holding my sister and brother's hands, staying close to bushes, and searching the nearby homes to determine which seemed safe for us to run to if necessary. At the movie theater, my anxiety subsided a little once we were seated and the movie began. But if one of my siblings needed to go the bathroom, we all went together. My lurking fear always made it difficult to relax and enjoy the show.

When I was 9, my world turned upside down when my parents divorced, and Mom moved 3,000 miles away. I missed her terribly and was so very sad. I went through my days feeling lost and alone. My stomach hurt frequently, and I could not articulate the feelings that often overwhelmed me. I prayed to God often to bring my mom back home because her absence left such a deep hole in my heart.

Instead, my parents each took other spouses. Dad remarried a woman with five children. She was a quiet, reserved Christian woman who read her Bible every morning and took to raising her new family of 10 admirably. With so many more brothers and sisters, I was distracted and kept busy with chores, homework, and playing games.

Mom also remarried. We met her new husband when they visited us one summer and took us to Disney World. Mom brought my sister and me two-piece bathing suits, which neither of us liked. I was an awkward and shy 12-year-old and was very embarrassed showing so much skin. Mom seemed much happier and laughed a lot more. The following year they took us to visit Mom's side of the family and then on to California for the summer. We kids spent a lot of time alone during the day while the adults worked. On the weekends, we helped with chores and sometimes went to the lake swimming, boating, and skiing with friends. The adults drank alcohol, laughed a lot, and sometimes argued loudly.

Mom would go to bed at the same time each night, and I would frequently stay up and watch whatever her husband was watching on TV until bedtime. One night, my mom's husband pulled my head down onto his lap while we were on the couch and began touching my chest. I was too terrified to move, ashamed, and very embarrassed by my intense feelings. He bent down and kissed me, putting his tongue in my mouth, and I began to cry. I distinctly remember the smell and taste of beer. That was the night that man, a father figure, robbed me of my innocence and took advantage of my naiveté and desire to be loved. He began visiting me in my bed that night and most nights thereafter, with my brother and sister asleep in the same room. I was only 13.

The summer ended, and we kids returned home. I was too embarrassed and scared to tell anyone what had happened. We were raised in a home where many subjects were taboo, including feelings and body parts. When my older step-sister began her period, our parents took her into their bedroom to show her a book and talk about it. Later, she told me, and, as we giggled, we were overheard and got in trouble. Another time, somebody brought up Germany, and I jokingly said, "I've been to Germany," having been conceived there out of wedlock. Dad got so angry with me, causing me to feel deep shame. Through many other situations like this, I learned to keep things inside.

My life began to spiral out of control as I grew. I was no longer innocent and felt smothered at home. I was angry and couldn't tell anybody why. Concerned, Dad eventually took me to a doctor who said, "Don't worry, she's 14. She'll grow out of it." In retrospect, I was severely depressed, but nobody talked about that back then. At least not in my family. My mother would often call or write, telling us how much she missed us and about all the fun things she was doing. Her husband would sometimes call me and tell me how much he loved and missed me and that he hoped to marry me one day. I was so confused and began spending as much time in my room as I could get away with, reading many books or writing poems where I poured out my pain. Many of which were about wanting to die. I felt such confusion, guilt, shame, and sadness. Even with a houseful of people around me, I was all alone. And I still missed my mom terribly. One day I told my dad that I wanted to go live with her. It broke his heart, but he reluctantly allowed it.

The next four years were tumultuous. I lived with my mom and her husband for about a year, and the abuse continued. I responded by rebelling and hanging out with the wrong crowd, smoking pot and cigarettes, cutting classes, and breaking rules. To make sure my mom's husband didn't take my virginity, since he had done everything else, I slept with an older boy who was quite willing to be my first. I thought we were in love, but he was just using me. When the folks found out about it, Mom put me on birth control, and her husband was angry and acted hurt. Soon after, he raped me and continued his almost nightly visits to my bedroom. Out of control by then, I was sent back to live with my dad. I remember feeling that all hope was lost and I would be better off dead.

Mom eventually left my abuser and moved to Montana to be closer to her biological father. I reasoned that now, with her husband out of the way, maybe Mom and I could have the close relationship I'd always wanted. I got up the nerve to ask once more if I could live with her, and she said yes. I was afraid to ask my dad but finally did, and, as expected, he was angry and hurt, but he allowed me to go.

I was now in the last half of 8th grade. I eventually worked up the nerve to tell Mom what had happened between me and her husband. She wanted specifics I wouldn't give, so she slapped me across the face and called me a liar. I again acted out, smoked pot, and slept with two more boys. Six months later, my mom and her husband reconciled, and we headed back to California. On that trip, I got drunk in a bar and Mom let me ride in a big rig when a trucker asked. Let's just say it wasn't a free ride. By then, I was primarily wearing my mom's hand-me-downs, so my wardrobe usually consisted of short shorts, tight jeans, halter tops, and other revealing clothing.

I felt as though I barely survived the next few years. I was still being sexually abused, had run away once, took an overdose of pills, and acted out sexually all the time. I somehow managed to graduate from high school at the age of 17. I took a job at a pizza restaurant and fell for a man three years older than me. I eventually worked up the nerve to tell him what was happening at home, and he immediately wanted me out of that environment. Because he supported me that way, I felt he was my knight in shining armor, and I fell head over heels in love with him. I ended up getting pregnant, and we married a few months later. I thought everything would be all better and I could finally be happy. But I overlooked my husband's baggage, not to mention my own.

I didn't know my husband was a drug addict and had unresolved issues from childhood. My self-esteem was low, and every decision I made was rooted in fear. I only wanted to be loved and have a happy marriage and family. My husband and I frequently argued because he didn't provide consistently for our family or do the chores while I worked. I was super responsible and worked full-time, sometimes multiple jobs, to support our family. I tried to be both mother and father to our two children. I wanted them to have a better life than I had, and I did everything possible to make that happen.

I went to counseling for over a decade to overcome my past trauma and learn how to have a healthy marriage. I kept pushing myself to attain a better life by doing such things as taking various courses to advance in jobs and attempting college. I focused on trying harder, never giving up, and never getting divorced - because I felt that my parents' divorce had led to my downward spiral so many years earlier, and I could not let my children go through that kind of pain.

One night, after years of struggling in my marriage, feeling unloved, and being overwhelmed with depression, I took an overdose of pills. As a result, I had my stomach pumped and stayed in a treatment facility for a few days. But even after that, my husband continued his practice of staying up for several days at a time and sometimes leaving and hanging out with friends all night. Then he would stay home sick for days, sleeping on the couch and yelling at us if we changed the TV channel to something we wanted to watch. I knew something wasn't right with him, but he kept telling me it was me. And I began to believe him. It was a crazy life; the kids and I often felt like we were walking on eggshells.

Our life together was going downhill quickly. One night, my husband finally admitted that he was using methamphetamines along with alcohol. I cried and offered to help in every way possible, including getting him into counseling. He said he would try to stop. But instead, he continued. And out of frustration, one day, I stupidly asked him if I could try some. I felt so much guilt and tried to keep my new coping mechanism hidden from my children. I wanted them to feel safe and know everything was okay. I always told myself I could stop and eventually did; however, I lost so much before that. My marriage was all but over, and I couldn't stand my husband anymore.

Then I got a new job and met a co-worker who began telling me about Jesus. When I saw her coming, I often went the other way because I didn't want to hear what she had to say. Sometimes, I would intently listen to her as she talked. I always watched her, though, waiting to see her slip up and say or do something inappropriate. But she never did.

I began feeling a tug on my heart. So, when my new co-worker invited the kids and me to church, we began to attend sporadically. Then, one day, she invited me to a women's retreat. During that weekend, I told her if I could know the Jesus she talked about, I wanted to. I had never met anybody who lived and breathed Jesus as she did, and I desperately needed a Savior. Still, the idea of letting go of everything, relying on this unseen Jesus, and living by faith was foreign to me. I didn't trust anybody and didn't think I ever could.

In May 1995, I surrendered everything and found Jesus. My co-worker became my best friend and began mentoring me. With her guidance and the help of the Holy Spirit, I began praying for my husband and even forgave him, though he continued to use drugs. The beginning years of my walk with the Lord were incredibly sweet as I began to learn I could trust Him. He answered my prayers and taught me to love my husband once again. I became a new person, learned Scriptures, sang praises to God, and a few years later, was baptized in the Holy Spirit and began speaking in tongues. The very first verse I memorized was Proverbs 3:5-6: *Trust in the Lord with all thine heart; and lean not unto thine own understanding. In all thy ways acknowledge him, and he shall direct thy paths.* (KJV)

My mom eventually divorced her husband. And I ultimately forgave her for not knowing the abuse was taking place and for putting me in threatening situations. I came to realize she, too, carries a lot of baggage and has many scars. We have both worked hard on our relationship, and I love her deeply.

Then, Jesus did what seemed impossible. He helped me to forgive my abuser.

Though I still carry the what-ifs, wondering if he abused others and wishing I'd been healthier to prosecute him before the statute of limitations was up, I have forgiven him. I have not sought him out and have no desire to do so. During the early years of my healing process, the Lord once put us in the same building together. The man who threw my life into such turmoil now opened the door for me as I entered the building. From the look on his face, he didn't recognize me, but my breath was taken away as I shakily sat down in the lobby and watched him leave. In that huge parking lot, his car was parked right next to mine. I marvel at how God orchestrates situations in our lives while continuing to emphasize healing and reminding us that we can trust Him.

After almost 22 years of marriage, my husband left me. That literally almost broke me, but I hung onto Jesus with everything I had. By then, I had enough spiritual battles under my belt to know what it meant to walk by faith, so I leaned in and trusted God to bring me out the other side. Psalm 126:5 truthfully says, *Those who sow with tears will reap with songs of joy.* (NIV)

I pray that anybody who struggles with feeling like they're all alone, that nobody loves them, that there is no hope, or that they are too far gone will surrender all that they are and discover all that He is. It seems so hard at the time, but it really is quite simple.

While we were still sinners, Jesus died on a cross for your sins and mine - because He loves us. His death was painful, but He willingly took on the pain to save us from eternal pain and loneliness. Then, He rose from the grave after three days and will return one day as promised, ready to take you and me home. If you let Him, Jesus will lift you out of your pit, just as He did for me. I pray that you will surrender to Him. Give Jesus your burdens, your scars, and your trials. He is strong enough to take them all away from you and replace them with joy and peace that only His presence can bring.

Surrender Your Bad Habits

By Julie T. Jenkins

The definition of a habit is "a settled tendency or usual manner of behavior; an acquired mode of behavior that has become nearly or completely involuntary."[1]

In other words, a habit is an action that likely began with intentionality and, over time, has become something we do without thinking. Habits, at their core, can allow us to operate on a higher level. Picture a child who is learning how to brush her teeth and bathe herself—those actions take much thought and intentionality. As adults, we move through those actions without thinking, giving our brains a break.

But just as a habit can be positive, we can also develop habits that are detrimental to who we are and who we are becoming. Therefore, we should take time to evaluate and consider our habits regularly. Only by recognizing the bad habits that have infiltrated our lives can we surrender them, giving room for intentional growth.

Romans 12:2 reminds us that we have a choice when it comes to our actions. *Do not conform to the pattern of this world, but be transformed by the renewing of your mind. Then you will be able to test and approve what God's will is—his good, pleasing and perfect will.* (NIV)

Bad habits can be glaringly detrimental to our health and well-being, such as smoking or mindlessly drinking alcohol, or they can be seemingly harmless patterns that, over time, rob us of the joyful life God has prepared for us.

Consider the habit of wasting time. This inclination is prevalent in society today as we carry smartphones connecting us to an endless stream of social

---

1   https://www.merriam-webster.com/dictionary/habit.

media and mind-numbing games. What started out as a convenience and even a diversion now often devours the time God has given us to grow and learn and connect with others.

Consider the habit of arriving late or canceling at the last minute. Our lives have become so jam-packed that we operate without margin, making it easy for us to excuse our own tardiness. But the habit of being late is disrespectful to others and declares, without words, "You aren't important to me."

Consider the habit of living a slothful lifestyle. We were given one body to carry us through this lifetime. When we get in the habit of not exercising or taking care of ourselves physically, our body grows weak and tired, keeping us from being able to do all that God has prepared for us.

And consider the habit of thinking poorly of ourselves. Small thoughts such as "I'm not good enough," or "I'm not smart enough," or "I'm too ugly" eat their way into our souls and cause corrosion that is difficult to repair.

The devil delights in using the mundane to entrap us. As Romans 12:2 tells us, our responsibility is to renew our minds and seek God's will regularly. We are to take stock of those things we do by rote, asking God if our actions are pleasing to Him. And then we are to put a stop to those actions that have morphed into bad habits that dishonor God.

When we don't renew our minds regularly, our bad habits can begin to control us and take us out of God's will. But when we take inventory and surrender to God the bad habits that have snuck into our lives, He will remove the power they have over us.

In the Bible, we don't read about any bad habits that Jesus had. Well, He is God—so He did lead a perfect life! But we DO read again and again about one habit that Jesus intentionally cultivated.

But Jesus often withdrew to lonely places and prayed. (Luke 5:16 NIV)

> *After he had dismissed them, he went up on a mountainside by himself to pray. Later that night, he was there alone.* (Matthew 14:23 NIV)

> *Very early in the morning, while it was still dark, Jesus got up, left the house and went off to a solitary place, where he prayed.* (Mark 1:35 NIV)

Perhaps Jesus didn't develop any bad habits as a human because He intentionally developed the *good* habit of going to God the Father in prayer. Now that's a habit we should get on board with! Why not begin now?

Dear Most Holy God,

We come to you today surrendering the bad habits that have become ingrained in us and are taking us away from all you have called us to be. Father, it is amazing that you have given us each a purpose, yet it takes the continual renewing of our minds in your presence to walk in that purpose. We recognize that the devil wants to pull us away from all you have intended for us. So, God, we come to you today asking for your protection and guidance as we surrender the bad habits we have allowed to grow in our lives. And we ask that you help us make prayer and fellowship with you our habit of choice. In Jesus' name, I pray. Amen.

. . . .

Nayilis Hernandez

Nayilis Hernandez was born and raised in Havana, Cuba. She grew up loved and cherished by her grandparents Mima and Pipo. She has now lived in Palm Beach County, Florida, for over 20 years with her dear husband and three daughters.

Nayilis loves spending her hours walking by the seashore, praying, and spending time with her family.

She also truly loves cooking Cuban food while worshiping—that is her Mojo! Praying has become the seasoning in her life. It is always her priority and the means by which she surrenders every single area of her life.

Nayi prays that you, her reader, will experience God's blessing to overflow!

Surrendering In Faith

By Nayilis Hernandez

We all battle different emotions every day, including loneliness, sadness, and fear. Fear affects us all at one time or another. And while it does have its place to protect us from danger, the enemy uses this emotion as one of his most potent means of persuasion to get us to stop, avoid, run, or even succumb to his strategies. The devil wants fear to be so tangible that the mere existence of any challenge does not just warn us of the threat but promises the certainty of it. But once we learn to put our trust in God and go forward by faith into the unknown, we will no longer be afraid of the things that come against us.

> I sought the LORD, and he answered me; he delivered me from all my fears. Those who look to him are radiant; their faces are never covered with shame. (Psalm 34:4-5 NIV)

In May 2019, I started a fierce battle with a sickness that destroyed my world and life as I knew it and changed my view of God forever. I had been walking through life with a desolate outlook on my circumstances and a mind saturated with discouragement. But, as I share my story with you today, God has taken my hand, and I now walk by faith with Him. In the middle of my battle, however, I was so sick and scared and, if I am honest, the loneliest I have ever been. I thought I was going to die, so I wrote letters to my husband and my kids.

> Be strong and of good courage, fear not, nor be afraid of them, for the LORD your God, He is the One who goes with you; He will never leave you nor forsake you. (Deuteronomy 31:6 NKJV)

I was scared for my husband and the uncertainty of him having to raise kids on his own. This is a little portion of what I wrote to him before I went on a seventeen-day trip to Cuba to find answers from different doctors:

"I feel like something bad is going to happen to me. I am so scared. I don't want to go anywhere, but rest assured, my love, as I write this letter, I want to believe that I will be fine. Even though the last few weeks have been the scariest days of my life, I have come to the realization that there is nothing I can do about what is making me feel this sick. The one thing I ask God is to help me control, resist, and fight these symptoms and the fear that this sickness has created in me. I promise you that I will not go down without putting up a big fight."

God, in His Word, tells us clearly that we do not need to be weighed down. *"Come to me, all you who are weary and burdened, and I will give you rest. Take my yoke upon you and learn from me, for I am gentle and humble in heart, and you will find rest for your souls. For my yoke is easy and my burden is light."* (Matthew 11:28-30 NIV)

I came back from my trip with more questions than answers. As the sickness progressed, I continued to go from doctor to doctor without answers or relief. I felt anxiety, and the desire to find a doctor who could tell me why this was happening to my body became an obsession. I had five to seven appointments every week, went to all kinds of specialists, and got poked and prodded, only to hear, "Everything is normal." "Your test is negative." "Your blood work is perfect." "Your heart is healthy." "Your MRI looks good." "The scans show nothing."

Sometimes, I thought, *This is good, right? If every test comes back normal, I am fine.* Yet I was getting worse by the day.

That is when the fear got real, and God began to transform my life from independence to being totally dependent on Him. As I learned to let God in, I realized I had always known about God but never truly knew who God was. I began to pray and ask God to help me on a daily basis. I couldn't walk straight, so I got a cane. I couldn't stand without getting dizzy, so I sat and listened to worship music for hours on end. My head hurt so much that I was hospitalized three times in two weeks and went home as sick as I went into the hospital. I lost 50 pounds in eight months because anything I ate would either raise my blood pressure or lower my blood sugar. I had panic attacks as I slept, and my husband would hold me until my body stopped shaking. All the while, every test showed that I was fine, but I was not.

I was so scared for my girls—I didn't want them to have to grow up without their mom as I had; and truly, I tell you, I had always seen myself growing old like my grandparents, having a house in the country full of grandkids, a dog, and some chickens. But I was losing all those dreams, and the reality that I was soon going to be with Jesus occurred to me suddenly and very unexpectedly. So, I wrote to my girls in fear that I would not be able to finish raising them:

"My first born, my star child, and my baby.

I just want you to know how much I love you and how deeply I care about you. I need you to be more than okay. When you were born, I fell in love in so many ways. I could have never guessed the love my heart could feel on those three miraculous days and every day thereafter. I was over the moon. Everything about you girls was so perfect—from your perfectly manicured hands and toes to your red lips, small bodies, and beautiful eyes. I knew that I would love you for the rest of my life. Three times my whole life transformed before my eyes, and I was so happy. There was a knowing inside me that my life was never going to be the same, and it has not been; you are a true, honest, harmless, pure love for me. I never thought of harming you or not loving you for a second. I strived to be a better mom than mine, but I know I failed many times. Let me tell you that I gave you the best of me and would do it all over again in a heartbeat. I am praying that God allows me to still my mind as it races and I lose my trend of thoughts. (Lord, help me surrender as I need to write the truth of my concerns and feelings to my girls before I die.)"

I was feeling pressed and depressed. Even as I tried to identify the causes, I surrendered my thoughts and asked God to reveal His causes to me. God did this for me, He helped me to know what I was fighting against, and I took it to Him in prayer.

> *The LORD is close to the brokenhearted and saves those who are crushed in spirit. The righteous person may have many troubles, but the LORD delivers him from them all.* (Psalm 34:18-19 NIV)

It has been four years since the day I first felt sick, but it feels like it was yesterday as I share my heart with you. I tell you the truth— my day-to-day life is now fearless. God has done a work in me that brings me peace and puts a smile on my face. Today I know *I can do all things [which He has called me to do] through Him who strengthens me [to fulfill his purpose-I am self-sufficient in Christ's sufficiency; I am ready for anything and equal to anything through Him who infuses me with inner strength and confident peace.]* (Philippians 4:13 AMP) This is one of the verses I knew but had to learn to live out.

These last four years, I was encouraged to get to know God in a deep and personal way, and as I asked Him to heal my mind, body, soul, and spirit, He gradually did just that. And I came to the conclusion that prayer and surrender to God are the keys to everything. For all things are possible with God.

Before my sickness, I knew about God, but I never really knew who God was until He was all I had to hold on to. I had to get almost to the point of death, so I could truly die to self and let God in and allow Him to change me. I am closer to God today than anyone I know; I am fully in love with who He is.

As a young woman, my thoughts of God were, *He is the rule enforcer. He is a Father you can only go to with good news, or you will be punished, or worse yet, He will not talk to you for weeks because you messed up.*

But please allow me to share with you how I see God today: He is a loving Father who is only a call away. He is a Father who wants to prosper me and not harm me, the One who gives me a future and hope. (Jeremiah 29:11)

Here are some scriptures that have helped me overcome my fear, sadness, and loneliness and allowed healing to take place.

This is what the Lord says—the Lord who made the earth, who formed and established it, whose name is the Lord. Ask me and I will tell you remarkable secrets you do not know about things to come. (Jeremiah 33:2-3 NLT)

He said, "If you will listen carefully to the voice of the Lord your God and do what is right in his sight, obeying his commands and keeping his decrees, then I will not make you suffer any of the diseases I sent on the Egyptians; for I am the Lord who heals you." (Exodus 15:26 NLT)

He is the Lord who healed me, and I am so grateful I get another chance in this life. So dear friends, I am not saying that I have it all figured out, but I, like Paul, can tell you that God keeps working in me, giving me the desire and the power to do what pleases him. Also, as Paul says in Philippians 3:12-13, *I don't mean to say that I have already achieved these things or that I have already reached perfection. But I press on to possess that perfection for which Christ Jesus first possessed me. No, dear brothers and sisters, I have not achieved it, but I focus on this one thing: forgetting the past.* (NLT)

I had to press on through my sickness and the fear, desperation, and anxiety that came with my illness and near-death battle. I experienced loneliness, depression, and feelings of worthlessness because some of my closest friends disappeared when I needed them most as my health worsened. I felt pure fright as I saw myself unable to do simple daily tasks like taking a shower on my own, walking without help, preparing a meal, or even washing my hair without screaming in pain. I had to face the disbelief that, from one day to the next, I became so sick that I could no longer drive my kids to school. My inability to make sentences that made sense made me cry all the time.

But looking forward to what lay ahead, I pressed on to reach the end of the race and receive the heavenly prize for which God, through Christ Jesus, was calling me. I can now take comfort in knowing I do not suffer alone anymore. Since I surrendered all to God and have my sights set on Him alone, I am able to draw all my strength from Him.

> But he said to me, "My grace is sufficient for you, for my power is made perfect in weakness." Therefore, I will boast all the more gladly about my weaknesses, so that Christ's power may rest on me. That is why, for Christ's sake, I delight in weakness, in insults, in hardships, in persecutions, in difficulties. For when I am weak, then I am strong. (2 Corinthians 12:9-11 NIV)

So now, I hold onto the progress I have made in the past four years. I can take care of myself—praise God! I drive my youngest daughter to school most days, no longer have excruciating pain, and can walk without assistance. And I can put a few sentences together—even writing these few paragraphs is a complete miracle.

I now have like-minded friends who I can call for prayer, and some of the friends that had distanced themselves are coming around. I know that I am not alone because God will never leave me nor forsake me. I trust God for every minute of my life; after all, He knows me by name, and I know him as my Father. He loves me more than I love my children—and I must confess, I LOVE MY KIDS more than words can express! In my distress, I found my God to be more merciful, kind, and close than even my best friends. He is my help in my time of need, my shelter from sickness and disease, the One I can fully trust, and my companion in the months of loneliness.

As I yielded my will, emotions, and craving for acceptance to God, I also surrendered my life to Him again, this time forever. I know that God would do a better job than me at helping my husband raise our three daughters. He protects and cares for my girls more than I ever could. God revealed that the Holy Spirit, whom Jesus had spoken about, was sent as my helper and comforter. The Spirit of Truth, that same Spirit that raised Jesus from the dead, now lives in me and is why I am alive today.

God works in mysterious ways; He delights in everything He does and wants to be glorified for all He does. In my natural state, I was feisty and always had a fight in me. But this time, it was different. My body responded by freezing, and I was unable to fight. But my God, in His unlimited power and strength, allowed me to let go of my own abilities and become dependent on His power and grace. God alone became my safe place, my refuge, my shelter from the storm. Holding onto my faith and walking daily with the Lord under His mighty hand makes my health improve daily. I don't want to let the unexpected creep in and distract me from God's ordained purpose in my life. My faith became stronger through difficult times, and I desire never to lose sight of God's Word or His promises. That is what keeps me in a state of surrender.

I have fully surrendered my kids, marriage, soul, spirit, and life to God. My husband and my girls never had to read these letters, but I have shared little glimpses with them as they deserve to know the truth about how I love them and how they will continue to be my joy and my delight. I thank God I was able to recognize that my family is a gift from Him, and I will let go and let God finish the work that He had already started in each of their lives as I pray and watch them grow into the freedom, love, joy, acceptance, healing, strength and peace that is in Christ Jesus! The blessing of the unconditional love of my family when I needed them the most, as well as the emotional and spiritual support and the acceptance, encouragement, and help they freely gave me, is proof of God's love for me.

Through this time, I have learned to be courageous because God has not given me a spirit of fear but of power, love, and a sound mind! (2 Timothy 1:7 in my own words) I pray I can encourage you to have the faith you need to accept God's plan for your life and know that His ways are better than yours, His timing is perfect, and He has ordained all of your days. I exhort you to put your faith in our Heavenly Father, and no matter the circumstances, to have perfect peace to overcome life's challenges.

Surrender your first step of faith to God, knowing He will carry you the rest of the way through all of life's cares, sicknesses, diseases, and times of loneliness and fear. *Faith shows the reality of what we hope for; it is the evidence of things we cannot see.* (Hebrews 11:1 NLT)

Surrender Your Parenting

By Julie T. Jenkins

I am the youngest of seven siblings, and my husband is the youngest of five. So, even before we had our own children, watching our nieces and nephews grow allowed us to witness many parenting styles. And as newlyweds, we had many discussions about what we imagined our parenting style would be. Now, after 22 years of raising children, I can say with hard-fought wisdom that each child deserves unique treatment. In other words, as we parent, we must surrender our own preconceptions and yield to God's unique design for each child.

The Bible has much to say about parenting in the general sense.

Ephesians 6:4 instructs parents to teach their children carefully and without anger. *Fathers, don't exasperate your children, but raise them up with loving discipline and counsel that brings the revelation of our Lord.* (TPT)

Deuteronomy 6:6-7 teaches the importance of raising the child under the banner of the Word of God. *These commandments that I give you today are to be on your hearts. Impress them on your children. Talk about them when you sit at home and when you walk along the road, when you lie down and when you get up.* (NIV)

And Proverbs 29:17 speaks of the outcome of parental discipline. *Discipline your children, and they will give you peace; they will bring you the delights you desire.* (NIV)

These are fundamental truths we can and should hold onto. But perhaps we can learn most effectively about parenting styles by recognizing and appreciating how our Father God parents us, His children. Thankfully, God doesn't have a cookie-cutter approach to parenting, but He meets each of us where we are.

One passage of scripture that speaks most clearly regarding God's individual care for each of us is Psalm 139 (NIV). When we examine these words, we recognize lessons that help us surrender a rigid parenting style and teach us to meet our children where they are.

Verse 1 reminds us that God has *searched me* and He *knows me.* God takes time with us individually. Some days, as a parent, I have to turn away from my work and simply be present with my children—listening as they process the joys and frustrations of the day. Other days, we ride quietly in the car because I recognize that, in that moment, my child needs to be alone with their thoughts.

You know when I sit and when I rise; you perceive my thoughts from afar. (v. 2) On those days when I don't want to get out of bed, my Father lovingly gives me rest, something to look forward to, or disciplines me with love—that is, He gives the appropriate response to what is going on in my head and heart. I, too, by paying attention to my child, can discern if he needs a day off, a boost, or a swift kick to get him moving.

You hem me in behind and before, and you lay your hand upon me. (v. 5) I am so grateful for God's protection and guidance in my life! Laying a hand, in this case, means protection, as the second clause modifies the first. But it is interesting to note that "laying a hand" can also be an act of discipline. The fact is that God knows when we need protection or discipline, or both. As a parent, it is my job to surrender my own emotions and ask God for His wisdom to respond in the best interest of my child. When we are in tune with the Holy Spirit, we quickly recognize that not only is each child unique in what he or she needs, but each situation each child encounters is unique. As parents, only God can provide our right response.

As you read Psalm 139, and I hope you will, you will recognize that this analogy falls apart. Because our God is the perfect parent, and you and I will never be perfect this side of heaven.

And yet, parenting, like life, is our God-given opportunity to be refined into the image of God. Surrendering allows us to grow and become who God has called us to be in all aspects of our personality. When we surrender rigid parenting styles that stem from the world or our emotions and instead respond lovingly by the power of the Holy Spirit to our children and what they are going through, God's heart will shine through us. Who could ask for anything more?

Kristy Furlow

 Kristy Furlow is President of Cloth & Clay Ministries, which cultivates surrender, healing, hope & rejoicing in the lives of believers experiencing pain and sorrow. After her husband Clay received a brain cancer diagnosis in 2016, Kristy began a blog, speaking, counseling, and encouraging believers to trust God amid difficult circumstances. God taught Kristy and Clay to rejoice in suffering; now, her ministry helps other believers do the same. Since Clay moved from death to life in 2017, she has committed to ministry, pursuing God's will as He brings life to others through her tragedy.

Kristy is the church administrator for First New Testament Church in Baton Rouge, Louisiana. She works closely with the founding pastors, Lee & Carla Shipp, and ministers as a counselor, teacher, preacher, and worship Leader.

In November 2020, Kristy purchased an 1800s Victorian home in St. Francisville, LA, and created The Hill at St. Francisville. Struggling and heartbroken women come to this serene retreat center to be refreshed, encouraged, restored, and gain endurance. Kristy ministers to small groups of women in this intimate setting, offering multiple retreat options each year.

www.thehillatsaintfrancisville.com
www.clothandclay.org
info@clothandclay.org

This Has To Be for the Glory of God

By Kristy Furlow

One Sunday morning in early 2016, our pastor came to the pulpit and asked for prayer for a man in our church named Leonard. That past week, Leonard had fallen from a tall ladder and landed flat on his back while working. He fractured his spine in several places; the situation was very serious. Pastor Lee was recounting his visit with Leonard, and as I listened to him tell this story, my life was literally changed.

Just hours after the incident, Pastor Lee received the phone call that Leonard was in the emergency room (ER), potentially paralyzed. He rushed over to be with him, praying that God would intervene and miraculously heal Leonard's back. I mean, of course, that is what we should pray for, right? Healing. He is hurt and potentially impaired for the rest of his life. We should be bombarding heaven for a miracle.

When Pastor Lee arrived at the ER, Leonard was flat on his back, unable to even raise his head to greet his pastor. Lee drew close and held Leonard's hand tightly, providing much-needed comfort. Just as he said, "Let's pray," Leonard stopped him.

And here it is. The one simple expression of faith that changed my entire perspective.

"You can pray, but don't pray for healing. Pray for God to receive His glory. Whatever that means! Just pray for God to receive His glory!"

.....

You should read that again. It's been years since I first heard it, and I've recounted the story numerous times. Yet, I still have tears rolling down my face as I type this to you.

Please, just imagine this man. He's about 60 years old. He has many years ahead of him to live, work, play, and enjoy life. He is too young to be paralyzed from his neck down. He is a hard worker, a loving husband, and a father. He needs his legs. He needs his mobility. He needs his strength. Wouldn't you expect him to be desperately crying out to God for healing? Wouldn't you assume that you would find this man lying on that ER stretcher bawling his eyes out and praying for God to do a miracle?

In walks his pastor. The man of God who is responsible for shepherding his spiritual life. And, as Pastor Lee begins to pray, Leonard has the faith to stop him and tell him what to do.

In the most critical moments of his injury, Leonard was fully composed and strengthened with a faith I had never seen before.

"Pray for God to receive His glory."

Those words changed me. Leonard understood something that I didn't. His testimony was teaching me that *God's glory is more important than my comfort.*

I was listening to Pastor Lee recount this story from the second-row church pew while snuggled up between my amazing husband and my three children. There we were—healthy, happy, and content. We basically had a perfect life, and I rarely considered it would ever change.

But when I heard those words that morning, I knew something had happened. In my memory, it is like a movie scene. Pastor Lee speaks the words, "Don't pray for healing. Pray for God to receive His glory." Instantly everything stops. The moment is frozen in time, and the sound of those words lingers in the air like an echo through a cavern. Everyone in the room is frozen in place except me. I'm there. The only one able to move or look around. I'm suspended in the moment.

The presence of God is so thick that all I want to do is fall flat on my face, but I can't get up from my seat. It is a divine encounter with God. He visited me there. He stopped me in that moment to make sure that the words would filter into my soul. This was not a message that I could hear and simply applaud. I couldn't be content to celebrate Leonard's faith and move on with my life.

God wouldn't allow me to escape the moment without burying the seed. He knew the absolute necessity of this lesson. He knew what was ahead of me. And He knew the life that this seed would produce. It *had* to live. It *had* to be planted deep and take root. This was a matter of life and death. God knew exactly how vital this lesson was for me. There I sat, with my cute little family and my perfect little life, and I couldn't have comprehended the magnitude of the moment.

There was a storm brewing, but I had no weather app alerting me of its projected path. I didn't know that within months my life could be wrecked by the biggest storm I had ever seen. The force of the coming winds would have the capacity to blow away every single thing in its path. A tumor was already in place. At this point, it had likely been growing for many months. A silent killer lodged in Clay's brain—invading his body as if it had some right to be there. Every ounce of my faith would soon be challenged, though I had no way of knowing.

But He knew. And, in His gentle grace, He had fully prepared the soil of my heart to receive this seed. There was rich, dark, moist ground in which it would be planted.

God had been tilling up the ground of my heart for quite a while. I knew He was working in me, challenging me to fully surrender. He was asking me questions about the state of my heart. He had been showing me more about Himself and more about the parts of me that I didn't want to admit existed. I didn't really understand why, but I knew He was preparing me for something.

And, on that day, in that suspended moment, He stopped time, so He could gently press that seed to the perfect depth in the soil of my heart. Then, He covered it back up, watered it, and waited.

The First Sign of Life

The first little sprout of life made it to the sunlight when the second most powerful statement to alter my life was spoken,

"Mr. Furlow, you have a significant abnormality in your brain."

Just a few months later, I had my own decision to make. As Pastor Lee walked through the door of *our* hospital room, what would I say? Would I demand that he declare healing? Would I box God in and give Him no other alternative in which to answer my prayer and be glorified?

Or would I, like Leonard, give God the liberty to do whatever He desired with my life? Would Clay and I truly be able to say, "Pray for God to receive His glory!"

The neurosurgeon gave us the news at around 2:30 pm on Tuesday, May 3, 2016. Clay and I were alone in the hospital room with him. Clay was lying in bed while I sat cross-legged right beside him. Dr. Scrantz pulled his chair up close to the bedside and leaned in.

As he began to describe the location and the size of the tumor, his eyes were filled with pity. The MRI revealed a massive tumor right in the center of Clay's brain, wrapped around the cerebral cortex. It was literally intertwined with the delicate brain stem and all the "wiring" of the brain to the rest of the body. Surgery seemed impossible. He labeled it as an "inoperable brain tumor" and gave Clay three months to live.

The doctor left the room, and we sat in silence for a minute—stunned. I wrapped my arms around Clay's head, resting my chin on his bald crown, and we both cried. His tears...my tears...both running down his face. I held him so tight. I never wanted to let go. I could have stayed in that room forever. I could have locked the real world away, banning the truth from re-entry, and lived in that 15x20 space with Clay for the rest of my life.

The hurricane had made landfall. It was blowing so hard against us in that moment. The winds carried so many emotions with them—anxiety, fear, doubt, anger, frustration, self-pity, hurt, shock, hate, questions, and panic. I could see the devil like a sorcerer, controlling the wind with his arms, waving that spiral into being. Telling those winds how to move and giving them speed as he directed them to blow harder. As I held onto Clay so tightly in that hospital bed, I could imagine his face filled with anticipation as the force of the winds blew against us.

I think he fully expected us to crumble. He must have been holding his breath as he waited for an explosion of emotions to be displayed. I think he was excited to watch as this house we had built would be torn apart—board by board—by the disastrous winds. He knew this storm had the power to pulverize us—to leave nothing but shreds of our past and splinters of our dreams strewn across the landscape of our bleak futures. He knew we didn't have the strength to stand. He had conjured up the perfect way to crush our lives and destroy our testimony.

But there was something he didn't know.

Remember that little seed planted only a few months earlier? That little seed of faith had sprouted something strong enough to withstand these winds. The enemy could never have known how deep that root had grown and that all the force of this hurricane wouldn't be able to uproot that newly planted tree.

Imagine the determination on his angry face as he directed the full force of those whipping winds at that little sapling. It waved in the wind, but he couldn't uproot it. I believe he was shocked when the first words out of Clay's mouth were, "Kristy, this has to be for the glory of God."

My heart is leaping inside of my chest as I tell you this. Y'all! It was so supernatural. The man had just been told he was staring death in the face, and after a few moments of tears and processing a ton of information, his first words were perfectly aligned with those that God had planted in my heart.

Following Leonard's example, we declared that we would not beg for healing. We would pray for God to receive His glory. We would pray for souls to be saved, believers to be strengthened in their faith, prodigals to come home, and revival to come.

I wish I knew all of you personally so you would know how deeply I mean what I am about to say.

There is nothing special about me. There was nothing special about Clay. God is no respecter of persons, and He loves you just as much as He loves me. I did nothing to accomplish this work, and neither Clay nor I deserve any credit or any glory for anything that happened. The only thing we did was agree with God. We said yes. That's it. He did everything else. And He can do the same for you.

You don't have to be smart enough, spiritual enough, or strong enough. You just have to say yes. You simply must be willing to allow God to receive His glory through your life. He does all the hard work—the tilling, the fertilizing, the preparation, the planting, the watering, and the nurturing. God does all of that. You simply give Him the ground of your heart. You have to say, "Yes, God. You can plant here."

And, in that simple surrender, you will soon find that God is a Master Gardener. He has the greenest of all green thumbs! You will never regret His work.

Treasure in Jars of Clay

I'm writing these words to you as I sit in the exact place I was when I heard Clay's very last heartbeat on this earth on September 12, 2017. He lived 16 beautiful months from the conversation I just re-lived for you. And those 16 months are the most glorious moments of my life so far. I know that sounds crazy, but it's true.

> 2 Corinthians 4:7-12 (NIV) says, *But we have this treasure in jars of clay, to show that the surpassing power belongs to God and not to us. We are afflicted in every way, but not crushed; perplexed, but not driven to despair; persecuted, but not forsaken; struck down, but not destroyed; always carrying in the body the death of Jesus, so that the life of Jesus may also be manifested in our bodies. For we who live are always being given over to death for Jesus' sake, so that the life of Jesus also may be manifested in our mortal flesh. So death is at work in us, but life in you.*

Those words became our reality. The Holy Spirit gave us a deep revelation of what Paul meant, and everything about our lives and our perspective changed. We were no longer living for us or for the things of this world. This death sentence was the means through which God gave us eternal perspective. It took complete devastation for us to understand Paul's words and to have the strength to live them, but God accomplished His work! He received His glory.

Many believers are called to show the world how to live, but Clay was called to show believers how to die. He willingly surrendered to the plan of God from the very first moment of his diagnosis, and I could never tell you all the ways God used him during those amazing 16 months. He ministered to thousands of people, but more importantly, he ministered to Jesus. He was a faithful servant who put his eyes on heaven and surrendered to God's plan. He truly allowed death to work in him for the good of the church, and many believers were strengthened because of his testimony.

Now, five years later, the Lord has allowed me the opportunity to open a retreat center near the city we live in. Just 45 minutes outside of town, there is the most beautiful 10-acre plot of land with a 7,000-square-foot 1800s Victorian home. Opened in July of 2021, The Hill at St. Francisville has now hosted hundreds of people who have come to meet with God and be healed. It is a place of restoration, a place of hope, and a place where many people have found their joy again.

Without Clay's sacrifice, this could never have happened.

My prayer for you is that this story will strengthen your resolve. That the strength to surrender, which God miraculously worked into our souls, will help you understand, accept, and rejoice in the trials of your life. You see, we all experience suffering. We all face hardship. We live in this fallen world, and we can't escape it. But we have a Savior. We have a high priest who is acquainted with our sorrow, who can sustain us through anything, and who promises to do so much more than we can think or imagine.

Trust in that God today. Put your faith in a God who promises to make good of all that happens in your life. Wholeheartedly love this Savior who holds your future in His hands.

He deserves your surrender. He deserves His glory.

Surrender Your Time

By Julie T. Jenkins

Our time is precious—marked by the minutes and years that tick by. And yet when it comes to the passage of time, as Christians, we can stand in surrender, limiting the anxiety and stress that threatens our joy as we lean on God's wisdom to direct our steps, recognizing that He holds all of time in His hands.

What does it mean to be a Christian? A Christian is someone who has submitted his or her life to Christ.

Sin is part of every human's life. But Jesus, fully God, came to earth as fully man to live without sin, despite wicked temptations that you and I can't begin to imagine. And then He died. Jesus was put to death on a cross, paying the wages of sin even though He Himself had never sinned.

Imagine a sinless man holding enough in His account to pay for a life of sin. Jesus took His full account and offered it to us. He was and is willing to use His credit to pay for our sins—all we have to do is hold out our hands and accept His free gift of salvation by believing that Jesus Christ has the power to offer us eternity with God.

Accepting that gift from Jesus of eternity with God is what makes a Christian.

You may have already known that. But read that sentence again. Christianity is accepting Jesus' gift of *eternity* with God.

Eternity!

If we have been granted eternity with God, why do we hold our time so tightly?

Surrendered: Yielded With Purpose

> *Whoever does the will of God lives forever.* (1 John 2:17 NIV)

When we look at time from God's perspective and recognize that our days are eternal, we can begin to understand that we will have plenty of time for anything and everything good and ordained by God.

Allow me to make another point. Not only is our time with God unending, but God is THE great organizer of time.

Reading through the whole Bible, we certainly see God's plan of salvation unfold: from the creation of man and the first sin, then to Jesus' death and offer of salvation for all who claim Him as their Lord and Savior, and finally to the glorious defeat of Satan in the end times. We also see God's plan orchestrated within individual books and chapters in the Bible. For example, in Genesis, we see the creation of the world—beginning with formlessness, and moving to the creation of light and water, then vegetation, followed by animals. Just check out the progression: animals couldn't exist without plants to eat, and plants couldn't grow without water and light. God had and orchestrated a perfect plan.

And Jesus, God in the flesh, was also organized. First, he called His disciples one by one. Then He taught them, and finally, He empowered them to teach and write His message. Jesus took His time, carefully taking the necessary steps to ensure His message would never die.

Our God is so smart! He has everything planned out, and we can trust His plans will succeed.

Recognizing, then, that we will spend eternity with God and that His carefully procured plans always succeed, we have the substantive grounds to surrender our time. We no longer have to stress about our minutes or days because God has gifted us with eternity. And when we seek God's wisdom in planning our days, we can live joyfully, trusting that He will provide us with a perfectly curated agenda.

Still, at times we may feel like we are wasting time, our time is out of control, or things are just moving too slowly. At those moments, we are to surrender in faith, trusting that God is in control and His ways are always perfect.

If you have accepted Jesus' free gift of salvation, you can look forward to eternity with God, understanding that today is part of your forever! And as God's child, you can trust Him with your minute-by-minute schedule— because He is the perfect coordinator and executor.

> I hear the Lord saying "I will stay close to you, instructing you and guiding you along the pathway for your life. I will advise you along the way and lead you forth with my eyes as your guide. So don't make it difficult; don't be stubborn when I take you where you've not been before. Don't make me tug you and pull you along. Just come with me!" (Psalm 32:8-9 TPT)

Let's pray together.

Father God,

We thank you for giving us the gift of eternity! We give our lives to you, accepting that gift. We acknowledge our sinfulness, and we come to you in repentance. Jesus, we recognize that you have already paid our debt of sin, and we simply can't thank you enough.

Father, as we walk through this life, we surrender our time to you. We ask you to orchestrate our days and guide us in your will. Grant us your perfect wisdom as our time here on earth unfolds. We look forward to spending forever with you and recognize that eternity begins today!

In Jesus' name, I pray. Amen.

Afterword

The many stories and teachings you have just experienced clearly establish that God is our provider and is in complete control. His scriptures are clear—we do not need to carry any weight on our own shoulders. *But my God shall supply all your needs according to his riches in glory by Christ Jesus.* (Philippians 4:19 KJV)

Each day we surrender our hearts to God, we give up. We let go completely, releasing our hands and feet, our minds and body and all we have, saying, "I'm done doing things my way." We submit to God and ask Him to take over our lives and make us who He wants us to be. We remember that His promises in scripture are true and good. And we embrace each day by declaring who we are in Christ.

- We are God's beautiful daughters.
- We are accepted and loved by God without conditions.
- We are forgiven through the blood of Jesus Christ.
- We are valued by God.
- We are totally surrendered to God, yielded to His purpose.

God wants your life to be one of complete success for His Kingdom's glory, which it will be when you yield to Him, reflecting the Holy Spirit that lives inside you. We are sisters in Christ on this journey and are here to empower you to live out God's purpose for you. God is our strength, but together, we can stand stronger. We would love to hear from you and walk with you as we commit to surrendering together.

Let's close in prayer, in the power of Jesus Christ our Lord, our Conqueror and Deliverer. It is in Him and Him alone that we trust and obey.

Dear Lord Jesus,

May each reader of this book arise daily with a grateful heart to serve You better. May she be fully surrendered, yielded with purpose, and ready to face each battle, giving You full control of her life. May she pray wholeheartedly, love unconditionally, trust You completely, and live her life with full, indescribable, unfiltered joy and perfect peace that surpasses all her human understanding! May her surrendered heart be held tightly in Your arms of strength. May she step out in unabandoned faith, giving herself in total commitment to You. As she is called out of her place of comfort, may she choose to run after You—Surrendered: Yielded With Purpose to serve her King and Your Kingdom, for Your glory alone.

In Jesus' name, we pray. Amen.